Pasta & Cheese

THE COOKBOOK

by Henry A. Lambert

Produced by James Wagenvoord

Designed by David Larkin

Published by Pocket Books
New York

Produced by James Wagenvoord Studio, Inc.

Editor in Chief — James Wagenvoord
Executive Editor — Patricia Coen
Design Associate — Rebecca Adams
Associate Editor — Lis Bensley
Research Associates — Jeanne Jensch, Ryah Parker
Art Assistant — Dave Cooper

Illustrations by Barbara Fiore and David Larkin

 POCKET BOOKS, a division of Simon & Schuster, Inc.
1230 Avenue of the Americas, New York, N.Y. 10020

0-671-53252-9 Hard Cover Edition
0-671-50857-1 Paperback Edition
First Pocket Books printing April, 1985

10 9 8 7 6 5 4 3 2 1

POCKET and colophon are registered trademarks
of Simon & Schuster, Inc.

PASTA & CHEESE is a trademark of Pasta & Cheese, Inc., and is used by permission.

Printed in the U.S.A.

Acknowledgments

This book offers recipes for an incredible array of dishes — it is not limited to those items that have been developed for, or can be purchased in, the Pasta & Cheese stores. Instead, the dishes come from a variety of sources.

Many, of course, were developed expressly for the Pasta & Cheese line, but others are based on dishes that I have experimented with during various cooking classes or samples with various chefs I have known; some are adaptations of meals that I have enjoyed in great restaurants or private homes throughout the world. They all share one characteristic — each one will unquestionably be an asset to any cook's repertoire.

It is obvious that assembling a collection of recipes of this magnitude requires the efforts, skills, and knowledge of more than one person. I have been aided by many experts, many of whom are also colleagues at Pasta & Cheese.

My associate, Steven Philips, is a knowledgeable young chef who has been instrumental in the development of many of the recipes in the book. He has also been extremely helpful to me in the exploration of ideas which have subsequently become recipes. His assistance has been invaluable.

Sarah Fortune, another young chef at Pasta & Cheese, has tested many of the recipes and has participated in the development of others. She has been of enormous assistance.

Paul Deneen, a great expert on pasta and its production, has been invaluable in the development of the pasta section of this book; Kathleen Kennedy, the buyer for our retail stores, has contributed her expertise to the development of the cheese section.

Tony Muncey, the chief chef for Pasta & Cheese, has lent his skills and his valuable time to the development of recipes for this book, and he has also offered valuable advice on the viability of recipes suggested by colleagues.

Jean-Claude Nédélec has from time to time consulted for Pasta & Cheese and helped us to develop dishes to add to the Pasta & Cheese menu. His knowledge and experience have been of great assistance, and I'm grateful that he's allowed me to include some of his recipes here.

And there are numerous other chefs, food experts, and helpful friends who have made contributions to the book. Some are mentioned later in the pages of this book; all have my gratitude. They include: Margaret Fortune (who contributed many southern-flavored recipes); Marion Lambert; Benjamin Lambert; Allison Brantley; Bill Grose; Fred Bridge; Carol Bernstein; Yvon Guillou; Roger Stephan; Jacques Rachou; Peter Kleiser; Linda Powell; Teresa Canderozzi; Ann Considine; Greg Usher; Lauren Kaye; Steve Heinzerling; Sir Walter and Lady Salomon; Paul Ehrlich; Adele Reilly; Phillip David; Mary Jane Hunter; Cezar Sola; Connie Villalonga; John Haessler; Lukas P. Georgiadis; Clair Milhalski; Stan Pulrang; John Stahl; Tom McLaughlin; Tim Fowler.

Contents

About Pasta and Cheese

This cookbook is about pasta and cheese. It's also about sauces, and pâtés, and curried chicken salad, and meal salads, and side salads, and hams, and vinegars, oils, spices and herbs, and dessert tarts and truffles, and sandwiches that make a meal, and pot pies, and still more. Mostly it's about creating and eating well-made food that incorporates the freshest and finest ingredients available in the marketplace. That's what we've been doing at Pasta & Cheese since I opened our first small shop on New York's upper east side in the spring of 1976. In the years since that opening our customers — busy, active people who understand and insist upon quality — have confirmed our original premise that many people want top-quality food, enjoy variety, and will pay the slight bit more that it costs to have or to be able to prepare fresh foods that are consistently of the first rank. The recipes throughout this book are a mixture, in much the way that the shelves and containers in the Pasta & Cheese stores are a mixture. Many of the dishes that have most pleased our customers, and until now have been available only in our stores and restaurants, are offered here. And in addition to the many Pasta & Cheese recipes, I've included many others. Recipes I've developed as a result of my life-long fascination with preparing and experiencing good food.

As is noted throughout the book, many of my recipes were inspired by memorable meals I've enjoyed at outstanding restaurants around the world. When I'm served a meal that I particularly enjoy, I often make a note of the ingredients in a specific dish (these are often listed on the menu, and I will sometimes confirm them with the waiter or headwaiter). Then, back in my own kitchen, I experiment and try to come up with a dish that resembles the one I enjoyed in the restaurant. Sometimes it simply doesn't work and I quit in despair; other times I come up with a result that is quite different, but very good. And other times I'm delighted because I feel that I've hit the recipe right on the nose. I think I reached an extreme one day during lunch in a Beverly Hills restaurant. I amazed the man with whom I was negotiating a real estate deal when I pulled out my camera and took pictures of the different layers of my sandwich. On reflection, I share his amazement. All things in moderation.

I had always looked for a way to be involved in the food business. I had the advantage, growing up in New York, of coming from a family that enjoyed food and frequently went to good restaurants. There's no question that this gave me an appreciation of the presentation and style that is so much a part of first class restaurants and food stores.

I've been in the real estate business on a full-time basis since college, and I've never considered leaving the real estate business. But in 1975 I became fascinated with the fresh pasta stores in San Francisco's North Beach section, and on Houston Street and Grand Street in New York. At the time I didn't actually appreciate what the difference was, but it was obvious that something special was happening. People from Manhattan's east side were making Saturday morning shopping trips to Raffeto's and the Piemont Ravioli Company on the lower east side to purchase something that wasn't available anywhere else. I started looking into the mystery of fresh pasta — the way it was manufactured as opposed to the national brand dry pasta manufacturing operations. I spent time at Raffetto's and at Piemont Ravioli on a regular basis, and on my business travels to cities such as San Francisco I looked more closely at the way fresh pasta was being received by customers and at how it was being produced and marketed. Several things were apparent. Fresh pasta was wonderful, people obviously were buying, cooking and enjoying it in increasing numbers, and setting up and overseeing a shop on the upper east side where fresh pasta could be made and sold would be interesting and fun and a good business venture.

I opened the Yellow Pages and found out where to buy pasta machines. Once the machines were located I began to look for a location for the shop. My sister-in-law Priscilla went from store to store and talked with a number of landlords. She learned that most people thought that pasta was pizza, and that there weren't many buildings in good neighborhoods that wanted to rent space to a pasta operation. Then she met the owner of a small cheese store. He had a great knowledge of cheese but was anxious to sell since there was no one in his family with an interest in maintaining the store. That store, on Third Avenue between 78th and 79th streets, was well located and seemed to be the right size for my purposes. A few weeks later two pasta machines were delivered and placed in the back of the shop, which was in the process of being completely renovated. And the first Pasta & Cheese employees, two young men, one an out-of-work mime and the other a recently graduated Phi Beta Kappa from Tufts, were hired through an ad in the New York Times.

In June, a few weeks after the shop opened, I had, with hindsight, the audacity to call Mimi Sheraton who was at the time the restaurant and food reviewer for the New York Times. Unbeknownst to either me or the staff, she then dropped in and looked at the store. She gave us a marvelous review: "Pasta cognoscenti who value the delicately tender delights of freshly made fettucine and related noodle dough variations should waste no time in getting over to Pasta & Cheese.

"In the bright white open kitchen of this sparkling new shop, two pasta makers roll out a day-long supply of white or spinach-tinted noodles, in widths that range from a standard fettucine size to the finest, most gossamer cappelli de angelli, angel's hair, generally served in broth.

"The same meltingly toothsome, freshly moist, egg-rich dough is shaped into ravioli, green or white, filled with creamy, buttery ricotta cheese or with a mildly spiced beef filling, equally good with a fresh tomato sauce, or gratinéed in a light wine and cheese sauce.

"Cheese, fittingly enough, is the companion specialty and an excellent array is impeccably displayed and stored in a wall-wide refrigerator case, spacious enough to allow for sufficient air-circulation around the cheese.

"Prices seemed about 10 percent higher than they should be, but the condition of every cheese appeared to be letter-perfect, which is saying a lot these days. Canned oil, tomatoes, jars of honey, jams, mustards and similar fancy food selections are also in stock."

The Times review was a spectacular kick-off for the store and the company. In the brief years since those first pasta machine lessons, we've opened 8 stores and 5 restaurants in New York City, a store in Wainscott, Long Island, and a fresh pasta kitchen, where we prepare fresh pasta and fresh pasta sauces, and soups and salads for the shops. Today, fresh pasta and fresh sauces from Pasta & Cheese are shipped daily from our kitchen to stores and supermarkets across the country.

My decision to learn how to cook had no great drama attached to it. A number of years ago H.L. Mencken, the mid-20th century American writer, pundit, and iconoclast, was interviewed concerning his beginnings as a writer. He explained that when he was a teenager he wrote a short school essay which a teacher submitted to the small weekly newspaper in his home town. A few days later the paper came out and there was the essay, shortened to about 10 lines. Said Mencken some 40 years later, "My name was printed right there on the page. I knew nothing about writing but I was so pleased with the way my name looked that that was the moment. I was a writer". When, shortly after using a cook book for the first time, I prepared and served a meal to my guests and heard some oohs and aahs, I was a cook. I knew that I would always enjoy cooking. It continues to be a marvelous experience to share with guests who enjoy food.

During those first experiences in the kitchen I became fascinated by the the chemistry and the mystery of food. How mayonnaise was made, how a vinaigrette was made, why a soufflé worked. I couldn't imagine having spent all those years without having excellent mayonnaise on my chicken sandwich because I hadn't known how easily and quickly one could prepare a good homemade mayonnaise.

I was amazed when I first learned how to emulsify oil and vinegar to make a good vinaigrette. It became clear to me that if you took some good mustard, a little egg, and some seasonings, whisked them, and then slowly added oil to the mixture, you could make a marvelous sauce which would grip lettuce and other ingredients. I suddenly realized that if I wanted a salad for lunch I could make one for myself that would be as good as any salad I could have at a fine restaurant.

My interest in cooking developed in the early '70s when I began attending a number of cooking courses. I was also lucky enough to get to know the owners of several New York restaurants. Yvon Guillou, one of the owners of Mon Paris, who had formerly been the saucier at Chambord, let me come into his kitchen for several months at 7 o'clock each morning until it was time for me to go on to my own office. Subsequently, Jacques Rachou, who then owned Manhattan's Lavandou Restaurant and now also owns La Côte Basque, was kind enough to let me come into his kitchen early in the morning for several months to observe. It was in these professional kitchens that I first learned that a delicate combination of ingredients, technique, and recipes turns good food into memorable dining experiences.

I've been fortunate. For the past 15 years I've been able to work with some of the finest and most imaginative people in the food industry. Throughout the brief history of Pasta & Cheese we've been able to attract chefs of distinction as consultants and as direct participants in the development of notable sauces and fillings and a variety of dishes featured in our own stores and restaurants. We've challenged each other, and we've shared solutions.

The recipes in this book are tested and proven. But they are not sacred. If they suggest a path to memorable food experiences, then this book will have most definitely served its purpose.

Henry A. Lambert

Essential Equipment

Matching the equipment to the task invariably makes cooking easier and produces better results. You needn't buy every cookware gadget on the market, though. I've found that the simple and traditional cooking implements are, in fact, the essential ones, and these are the items I've called for in the recipes in this book. They will enable you to prepare virtually any recipe with confidence. The list that follows is based on the recommendations of Fred Bridge of Bridge Kitchenware in Manhattan.

MEASURING AND MIXING

1 Set Dry Measuring Cups
Liquid Measuring Cup
1 Set Measuring Spoons
1 Spatula (7-inch blade)
Mixing Bowls (Assorted Sizes)
Wooden Spoons

PREPARATION UTENSILS

Food Processor
Cutting Board
(white plastic)
Cutlery Set
(including:
carving knife
bread knife
3¾-inch paring knife
4½-inch utility knife
10-inch chef's knife
10-inch slicer)
Knife Sharpeners, Steel
and Stone
8-inch Strainer
Ladle
Basters
Colander
Long-handled Fork
Vegetable Peeler

Slotted Spoons
Wok Strainer
Tongs
Can Opener
10-inch Revolving Rolling Pin
Pasta Machine with Rollers
Cheese Grater
10-inch Sauté Pan
8-inch Frying Pan
Covered Saucepans
(2 quarts, 3 quarts)
Double Boiler
Broiling Pan
Roasting Pan with Rack
11-inch French Loaf Pan
1½-quart Soufflé dish
12-inch Wire Whisk

MISCELLANEOUS

Pepper Grinder
Salt Shaker
Casserole
Meat Thermometer
Oven Thermometer
Long-Handled Spoon
9½-inch Quiche Pan
(with removable bottom)
Tarte Tatin Pan
Pastry Brush

About Pasta

No pasta can ever be better than its ingredients. Pasta in its simplest form is dough created by mixing flour with eggs or water. Since flour is the primary ingredient, the type of flour used significantly affects the flavor and texture of the pasta. The highest quality pasta begins with durum wheat, which is coarse ground into "semolina," or into fine flour, called extra-fancy durum. This durum flour is the basis of a firm, resilient pasta with a slightly nutty flavor. Durum-based pasta is ideal for "al dente" preparation, and the best commercially available pasta begins with durum wheat. If you prefer, you can also choose pasta made from whole wheat flour. Whole wheat pasta has a soft texture, a brownish color, and contains bits of bran and wheat grain. There is also soy flour-based pasta, which is exceptionally high in protein, very soft, and slightly gray.

Moisture is required to form the flour into pasta dough. Water can be used, of course, and much of the pasta available is made from just flour and water. When making fresh pasta at Pasta & Cheese we use fresh eggs and no water. Historically, in the south of Italy, where eggs were not easily available, pasta was usually made with flour and water. In northern Italy, however, where the economy was markedly stronger, eggs were available and were considered

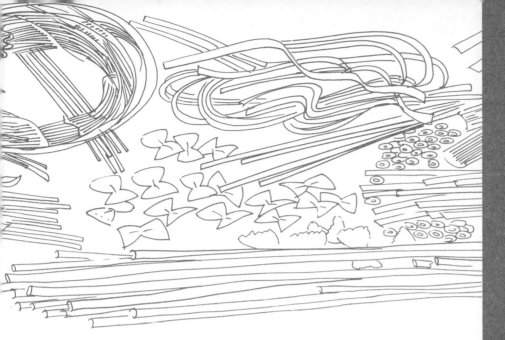

an important ingredient in pasta. Eggs are added for their taste — the presence of eggs is not necessary in order to make fresh pasta. It does however, make the pasta a richer, better tasting product. At Pasta & Cheese, the result is a rich tasting, golden yellow pasta of the highest quality. There are no preservatives, additives, fillers, sweeteners, or artificial flavorings in any of our products.

Fresh pasta which is kneaded, stretched, and flattened through rollers differs in taste from "extruded" pasta which is forced through shaping dies under high pressure. The more laborious process of kneading and stretching and flattening develops the gluten in the flour, giving the finished pasta its characteristic "al dente" quality. At Pasta & Cheese, we use Italian-made kneader-sheeter machines which are larger versions of the roller-type home pasta machines. The level of production per man and machine is miniscule compared to the 4,000 pounds per hour produced by the large extruding press used by most commercial pasta manufacturers. But our method gives us quality control and it gives our pasta the "artisan's touch" of consistently good dough with proper gluten formation. It is not overworked and tired but has good tensile strength; it is thin but not brittle; and it has the proper moisture content and texture — not too wet, too dry, too rubbery, or too soft.

Varieties and Shapes

Pasta is made in a wide range of shapes, each of which is made in an even wider variety of sizes, thicknesses, and textures. To make a broad subject even more difficult to define, the names change from region to region in Italy. The pasta shapes I see most frequently in shops and supermarkets and restaurants in this country tend to be the more common varieties. Those readily available include:

ANGOLOTTI — sometimes available commercially, these crescent shaped small dumplings are usually stuffed with cheese or meat.

CAPELLI D'ANGELO — this is "angel's hair," the thinnest of the flat pastas.

CAPELLETTI — "little hats" are dumplings shaped like a small peaked hat. They are usually stuffed with chicken, ham, or cheese.

CONCHIGLIE — "sea shells" shaped like a miniature, open scallop are available with either smooth or ridged surfaces. The shape is excellent for gripping thick sauces.

FARFALLE — the tiny bow-tie shaped pasta, also excellent with thick sauces.

FETTUCCINE — the basic Roman egg noodle. In Bologna a similar flat pasta, slightly wider and thinner, is called tagliatelle.

FUSILLI — a spiral, "spring-shaped" pasta similar to rotelle.

LASAGNA — the largest of the pasta noodles, lasagna is 2 — 2½ inches wide and is made smooth or with ridges that aid in gripping sauces.

LINGUINE — a thin, flat noodle.

PASTINA — a generic term for a number of tiny pastas, such as anellini and ditalini, that are frequently used in soups.

PENNE — short, hollow tubular pasta aproximately 1½ inches long and ¼ inch in diameter.

RAVIOLI — a square pasta dumpling usually filled with cheese, meat, chicken or spinach.

RIGATONI — similar to penne but larger, this ridged macaroni type noodle is usually about 2 inches long and ½ inch in diameter.

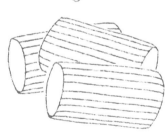

SPAGHETTI — called vermicelli in southern Italy, this thin, solid, round pasta noodle is the most widely known pasta type.

TORTELLONI, TORTELLINI — these small ring-shaped dumplings are usually stuffed with cheese, chicken, or meat. Tortellini is the smaller of the two, approximately half the size of tortelloni.

ZITI — similar to rigatoni, although a bit smaller and with a smooth surface.

Cooking Pasta

The equipment is simple. All you need is a large pot, a stove top burner, a wooden spoon for stirring, and a strainer. Many people transfer the cooked pasta from the boiling water by draining it in a colander. I've found that one of the most useful pieces of equipment I have is a wok strainer. Shaped like a skimmer, it is basically a shallow wire basket attached to a 10-inch wooden handle. I use this to scoop the pasta from the water. It allows me to remove all of the pasta from the water at the same moment, ending the cooking simultaneously for each piece of pasta. It also makes it possible to drain the pasta over its own cooking water, resulting in one less utensil to clean.

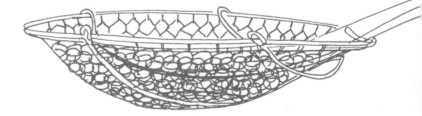

My personal rule of thumb for cooking pasta is to add to a large pot 4 quarts of water for each pound of pasta and bring the water to a rolling boil over high heat. It is important to cook the pasta in a lot of water, which will keep the strands or pieces from sticking together. To help develop the flavor of the pasta, add 3 teaspoons of salt for each gallon of boiling water.

When the water has reached a rolling boil, gently add the pasta to the pot. Then, using a wooden spoon, stir the pasta once to separate the individual pieces.

4 Quarts

If there's one pasta-making rule I feel strongly about, it is **do not overcook**. Timing is critical and, with one exception (angel's hair), you can only gauge the actual state of the pasta by tasting. Throughout the book I refer constantly to cooking the pasta until it is "al dente," which literally means "to the tooth." The cooking time for fresh pasta is incredibly short. For fresh capelli d'angelo (angel's hair) made by Pasta & Cheese, the cooking time is only 30-40 seconds (this doesn't allow time for tasting). Then it's ready to be drained, blended with sauce, and served. For our fresh linguine, the cooking time is 60-90 seconds, by which time the noodles are cooked through but still a little firm at the center. For fresh fettucine, the cooking time is 2 minutes.

Dry pasta requires a longer cooking time. From experience, I have found that most pasta cooks faster than the time indicated on the package, and I always begin tasting the pasta for doneness well before that time has elapsed. Just drain and serve the pasta when it is cooked to your taste. Before I add pasta to a cooking pot, I always have the sauce prepared and ready in either a saucepan or a bowl. When the pasta is "al dente," you need only turn off the heat under the pasta and, using the wok strainer or a pasta strainer, lift the pasta from the water, allow it to drain over the pot, and add it directly to the warmed sauce. I mix it gently to coat the pasta noodles with the sauce, divide it among warmed individual plates, and serve.

Making Fresh Pasta

Although Pasta & Cheese makes and sells marvelous fresh pasta, it is still fun to make it at home occasionally. I usually make fresh pasta when I want a ravioli filling other than those made by Pasta & Cheese. Fresh pasta is traditionally made by hand. Most dough recipes call for placing a mound of flour on a work table, making a hole in the middle of the mound, cracking eggs (if they're being used) into it, and adding salt and olive oil to the egg. The ingredients are mixed with a fork and then kneaded by hand for 5-10 minutes. Through experimentation we've come up with a way to make an outstanding pasta dough in a food processor. It's very simple — it takes approximately two minutes to make the dough and 10 minutes to rest it. And it's very easy to roll out with either a rolling pin or a pasta machine with rollers.

Use this rolled dough to make cut pasta, p. 23; ravioli, p. 98; canneloni, p. 94; manicotti, p. 97; or lasagna, p. 95 .

FOR APPROXIMATELY 1 POUND OF FRESH EGG PASTA:

3   extra large eggs

1½ teaspoons olive oil

2⅔ cups all-purpose flour
    (2⅓ cups for the pasta,
    ⅓ cup for dusting)

Salt

TO MAKE THE DOUGH:

1. Place the eggs, ¾ teaspoon salt, and the oil in the bowl of a food processor fitted with either the plastic or the steel blade. Add 1 cup of flour and process for 5 seconds. Stop the machine and scrape down the sides with a rubber spatula. Begin to process again, and slowly add more flour. The dough should form a ball that pulls away from the sides of the bowl. Continue to add the remaining flour, a little at a time, through the feed tube until the ball of dough becomes just dry enough to break apart into small pieces. There may be some flour left over.

2. Remove the dough from the processor and use your hands to shape it into a ball. Knead the dough two or three times by folding it in half and then pressing it out flat. Cover the dough tightly with plastic wrap and let it rest for at least 10 minutes in the refrigerator.

FOR APPROXIMATELY 1 POUND OF FRESH GREEN (SPINACH) PASTA:

½ pound fresh spinach,
stems removed,
thoroughly rinsed

2 extra large eggs

1½ teaspoons olive oil

2 ½ cups all-purpose flour
(2 cups for the dough; ⅓ cup
for dusting)

Salt

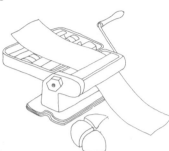

TO MAKE THE DOUGH:

1. Bring 4 quarts of water and 3 tablespoons of salt to a boil over
   high heat. Add the clean spinach leaves and boil for 5 minutes.
   Drain the spinach in a colander and rinse with cold running water
   until cool enough to handle. Use your hands to squeeze all of the
   water from the spinach. You should get about ¼ cup of spinach.

2. Place the eggs, spinach, ½ teaspoon of salt, and the oil in the bowl
   of a food processor fitted with the steel blade. Purée for 15 seconds.
   Add 1⅓ cups of flour and process for 20 seconds. Then stop the
   machine and scrape down the bowl with a rubber spatula. Begin
   to process again, gradually adding more flour. The dough should
   form a ball that pulls away from the sides of the bowl. Continue to
   add the remaining flour, a little at a time, through the feed tube
   until the ball of dough becomes just dry enough to break apart
   into small pieces.

3. Remove the dough from the processor and use your hands to shape
   it into a ball. Knead the dough two or three times by folding it in
   half and then pressing it out flat. Place the dough in a plastic bag
   or cover with plastic wrap and let it rest for at least 10 minutes in
   the refrigerator.

Rolling with a Pasta Machine

When making fresh pasta, I prefer using a manual or electric machine with rollers. Most pasta machines consist of three sets of rollers. One pair is smooth with an adjustment for rolling the pasta in varying widths. The other two pairs of rollers are equipped with cutters that slice the pasta sheet to the width of the pasta desired. These machines can be purchased at most major department stores and gourmet cookware shops throughout the country.

1. Divide the ball of dough into four pieces. Dust each piece with a little flour, then press each into the shape of a flat disk (approximately ½-inch thick). Cover three of the pieces with a slightly damp cloth and put aside.

2. Adjust the rollers on the machine to the widest setting. Roll the first piece of dough through the machine. Fold the dough in half lengthwise, dust it with flour if it feels sticky, and roll it through the machine again. Repeat this until the dough becomes smooth and elastic (about four or five times). Then adjust the rollers one notch closer, dust the dough with flour, insert the dough and roll it through the machine again. Continue rolling the dough, tightening the rollers one notch each time you put the dough through, until the desired thickness is reached. (I find that the thinner the dough, the better.) Repeat with the remaining three pieces of dough.

ROLLING BY HAND

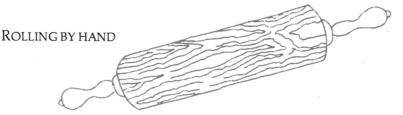

Dust a work surface and a rolling pin with a little flour. Begin rolling out the dough in one piece. Dust the dough with flour and roll away from you. Turn the dough often so that both sides are evenly dusted with a light sprinkling of flour. Continue to roll the sheet of dough until it is very thin, or until it has reached the thickness called for in the recipe.

Cut Pasta

(FOR FETTUCINE, LINGUINE, CAPELLI D'ANGELO, SPAGHETTI)

FOR FLAT PASTA:

Roll out the pasta dough as thinly as possible by hand or with a pasta machine. If you're using a machine, cut the sheets of dough into 12-inch pieces and let them dry for five minutes. Then roll them through the cutting attachment of the machine set for the desired width.

TO CUT PASTA BY HAND:

1. Sprinkle the pasta sheets evenly with ¼ cup of flour. Then fold the dough in half and sprinkle the top with a little additional flour. Fold the dough again, being careful to keep all the folded edges parallel so that the finished noodles are straight. Sprinkle the outside of the dough with the remaining flour and cut across the folds to the desired width.

For fettucine, cut the dough into ¼-inch strips.

For linguine, cut the dough into ⅛-inch strips.

For capelli d'angelo (angel's hair), cut as thinly as possible.

For spaghetti, instead of rolling the dough as thin as possible, roll it ⅛-inch thick. Then cut it by machine or hand to a width of ⅛ inch. If you toss the noodles in a mixing bowl for a minute or two, the square edges will smooth out, creating round, spaghetti-like pasta.

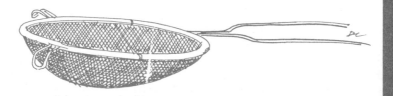

2. Place the cut pasta in a large dry strainer and shake to remove all excess flour. You can cook the pasta immediately or let it dry on a rack or on lightly floured paper towels. If the pasta dries completely, it may be stored in an airtight container for several weeks.

About Cheese

I became interested in good cheeses shortly before opening the first Pasta & Cheese store. It's fascinating to see how many dishes come alive only when they've been enhanced with a complementary cheese and to discover those cheeses that make superb appetizers and desserts all by themselves. My "discovery" was, in fact, something the Europeans have always known.

In Italy, for example, cheese is part of everyday life. It's not unusual to see shoppers purchasing five-pound wedges of Parmesan—and you know that in another week they'll be back for five pounds more. Cheese is eaten for breakfast and throughout the day. Most Americans are not as comfortable with cheese and its many uses as are Europeans.

There's no mystery to learning about cheese, just as there's no mystery to learning about wines. In fact, in terms of origins and names, the two have many similarities. For instance, true Burgundy wine comes only from the French province of Burgundy. Wines that are made in America but carry the Burgundy label usually resemble the original in color only, having assumed its renowed name in order to identify with the unique original. A similar situation exists throughout the cheese world. Roquefort cheese is a good

example — although there are many blue-veined cheeses, true Roquefort is a product of the French town of Roquefort-sur-Soulzon, and no other cheese can legally carry its name.

I think that the best way to learn about cheeses is to do it systematically — that is, choose a category, pick five or six different cheeses from within that category, and taste just those cheeses for a week or two to give yourself a chance to compare their traits and characteristics. Keep notes of your impressions — which flavors and textures are most appealing to you? Which foods do the cheeses taste best with? How would you describe the flavors? You may even want to devise your own numerical rating system so you can quickly refer back to your impressions of a certain cheese. As with wines, your palate will gradually learn to distinguish the subtle flavor nuances in different types of cheeses and to appreciate the complex flavors of the more sophisticated cheeses. All it takes is a little practice.

Whether you want to begin learning about cheeses or simply make more educated choices in your local cheese shop, my list of favorite cheeses and buying tips for each should help.

The Blue-Veined Cheeses

All blue-veined cheeses (also called blue cheeses or blue mold cheeses) have had air or a penicillin strain injected or stirred into them at some point during the cheese-making process. The needles used put holes in the cheese and allow air to enter it. As air enters, the naturally-occurring or injected penicillin turns into mold. Depending upon the type of cheese and the strain of penicillin present, the flavor of blue-veined cheeses varies tremendously. These cheeses keep well in the refrigerator for up to five to seven days. It's best to keep them wrapped in damp cheesecloth, but plastic wrap will do. Use fresh wrapping after each use, and serve at room temperature.

MAYTAG BLUE:

My favorite American blue cheese, this is very white and looks something like a Roquefort. It is generally less expensive than Roquefort and has a pleasant, mild flavor.

SAGA BLUE:

This Danish cheese is a "double-creme," which means its dry matter contains 60% butterfat. It has a few blue veins running throughout and is mild and spreadable. While I think Saga Blue pales in comparison to Stilton, Roquefort, and Gorgonzola, it is very popular.

ROQUEFORT:

Authentic Roquefort cheese, made from sheep's milk in the town of Roquefort-sur-Soulzon, bears little resemblance to pre-packed supermarket American blue cheeses. True Roquefort has been ripened in limestone caves on Mont Combalou and should be white with greenish-blue veins running throughout. Roquefort's flavor, which is an excellent complement to salads, varies somewhat from brand to brand and can be salty, so be sure to ask to taste it before you buy. I prefer the Coulet and Papillon brands.

STILTON:

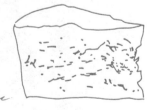

The English "King of Cheese" has an almost pasty, crumbly texture and a pungent taste. Made from cow's milk, it should have a yellowish color and a natural brown rind. Stilton, the traditional accompaniment to a glass of Port, is often served after a meal.

GORGONZOLA AND GORGONZOLA DOLCELATTE:

Italy's most famous blue cheeses come from the Lombardy region and are very creamy with delicate blue veins. The sharp flavor of Gorgonzola is ideal for many cream sauces while the milder Dolcelatte Gorgonzola is very often found in tortas.

CABRALES:

This Spanish cheese is made from a combination of cow's, sheep's and goat's milk. It should be yellowish with a natural brown rind, and it smells more aromatic than it actually tastes.

Other fine blue-veined cheeses include Bleu d'Auvergne, Bleu-de Gex, Bleu du Jura, Bleu-de-sept-Moncel, Pipo Creme, La Fourme d-Ambert, Blue Chesire, and Danish Blue.

Chevres

A chevre is simply a cheese that has been made from goat's milk and is therefore highly nutritious and more easily digested than cow's milk cheese. In the past few years, chevres have become very popular at Pasta & Cheese. We usually carry farm-made goat cheeses, because these have often been made by hand and are of superior quality. Chevres are not usually aged, so they are fresh and creamy looking with a fairly mild, salty flavor. If you're used to cow's milk cheeses, you may have to acquire a taste for chevres. It's worth the effort. Older chevres taste less salty and may develop what some people call a "barnyard" flavor. Chevres will keep well in the refrigerator for at least a week wrapped in fresh, damp cheesecloth. Never wrap chevres in plastic if you can possibly avoid it — they can stand unwrapped for a day or two. Remove them from the refrigerator about 20 minutes before serving.

CROTTIN DE CHAVIGNOL:

This is a small, hard cheese that comes from central France. I especially like it crumbled into a salad with watercress, endive, walnut oil, and raspberry vinegar. You may also try marinating Crottin for a week in this excellent marinade. Use an aged, dried Crottin.

Crottin Marinade

Virgin olive oil (enough to completely cover the chevres)
6 black peppercorns
15-20 juniper berries
6 cloves of garlic
2 tablespoons rosemary
2 tablespoons oregano
1 teaspoon dried thyme
Marinate 4-6 crottin for at least 7 days before serving.

MONTRACHET:

These mild, creamy, factory-produced logs (available with and without an edible ash covering) are a good introduction to chevres. These are spreadable, and can also be served with olive oil and herbs de Provence sprinkled on them.

CLOCHETTE DU CHAPUT:

These smooth and mild chevres are shaped like bells, which makes them a lovely addition to any cheese board.

POULIGNY ST. PIERRE:

Although this pyramid-shaped cheese looks most attractive when it's fresh, it tastes much better if you let it sit in the refrigerator for a week or so until the rind is nearly dry.

BOUCHERON:

I prefer the "fermier" (farm) buche or log, because its taste is far superior to the bland and usually uninteresting factory-produced versions. This cheese should have a chalky texture, and beware of those with gray or brown rinds that appear to be penetrating the cheese.

SELLES-SUR-CHER:

This small round cheese from the Berry and Orleanais regions of France is one of the finest chevres you can buy. Its natural rind is covered with harmless charcoal ash.

Sheep's Milk Cheeses

These are generally sharper than both cow's and goat's milk cheeses. The production of fresh ewe's milk cheese is seasonal, though you can always find harder, aged cheeses in most specialty shops. I am particularly fond of ewe's milk cheeses from Italy, Spain, and France.

BRIN D'AMOUR:

Many people associate this French sheep's milk cheese with chevres. It is semi-soft cheese covered with rosemary, savory, and sometimes Juniper berries. It should be very white with a smooth texture; avoid those that are yellow and hard.

MANCHEGO:

From Spain, this is one of our most popular ewe's milk cheeses. The rind of this cheese is imprinted with the pattern of the cheese press, and the color of the cheese varies from light to dark yellow depending upon its age. It has a pleasant flavor and is a good introduction to ewe's milk cheese.

ROMANO:

This white Italian cheese is generally covered with a black wax. My favorite is Pecorino Romano. Older Romanos (8-12 months) are generally used as a grating cheese; younger ones (4 months) as a dessert cheese.

TOSCANELLO:

I like this Italian cheese when it is young and firm. Toscanello is yellow with a smooth rind, and it is a marvelous cheese to use with an antipasto platter.

RAVIGGIOLO:

This very white ewe's milk cheese from Tuscany is sold wrapped in chestnut leaves. Beware of any discoloration in this cheese, and eat it very soon after you buy it.

Other sheep's milk cheeses include Brebis Pyrenees, Canestrato, Burgos, Caciotta Marella, Marzolino, and Camargue.

Soft Ripened Cheeses

This category, which ranges from the creamy, mild Brie to the pungent French Muenster, includes all quick ripened cheeses that are sprayed with surface molds after the cheese has been separated from the whey. It's best to eat these cheeses the day you buy them, although they can be held for up to three days wrapped in damp cheesecloth or plastic wrap. Make sure you re-wrap them in fresh plastic after each use. Remove them from the refrigerator about 20 minutes before serving.

CAMEMBERT:

One of Normandy's most renowned cheeses, Camembert is now also made throughout Europe and the United States. A true Camembert has a fairly strong flavor, a plump, full appearance, and should be pliable to the touch. Avoid Camemberts that are hard and cracked as well as those that have an ammonia-like odor. Always examine the Camembert before you buy it. The rind should have brown flecks along its edge, and the cheese should feel uniformly soft to the touch.

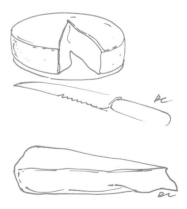

BRIE:

Soft, mild Brie is produced throughout France, although the best cheeses are those that have retained the names of their regions of origin, such as Brie de Meaux. Like Camembert, Brie should be plump with a creamy yellow paste. Avoid those that are runny and ammoniated (overripe) as well as those that have a chalky core (underripe). Once Brie and Camembert have been cut, they cease to ripen so be sure to buy a fully ripened piece of cheese. I like to serve baked Brie as an hors d'œuvres.

TRIPLE CREAM CHEESES

These cheeses, which include St. Andre, L'Explorateur, and Brillat Savarin, have a mild and buttery flavor. They are spreadable and are a good addition to cheese boards and buffets. Don't worry if these cheeses have a yellowish cast, but avoid those that have separated from their rinds and those with rinds that are gummy and gray.

PONT L'EVEQUE:

A great cheese from Normandy, Pont L'Eveque is a washed-rind cheese, which means the rind has been brushed with brine to give it a sticky, slightly hard protective surface. The cheese should be dark yellow; the rind should be tan or golden. Pont L'Eveque is aromatic but should never have a bitter flavor. Like Camembert, it is often packaged in a small chipwood box.

FRENCH MUENSTER:

This is one of the Alsace region's strongest cheeses. It should be golden yellow, tangy, and have a very creamy paste. Its rind is orange and slightly sticky.

You may also want to try Livarot, Chaource, Maroilles, Corolle, Pont d'Auge, and Rollat.

Semi-Soft Cheeses

As with the soft-ripening cheeses, there is a wide range of flavors available in semi-soft cheeses. These can be kept in the refrigerator a bit longer than the soft-ripening cheeses — up to five days. Just wrap them in damp cheesecloth or plastic wrap, using fresh wrap after each use. Remove them from the refrigerator about 20 minutes before serving.

REBLOCHON:

This, from the Haute-Savoie region of France, is one of my favorite cheeses. It should be yellowish white with a light brown rind and a nutty flavor. Beware of those with cracks in the rind which mean they may be on their way to becoming bitter. Reblochon is available in two sizes — the traditional one-pound paper-wrapped package and the half-pound "petite" Reblochon.

MORBIER:

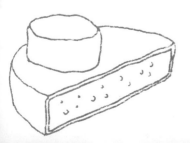

This mild yet flavorful cheese has blue ash running horizontally through it and works well as a snack or on a cheese platter. I prefer farm-made Morbier to the factory-produced version.

PORT DU SALUT:

One of the best-known Trappist cheeses, Port Salut is extremely flavorful — don't be put off by its sometimes aromatic odor.

ST. NECTAIRE:

This golden, mild cheese should have a natural reddish rind. Avoid those with cracked, dry rinds.

FONTINA VAL D'AOSTA:

This cheese, from the Val d'Aosta region of Italy, is the real Fontina. It has a nutty flavor, characteristic of the mountain cheeses of that region. It should be yellowish-white with a brownish-gray rind. Avoid Fontinas that are yellow or hard — they probably haven't been properly handled. The consistency and flavor of Fontina makes it perfect for lasagna.

Some other semi-soft cheeses are Doux de Montagne, Pre Clos, St. Jouvain, Tomme de Rouergue, Tetilla, La Selva, and Tomme Savoie.

Fresh Cheeses

Fresh, unripened cheeses are usually very white, very creamy, and very mild. They look a little bit like soft butter and have a yogurt-like texture. I find that they can easily be eaten with breakfast. Fresh cheeses are best eaten on the day you buy them — never hold them for more than two days. If you do hold them for a day or two, keep them in a plastic container or wrapped in aluminum foil. Remove them from the refrigerator about 20 minutes before serving.

MASCARPONE:

Originally from the Lombardy region, this can be called Italy's cream cheese. It is rich, mild, and slightly yellow. It works as well in desserts and tortas as it does in pasta dishes.

STRACCHINO:

This cheese, also from Lombardy, is somewhat similar to Mascarpone in texture and taste although it is not as rich. It is also excellent in desserts.

PETIT SUISSE AND FONTAINBLEAU:

These unsalted double creme cheeses can be served with fruit to make a fine dessert.

Semi-Hard and Hard Cheeses

These cheeses have been pressed to remove most of their moisture. They keep well — up to two weeks — and can be used in many types of cooking. Wrap them in plastic wrap and change the wrapping after each use. Because these hard cheeses take slightly longer to reach room temperature, remove them from the refrigerator about 40 minutes before serving.

PARMESAN:

Any true imported Parmesan is very different than what you're likely to find bearing that name in a supermarket, but when I think of Parmesan, I think of Parmigiano Reggiano. Like true Champagne, Parmigiano Reggiano is government controlled — it can only be made in certain regions, it can only be made certain times of the year, and every cheese is labeled and numbered. Producers can't make too much, yet they are obligated to reach a certain level of production. And they are strictly regulated as to the amount they may export to different countries.

Parmigiano Reggiano is the Rolls Royce of Parmesans. It looks distinctly different from other Parmesans and is easily recognizable by the bright white dots that look almost like mold running through it. It is unpasteurized and is usually imported to the United States when it's about two years old. Reggianos three years old or more are very difficult to find. The excellent Reggiano is best reserved for those dishes in which the cheese flavor is critical, such as a good veal dish or a delicate sauce. If you simply want good grated Parmesan to serve with pasta, choose a Grana Padano.

When you're adding grated Parmesan to a pasta dish, don't smother the dish with the cheese, as I see so many people in Italian restaurants do. You just need a little bit — you want to enhance the pasta's flavor, not cover it up.

EMMENTALER:

This is *the* Swiss cheese — "Switzerland" is stamped directly on its rind. It is made from unpasteurized milk and has eyes (holes) throughout. There is simply no comparison between this marvelous cheese and the dozens of imitations that are available. It is especially good in fondues, quiches, and omelets.

CANTAL:

This is regarded as the French Cheddar. It has an even yellow color and a dry, gray rind. Farm-made Cantal is creamier and tastier than factory-produced Cantal.

GRUYÈRE:

Like Emmentaler, Gruyère is imported from Switzerland and you should look for the Swiss stamp on the rind to be sure you're getting the real thing. Gruyère has a clean, nutty flavor. Instead of eyes, it has small slits running throughout — don't be put off by this, they're supposed to be there. Like Emmentaler, Gruyère is excellent in sauces and fondues.

Other excellent hard cheeses include Mimolette, Wensleydale, Comte, Farmhouse Red Leicester, Romano, Aged Gouda, and Beaufort.

Cheddars

Many countries produce good Cheddars, but I have my favorites. Farmhouse Cheddar from England is more mellow than sharp, but it has an exceptionally fine flavor. Canada's Black Diamond Cheddar is a sharper, white, crumbly Cheddar. The United States produces several good Cheddars, including two Vermont Cheddars — Shelbourne Farms and Cabot Farms — that are very popular in our stores.

Cheese and Fat Content

Most people are confused about the fat content of cheese. When our customers shy away from cheeses because of their their "fat content," we explain that the fat content is determined by the percentage of fat in the dry weight of the cheese, without its moisture content. But the cheese you buy *does* have moisture; therefore the actual fat content is lower than indicated. With very few exceptions, cheeses contain approximately 19% to 33% fat. The harder cheeses, such as Emmentaler and Gruyère, have the higher fat contents because they contain less moisture, but these also tend to be higher in nutrients such as calcium, vitamins A, B-2, C, and D than cheeses containing more moisture.

Shopping for Cheese

I think it's a good idea to get to know the people who work in your local cheese shop and draw on their expertise. They work with cheeses from all over the world day in and day out — they know its flavors, and what it goes well with, and will more than likely be happy to share their knowledge with a curious customer. If you find that your opinions of cheeses don't mesh with what the seller told you, or if you find that the staff of one cheese shop isn't knowledgeable or seems unwilling to share their knowledge, try another shop. It's important to find someone with tastes similar to your own to advise you.

When you're in a cheese shop, don't hesitate to ask to sample cheeses that interest you. Most cheese shops are willing to give tastes — at Pasta & Cheese it's customary.

If you're buying cheese for a party, don't buy it too far in advance, and don't overbuy. (A good rule of thumb is two to four ounces of cheese per person.) Purchase only what you need for your guests, and plan to visit the shop again if you want to buy certain cheeses to keep on hand.

Serving Cheese

Allow cheese to reach the proper temperature before you serve it. Take harder cheeses out of the refrigerator about 40 minutes before you plan to serve them; softer cheeses should be removed 20-30 minutes before. Arrange them on a large platter with clean knives and spoons next to each one so that the flavors of each aren't transferred by the utensils used to sample them. Suggest to your guests that they taste the milder cheeses first and then work up to the stronger ones — it's a bit too jarring to taste a really pungent cheese and then go back to a very mild one.

The presentation of the cheese is as important as the presentation of an entree. The best complements to cheese are the traditional ones — good crusty bread, plain crackers, and fresh fruit. We very often use fruit to enhance the presentation of cheese in the stores, and I sometimes use it at home. Make sure that you mass the fruit to achieve the proper effect — don't use just a single apple or a few grapes.

Herbs, Spices and Oils

Herbs and spices are an important addition to any dish, and I firmly believe that learning to season foods properly is essential to being a good cook. I've always made sure that the Pasta & Cheese stores carry an ample selection of these flavor enhancers, which can subtly intensify and accent the flavor of nearly any meal.

Most spices are imported from the Far East, where they're extracted from the bark, leaves, flowers, and roots of tropical plants. For example, it takes approximately 4,000 flowers to yield one ounce of saffron, which consequently can cost as much as $500 per pound. (Fortunately, most recipes that call for saffron require only a tiny amount.) Other spices aren't nearly that costly, and most dishes require only a small amount of any spice.

Herbs are plants (or parts of plants) and are most flavorful when fresh. When fresh herbs are unavailable, try simmering dried herbs briefly in butter to reactivate their flavor. Drain the butter and use the herbs as called for in the recipe.

Herbs are a tradition in pasta recipes because fresh herbs have always been plentiful in Italy. Creative Italian cooks have been using them for hundreds of years. Like good cheeses and fine wines, the quality of an herb or spice is determined by its origins. For example, there are two kinds of oregano — one herb is native to the United States and Mexico, the other to the Mediterranean. The North American oregano is bitter and sharp, but well-suited to strongly flavored dishes. The Mediterranean oregano, on the other hand, is mild and sweet and ideal for classic pasta dishes. The very best oregano grows in Greece.

Essential Herbs and Spices

Basil

BASIL: This robust herb lends itself especially well to tomato, fish, and egg dishes. It is the primary ingredient of pesto. When fresh basil isn't available, I prefer basil imported from Italy.

BAY LEAVES: This strongly flavored herb can easily overwhelm the flavor of a delicate dish, so never use a whole bay leaf if the recipe calls for less. The leaf should always be removed before the dish is served to prevent the possibility of accidentally choking on or swallowing it. Place the leaf in a cheesecloth bag before you add it to the dish so that you can remove it easily later.

CAYENNE: An intense and hot herb derived from the red pepper (*Capsicum annum longum*), cayenne should be used only in small quantities

CLOVES: This spice is the intensely flavorful unopened bud of the clove tree native to Madagascar and Zanzibar. It is available whole or as an oil or a powder.

CUMIN: I consider cumin a basic cooking spice. It is a principal ingredient in many curries. The best cumin comes from tropical climates.

CURRY POWDER: This is not one spice but a combination of many. The flavor of the powder depends upon its ingredients, which may vary. For example, curry powder from Madras is hot, while curry powder from Indonesia tends to be mild.

JUNIPER BERRIES: This sharp and flavorful spice is the berry of the *Juniperus communis* plant which grows wild throughout the northern hemisphere.

Cumin

MARJORAM: A pungent herb, marjoram is a member of the oregano family.

NUTMEG: Nutmeg is an essential cooking spice — I like to keep it in a special nutmeg grinder that grinds it fresh whenever I need it. It adds zest to vegetable and meat dishes as well as baked items. If you choose to grind whole nutmegs yourself, remember that one grated whole nutmeg is the equivalent of 2-3 teaspoons of ground nutmeg.

OREGANO: Like marjoram, oregano is an aromatic herb that works well in stews, sauces, and strongly flavored dishes.

PEPPERCORNS, BLACK & WHITE: Whole peppercorns, black pepper, and white pepper are all spices that come from the *piper nigrum* plant. Peppercorns are the plant's whole berries; black and white pepper are made from the ground peppercorns. White pepper is made from a ripened berry that has had its shell removed; it is slightly more aromatic and intensely flavored than black pepper, which is derived from underripe berries. White pepper is, of course, esthetically more pleasing in light-colored dishes.

ROSEMARY: A strong herb, rosemary should be used sparingly. It lends a distinctive flavor to sauces and marinades. Top-quality rosemary is imported from France, England, Spain, and Portugal.

SAFFRON: As mentioned, saffron is one of the world's most expensive legal crops. A small amount of saffron lends color and flavor to a variety of dishes. it is harvested from the petals of crocus plants in India and is a valuable addition to many soups, stews, and desserts.

SAGE: Fresh sage is vastly superior to dried sage, which has lost most of its oil and most of its flavor. Sage is a traditionally American seasoning for fatty meats, such as pork and sausages.

TARRAGON: I think that fresh tarragon imported from France is far superior to any other. This herb also grows in the United States and the Soviet Union.

THYME: This herb goes especially well with chicken, veal, and pork. Good thyme is grown in California, but I think the very best thyme comes from France.

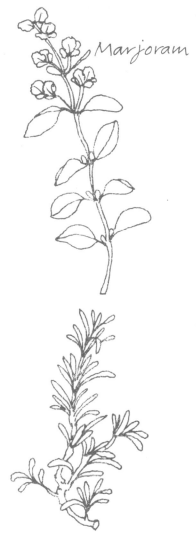

Marjoram

Rosemary

Sage

Shopping for Herbs and Spices

When choosing fresh herbs, look for rich green leaves that are whole or nearly whole. Because the commercial availability of fresh herbs depends upon season and location, you might want to try growing your own. Many varieties will thrive in a backyard garden or a windowbox.

When fresh herbs are unavailable, dried herbs — not powdered herbs — are an acceptable substitute. A good rule of thumb to remember is that 1 tablespoon of a fresh herb is equivalent to 1½ teaspoons of a dried one, a 2:1 ratio. Never overbuy fresh or dried herbs — take only what you need for the near future.

When buying spices, select those that have been freshly ground because a spice's flavor diminishes after it's been ground. Choose richly colored spices and buy only as much as you need. Spices lose flavor as they grow older.

Storing Herbs and Spices

Although little bottles of colored herbs and spices can be an attractive addition to your kitchen, it's not the best way to store them. Heat, air and light cause them to lose flavor rapidly. Instead, store herbs and spices in air-tight jars in a dark, cool cupboard.

Using Herbs and Spices

When you're using dried herbs, crush the amount you need between your palms and rub until it feels warm. This heats the herb's natural oils and releases its flavor and fragrances.

Be selective when experimenting with herbs and spices. Too many kinds, or too much of one kind, can overwhelm and smother a dish. Add a little at a time — you can always add more if you feel it's needed.

Oils

Never overlook the oil you use to cook pasta and other dishes — like herbs and spices, it can have a strong effect on the flavor of the finished dish.

Olive oil is, of course, the traditional oil of choice for Italian dishes. It is the richest and most flavorful of all oils, a fact reflected by its deep golden-green color and full, fruity aroma.

The best olive oil is labeled "Extra-Virgin," which means that it comes from the first pressing (often carried out by hand) of high quality olives. "Virgin" olive oil, the result of the first pressing of less-than-top-quality olives, is also excellent.

"Pure" olive oil results when the pulp left over from the first pressing is pressed again, usually by machine. This is often mixed with oil from other olives before it is bottled. It is not as desirable as oil from the first cold pressing.

All olive oils are subject to rancidity, so it's best to buy oil in fairly small quantities. If, for the sake of economy, you decide to buy a large amount, store it in the refrigerator and periodically pour small amounts of it into a decanter kept at room temperature for everyday use. Refrigerated olive oil will become cloudy, but an hour or so at room temperature will clear it.

When you buy oil, make sure that it hasn't been kept on display near a window or glass door — it shouldn't be exposed to light or heat. Also avoid oils with a coppery color, which indicates that the oil has probably gone bad.

For some cooking purposes, rich olive oil is too overwhelming and, practically speaking, too expensive. When a recipe simply calls for the light flavor of a vegetable oil, I prefer safflower oil. It has a delicate flavor and is low in saturated fats.

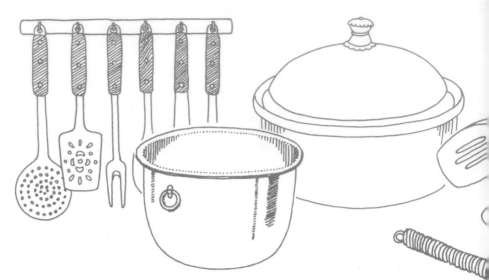

Thickeners and Brown Sauces

There are several techniques for thickening sauces and stews used throughout this book. They are detailed within the individual recipes but, because of the importance of these techniques in the creation of outstanding dishes, I feel it makes sense to consider each individually.

REDUCTION

A really outstanding sauce is one that is thick, rich, and flavorful. Reduction, one of the surest ways of achieving this concentration of flavor, works on the principle of evaporation. When any mixture is simmered, the water and/or alcohol it contains evaporates, leaving behind diminished liquid with intensified flavors. When you use reduction to create a sauce, it's necessary to begin with a greater amount of liquid than you will need in the finished dish.

THICKENING WITH STARCH

Of the three types of starch most frequently used in sauces — arrowroot, potato starch, and corn starch — I prefer arrowroot for several reasons. It is readily available; only small quantities of it are needed for adequate thickening; and it intensifies but does not alter the flavor of a sauce. Arrowroot is often used for thickening dark sauces, which must be thickened at the last minute (a sauce thickened with arrowroot will thin out if simmered for more than a few minutes). Unlike reduction, thickening with arrowroot does not diminish the sauce's volume.

TO THICKEN WITH ARROWROOT: Dissolve 1 heaping teaspoon of arrowroot in 1 tablespoon of cold liquid (water, wine, or stock) for each cup of liquid to be thickened. Slowly whisk this mixture into the boiling sauce. Return the sauce to a boil, simmer for 1-2 minutes, and serve.

THICKENING WITH FLOUR

I use flour as a thickener for white or light colored sauces and soups and in dishes that are cooked in the oven. To prevent lumps, flour is usually mixed with butter (or another fat, such as margarine or chicken fat) before it is added into a sauce. When there's time, I use flour as the base for a roux. When pressed for cooking time, I use flour to prepare a buerre manie.

TO THICKEN WITH A ROUX: To make enough roux to thicken 2 cups of heated sauce to a medium consistency, in a small heavy-bottomed saucepan melt 3 tablespoons of unsalted butter and add 3 tablespoons of flour. Cook over medium-low heat, stirring constantly, for 4-5 minutes, or until the roux is hot and bubbling but not brown. Allow the roux to cool for a few minutes, then whisk in the hot sauce all at once. Return the sauce to the heat, bring it to a boil, and simmer for a few minutes until the sauce is thick and smooth.

PREPARING BEURRE MANIE : When you don't have time to prepare a roux and then simmer the sauce for a few minutes, you can still use flour as a thickener by making a beurre manie. Unlike roux, beurre manie is uncooked. Its disadvantage is that it may separate if the sauce is allowed to simmer too long, causing the sauce to pick up the taste of the flour. To make enough beurre manie to thicken 2 cups of heated sauce to a medium consistency, combine 3 tablespoons each of flour and unsalted butter, kneading together until it is smooth and well mixed. Then slowly whisk the beurre manie into the boiling sauce. The sauce should be returned to a boil and then simmered for 2-3 minutes before serving.

Brown Sauce

Many sauces and stews require a base of brown sauce, a primary sauce similar to the classical French *fond brun*. It is prepared from a stock that cooks for five to six hours and is then reduced and thickened, which requires even more time. The classic brown sauce is available in Pasta & Cheese stores. If, however, you don't have access to a Pasta & Cheese store and you don't have five or six hours to spare, I've developed a quick and extremely good easy brown sauce that uses vegetables, canned beef broth, tomato paste, gelatin, and flour to create a flavor very similar to that of classic brown sauce. The preparation time for this easy brown sauce is 20 minutes, and it cooks for 1½ hours. The recipes for classic brown sauce and easy brown sauce follow.

Classic Brown Sauce

MAKES 2 QUARTS

FOR THE BROWN STOCK

5 pounds veal bones, cut into 2-inch pieces by a butcher	1 tablespoon thyme
5 tablespoons safflower oil, for bones	2 bay leaves
8 cups chopped yellow onions (3-4 large onions)	2 teaspoons coarse ground black pepper
3 carrots, chopped	5 large cloves garlic, chopped
3 stalks celery, chopped	¼ cup parsley stems
1 32-oz. can peeled tomatoes, drained	

NOTE: *If you have a large enough pot, you can double this recipe*

1. Preheat the oven to 450°. In a roasting pan, combine the veal bones with 5 tablespoons of safflower oil and roast them in the preheated oven for 20 minutes. Add the onions, carrots, and celery and continue to roast until the bones and vegetables are well browned (about 25-30 minutes). Add the drained tomatoes to the pan and return it to the oven for 10 minutes. Then remove the pan and transfer its contents to a large stockpot. Add 1 quart of water to the pan and use a wooden spoon to deglaze any bits that are stuck to the pan's bottom. Add to the stockpot.

2. Add enough water to the stockpot to cover the bones by 5 inches and bring to a boil over medium-high heat, skimming often. Then, lower the heat immediately to just below a simmer (the surface of the water should be barely moving), and continue to skim any grease that has risen to the surface.

3. After the stock has simmered for 4-6 hours, gently add the thyme, bay leaves, pepper, garlic, and parsley stems to the stockpot without stirring them in. Stirring will cloud the stock. Continue simmering for 45 minutes more. Strain the stock through a colander lined with several layers of dampened cheesecloth and let it cool.

4. If you're using the stock immediately, ladle the fat from its surface and discard. If you're reserving the stock for future use, cool it to room temperature and then refrigerate. The fat on its surface will solidify and can be easily removed. You should have about 3¾ quarts of stock.

To THICKEN AND REDUCE THE STOCK

Brown stock	1⅓ cups flour
10 tablespoons (1¼ sticks) unsalted butter	Arrowroot (optional, for thickening)

1. Skim all fat from the surface of the brown stock. Divide the stock between two large saucepans. Reduce over high heat by ⅓, so that a total of about 2½ quarts remains in the two pans (1¼ quarts in each). It isn't necessary to stir the stock during reduction.

2. While the stock is reducing, melt the butter in a small saucepan over medium heat. Add the flour to the melted butter, mix well with a wooden spoon and cook, stirring constantly, until the mixture (or roux) is a medium-brown color throughout. Remove the roux from the heat and let it cool.

3. When the stock has reduced, combine it in a single large saucepan and return it to a boil. Whisk ¼ cup of the cooled roux into the boiling stock. Allow the stock to return to a boil, then add another ¼ cup of roux and return the liquid to a boil. Continue adding the roux, ¼ cup at a time, and returning to a boil after each addition until all the roux has been added and the sauce has thickened a bit. Then lower the heat to a slow simmer.

4. Simmer for 20 minutes, skimming the foam that rises to the surface every 5 minutes. This is a finished brown sauce that's rich in flavor. If you would like a thicker sauce, dissolve 1 tablespoon of arrowroot in 2 tablespoons of water and whisk it into the boiling sauce.

5. Allow the sauce to cool, then refrigerate. For convenience, the sauce may be divided into small plastic containers and refrigerated or frozen. The sauce will keep for up to 2 weeks in the refrigerator, and up to 1 year in the freezer.

Easy Brown Sauce

MAKES 1 QUART

This is a simpler version of the classic French *fond brun*, or brown sauce. In the classic version, which takes several hours to prepare, veal bones are browned to extract their marrow. Here, gelatin is used for thickening, and the resulting sauce has a flavor that strongly resembles the classic version. The sauce can be kept in the refrigerator for a few weeks and is used in a variety of recipes. Because it can be used in so many dishes, you may want to double the quantities given in this recipe.

3	tablespoons unsalted butter	3½	cups beef broth (preferably College Inn)
4	cups chopped yellow onion (1 large onion)	1	bay leaf
3	large carrots, peeled and chopped	2-3	cloves garlic, crushed
3	stalks celery, chopped	8-10	black peppercorns
2	leeks, thoroughly rinsed and chopped (optional)	¼	teaspoon thyme
		4-5	sprigs parsley
¼	cup flour	¼	cup hearty red wine
3	tablespoons tomato paste	1	½-ounce package gelatin

1. Melt the butter in a large heavy pan over medium-high heat. Sauté the onions, carrots, celery, and leeks in the butter over medium heat for 15-20 minutes or until they are well browned. Stir in the flour. Then add the tomato paste, mix well, and cook, stirring constantly, for 1 minute. Transfer the mixture, scraping the pan carefully, to a large saucepan.

2. Add the beef broth, 1 cup of water, the bay leaf, garlic, peppercorns, thyme, and parsley to the vegetables. Whisk until smooth. Bring the sauce to a boil, then lower the heat and simmer for 45 minutes, stirring frequently. Skim off any residue that rises to the surface.

3. Strain the mixture into a bowl, using a wooden spoon to press all the liquid out of the vegetables. Discard the vegetables. Clean the saucepan, then add the wine to it. Sprinkle the gelatin over the wine and let it rest for 1-2 minutes. Strain the sauce back into the saucepan through a very fine strainer (or a heavy strainer lined with several layers of cheesecloth). Return the sauce to a boil, whisking constantly. When the gelatin has dissolved completely, remove the pan from the heat. This sauce may be used immediately or stored in the refrigerator for up to two weeks.

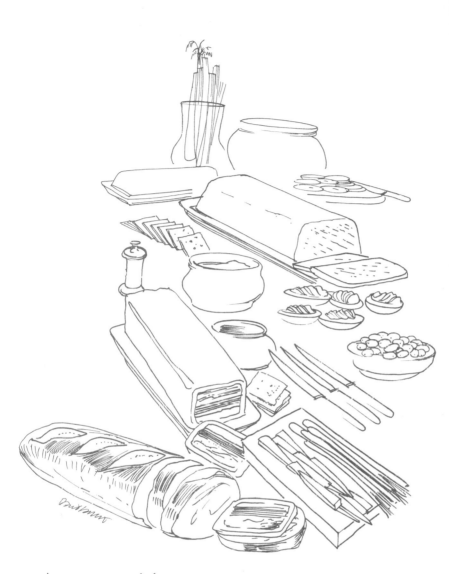

Hors d'œuvres

Choosing the hors d'oeuvres is the first major decision in
giving a party, and it's an important one. If you're having a
large party with a lot of guests, it's best to serve finger
foods that can be passed around easily on a tray. At smaller
gatherings, with four or six people, I've found it's just
as easy to serve crusty breads, crackers, and spreads. For a
huge party, I like to set out several tables with a complete
range of finger foods, cheeses, and pâtés for guests to enjoy.

Salmon with Dill Toast

MAKES 32 CANAPÉS

As the salmon cooks, the cream-dill topping browns. The result is a compellingly different hors d'oeuvre.

FOR THE DILL MIXTURE:

½ cup heavy cream

1 egg yolk

½ tablespoon Dijon mustard

1 teaspoon sugar

1 tablespoon balsamic vinegar

1¼ teaspoons fresh lemon juice

1½ tablespoons finely chopped fresh dill

8 thin slices white bread, crusts removed

3 tablespoons unsalted butter, softened

½ pound boned and skinned fresh salmon, thinly sliced

Salt

White pepper

1. Preheat the broiler. In a mixing bowl, whip the cream until it holds soft peaks.

2. Using a whisk, blend the egg yolk, mustard, sugar, vinegar, lemon juice, dill, ¾ teaspoon salt, and ¼ teaspoon white pepper, then fold the mixture into the whipped cream.

3. Lightly toast the bread, then butter it. Place the salmon slices neatly on the toast and spread the dill mixture over the top to just cover the salmon.

4. Place the salmon toast under the broiler for 2-3 minutes, until the topping starts to brown. Remove from the broiler, cut each slice into quarters, and serve.

Asparagus Rolls with Three Cheeses

MAKES 30 CANAPÉS

This easy-to-make baked canapé is always welcomed by my guests. The crunchiness of the asparagus is wonderfully enhanced by the cheeses that surround it in a blanket of thin toasted bread.

10 fresh asparagus spears

4 ounces Roquefort cheese

1 ounce cream cheese

½ cup grated Parmigiano cheese (Reggiano or Grana Padano)

16 tablespoons (2 sticks) unsalted butter (1 stick softened; 1 stick melted)

1 teaspoon grated onion

10 thin slices white bread

Salt

1. Preheat the oven to 350°. Trim the ends off the asparagus. Bring 2 cups water and ½ tablespoon salt to a boil in a large heavy pot. Add the asparagus, cover, and steam until the asparagus is barely tender (about 3-5 minutes).

2. In the bowl of a food processor fitted with the steel blade, combine the Roquefort, cream cheese, softened butter, and grated onion and process until they are well blended. Reserve.

3. Trim the crust from the bread. With a rolling pin, roll each slice out until it is ⅛-inch thick.

4. Spread a thin layer of the cheese-onion mixture on the bread, place an asparagus spear in the center, and roll up. Trim any spears that extend past the bread. Brush the rolled bread with melted butter and roll in the Parmigiano until well coated.

5. Bake the rolls for 15-20 minutes or until lightly browned. Remove the rolls and cut each into thirds. Serve.

Deviled Crab Toast

MAKES 32 CANAPÉS

As a deviled crab afficionado, I've tasted many versions of this dish. This is one of my favorite finger foods.

1 pound lump crabmeat

1 cup mayonnaise, p. 168

2 teaspoons fresh lemon juice

1½ teaspoons Worcestershire sauce

1 teaspoon Dijon mustard

2 tablespoons grated Parmigiano cheese (Reggiano or Grana Padano)

1 cup plus 2 tablespoons grated Gruyère cheese (1 cup for the topping; 2 tablespoons for the deviled mixture)

8 slices thin white bread

4 tablespoons (½ stick) unsalted butter, softened

Salt

Pepper

1. Preheat the broiler. Pick through the crabmeat and remove any pieces of shell or cartilage.

2. In a mixing bowl, blend the mayonnaise, lemon juice, Worcestershire sauce, mustard, 1 teaspoon salt, ½ teaspoon pepper, Parmigiano, and 2 tablespoons Gruyère. Add the crabmeat and stir until the mixture is thoroughly blended.

3. Trim the crusts from the bread. Toast the bread lightly under the broiler, then spread each slice with ½ tablespoon softened butter.

4. Spread the crab mixture over the toast, top with the remaining Gruyère, and place under the broiler for 2-3 minutes, until the cheese melts and begins to brown.

5. Remove the toasts from the broiler, cut each into quarters, and serve.

NOTE:
Mustard, a blend of mustard seeds, vinegar or white wine, and spices, can be sweet, mild, bitter, or pungent. Dijon, one of the best all-purpose mustards, is noted for its sharp flavor and smooth texture. It is made in the town of Dijon in France's Burgundy region.

Pita Hors D'Oeuvres

This attractive and easy to prepare baked hors d'oeuvre was created by Cezar Sola.

1 cup mayonnaise, p. 168	4 tablespoons grated Parmigiano cheese (Reggiano or Grana Padano)
4 teaspoons minced onion flakes	2 small (4-inch) pita breads

1. Preheat the oven to 400°. Combine the mayonnaise, onion, and Parmigiano in a bowl and blend well. Split the pita breads into halves and lay them, inside facing up, on a baking tray.

2. Spread each pita half smoothly with ¼ of the mayonnaise-cheese mixture. Bake them in the preheated oven for 10-15 minutes, until the mayonnaise bubbles and the edges of the pitas begin to brown. Transfer to a cutting board and slice each into 8 wedges. Serve.

Cheese Bites

MAKES 30 TO 40 CANAPÉS

We've been experimenting with cheese puffs for quite some time with the intention of adding them to the menu in the Pasta & Cheese stores. This recipe for a cheese bite accented with crisp bacon stands out among the many we've developed.

8 tablespoons (1 stick) unsalted butter, softened	1¼ cups flour
½ pound sharp Cheddar cheese, grated	½ pound bacon, cooked until crisp, drained, and crumbled (about ½ cup)
	Cayenne pepper

1. In the bowl of a food processor fitted with the steel blade, cream the butter and cheese together. Add the flour and cayenne pepper to taste and process until thoroughly blended. Add the crumbled bacon and process for a few seconds more.

2. Shape the cheese mixture into 3 rolls, each 1-inch in diameter, wrap in plastic, and chill for 15-30 minutes. Preheat the oven to 375°.

3. Slice the rolls into ¼-inch pieces. (If you'd like, you can squeeze the dough through a cookie press to make individual cheese straws.) Place the slices on an ungreased baking sheet and bake for 10-12 minutes in the preheated oven. Remove and serve immediately or let cool. Cheese bites may be prepared up to one day in advance and stored in an airtight container.

Deviled Eggs Parmigiano

SERVES 16 AS AN HORS 'DOEUVRES

This is a delicious change of pace from the usual deviled egg mixture. In this recipe, the finely grated Parmigiano blends with fresh mayonnaise to offer a subtle accent that gives fresh flavor to an old standard.

NOTE: *There's a simple technique that will usually prevent cracked egg shells. As eggs cook, the air inside them expands. This air usually escapes through the natural pores in the shell, but if the air pocket heats faster than the air escapes, the internal pressure will crack the shell. If you pierce a hole in the large end of the shell with a needle, the air will have an outlet and pressure is less likely to crack the egg.*

8 eggs	Salt
½ cup fresh mayonnaise, p.168	Pepper
⅓ cup finely grated Parmigiano cheese (Reggiano or Grana Padano)	

1. Pierce the large end of each egg with a needle. Place the eggs in a large saucepan and cover with 2 quarts of water. Bring the water to a boil over high heat and then reduce to a slow simmer. (This guarantees that the temperature of the eggs rises slowly so that the egg whites do not cook too quickly and get tough while the yolks are still raw.) Cook the eggs 12-15 minutes, depending on their size.

2. Cool the eggs in cold water. When they are cool to the touch, crack them gently against the side of the saucepan. (This allows water to seep into the shell and separate it from the egg to prevent sticking during peeling.)

3. Peel the eggs and cut them in half lengthwise. Remove the yolks and combine them in a bowl with the mayonnaise, Parmigiano, and salt and pepper to taste. Mash the yolks to form a smooth paste.

4. Fill each egg half with the yolk mixture, using either a small spoon or a pastry bag. Arrange the eggs on a platter and cover with plastic wrap. Chill until ready to serve.

Garlic and Herb Dip

SERVES 4

This flavorful dip takes just a few moments to prepare, making it ideal for those occasions when friends drop in unexpectedly. It was given to me by Nancy Bradford.

1 package (3 ounces) cream cheese, softened	½ teaspoon dried tarragon
1½ tablespoons sour cream	1 teaspoon minced garlic or garlic powder
1 teaspoon chopped parsley	

Combine all the ingredients in the bowl of a food processor fitted with the steel blade and purée until smooth. Transfer the mixture to a small bowl or ramekin and serve. If you are making this dip in advance, store it in the refrigerator. To serve, first let it reach room temperature to soften.

Anchovy Sauce for Raw Vegetables

MAKES 1¾ CUPS

I enjoy uniquely flavored hors d'oeuvres. This recipe fits that description.

6-8 anchovies (according to taste)	4 teaspoons balsamic vinegar
3 scallions, minced	½ cup chopped parsley
2 tablespoons finely chopped fresh tarragon (1 tablespoon dry)	1 cup mayonnaise, p. 168
	Black pepper, freshly ground

NOTE: If you use less than 8 anchovies, add salt to taste.

Mash the anchovies on a cutting board with the side of a knife. Combine the mashed anchovies with the scallions, tarragon, vinegar, parsley, mayonnaise, and ½ teaspoon pepper in a bowl and mix well. Cover and refrigerate 1 hour or longer to allow the flavors to blend. Serve with raw or blanched vegetables.

Barbeque Dip

MAKES 1 CUP

This tangy dip goes especially well with cold poached shrimp or raw or blanched vegetables.

½ cup mayonnaise, p. 168	½ cup plus 2 tablespoons barbeque sauce, p. 134

Combine the mayonnaise and barbeque sauce in a bowl and mix well. Refrigerate at least 1 hour to allow the flavors to blend. Serve.

Tonnato Spread

MAKES 1¼ CUPS

This dip, which doubles as an excellent filling for stuffed tomatoes, p.188, is good with crackers, crusty bread, or raw vegetables.

1 7-ounce can tuna, drained	1½ teaspoons lemon juice
2 tablespoons Dijon mustard	4-5 anchovies, mashed (or 2 teaspoons anchovy paste)
⅜ cup mayonnaise, p. 168	2 cloves garlic, minced
2 scallions, coarsely chopped (with root and much of the green removed)	¼ teaspoon white pepper

Add all of the ingredients to the bowl of a food processor fitted with the steel blade. Pulse until blended. Refrigerate until ready to serve.

Liver Pâté

MAKES ONE 3-POUND LOAF OR TWO 1½ POUND LOAVES

Although this pâté is slightly less elaborate than the pâté de compagne, the addition of truffles gives it a distinct, more pronounced flavor. This recipe makes a three pound loaf that will keep in the refrigerator for several weeks.

1	pound pork liver	2	tablespoons cognac
2	cups milk	⅛	teaspoon ginger
¾	pound pork fat, cut into small pieces	⅛	teaspoon nutmeg
1	cup chopped yellow onion	⅛	teaspoon cloves
1	egg	¼	cup truffles (if unavailable, substitute chopped black olives)
1	egg yolk	½	pound fresh fatback, very thinly sliced, or bacon
⅓	cup flour		
½	cup heavy cream		Salt, pepper

1. Wash the slices of pork livers under cold water and trim away their membranes and fat. Place them in a bowl, add the milk, cover with plastic wrap, and refrigerate for at least 1 hour.

2. Drain the liver, discarding the milk. Cut the liver into 1-inch pieces and mix with the pork fat. Place half the mixture in a food processor fitted with the steel blade, add half the onions, and purée until you have a smooth paste. Scrape into the bowl in which you soaked the liver, and purée the remaining liver, pork fat, and onions.

3. In a separate bowl, beat the eggs, egg yolk, and flour together until they are well blended. Add the cream and mix well. Then stir in the cognac, 1 teaspoon salt, 1 teaspoon pepper, and spices.

4. Preheat the oven to 325°. Shave the truffles into small flakes.

5. Stir the truffles (or olives) into the pâté until they are evenly blended. Line a 8½ x 4-inch loaf pan across its width with slices of fat back or bacon, letting the ends drape over the edges of the pan. Fill the pan with the pâté mixture and fold the fat ends over the top. Cover with aluminum foil.

6. Make a water bath for the pâté by partially filling a medium-size roasting pan with boiling water. Place the pâté pan in the water bath and bake in the 325° oven for 2-2½ hours, or until the internal temperature is 160°.

NOTE:
Ginger, a spice, is actually the root of the zingiber officinale plant, which is a member of the lily family. Fresh ginger has smooth, evenly colored skin without any sprouts. Although it can be placed in kitchen wrap and refrigerated for up to a month, it tastes its best when freshly harvested. Ginger that's past its prime has a bitter flavor.

Ginger

7. Remove the pâté from the oven and let it cool. Cover the top of the pâté with a board or a piece of heavy cardboard cut to fit into the pan. Refrigerate overnight to let the flavors blend. To serve, remove the pâté from the pan by inverting it onto a platter. Let the pâté reach room temperature, and cut into thin slices.

Rillettes

SERVES 16-20

There are several ways to serve this versatile dish — I particularly like to present it to my guests thinly sliced and accompanied by celery remoulade, p.175, as a first course. It also makes an excellent hors d'oeuvre when spread on crackers or crusty bread. This recipe was developed for Pasta & Cheese by Tony Muncey.

1	5-pound boneless pork butt or fatty shoulder	1	cup minced yellow onions
6	bay leaves	6	cups chicken broth
8	whole cloves	1	cup white wine
¾	teaspoon dried thyme	Salt	
2	teaspoons minced garlic	Pepper	

1. If there is skin left on the meat, trim it off. Cut the meat into 1–1½-inch cubes. Tie the bay leaves and cloves into a small piece of cheesecloth to create a sachet that you can easily remove when the pork is cooked. Combine all the ingredients except the salt and pepper in a heavy Dutch oven or covered casserole.

2. Preheat oven to 375°. Bring the liquid to a boil over high heat, then cover the pot and bake in the oven for 2½ hours. Test the meat — if it can be crushed easily with a fork, it's done. If not, return it to the oven.

3. Remove the pot from the oven and discard the sachet. Transfer the meat to a bowl and let it cool. Strain the liquid into another bowl and let it cool as well. As the fat rises to the surface, skim it off and reserve.

4. When the meat is cool, crush it into small flakes with a fork or your fingers. Add ¾ of the fat and enough of the cooking liquid to moisten the meat and mix well. Season to taste with salt and pepper. Pack the rillettes tightly in a terrine and chill until ready to serve.

Pâté de Campagne

MAKES ONE 3-POUND LOAF OR TWO 1½ POUND LOAVES

1 pound boneless pork shoulder	5 cloves garlic, minced
1 pound fresh pork fat, unsalted	2 teaspoons Chinese five-spice powder
1 pound beef or pork liver	1 teaspoon dried thyme
1 onion, chopped	½ pound bacon
⅓ cup fresh chopped parsley	4-5 bay leaves
2 eggs	½ cup white wine
1 egg yolk	1½ cups beef broth
¼ cup flour	2 envelopes unflavored gelatin
⅓ cup cognac	Salt, pepper

1. Cut the pork and the pork fat into small chunks. In a food processor fitted with the steel blade, process equal amounts of pork and fat in small batches until they are finely ground but not puréed. Transfer the batches to a large mixing bowl.

2. Cut the liver into small chunks. Combine the liver, onion, and parsley in the bowl of the processor and purée. Add the eggs, egg yolk, flour, brandy, garlic, 1 tablespoon salt, 1 teaspoon pepper, thyme, and five-spice powder to the liver mixture and process 30-40 seconds. Transfer this mixture to the bowl containing the ground pork and fat and mix thoroughly.

3. Line a large 5 x 9-inch loaf pan or each of two 8 x 4-inch loaf pans across the length with bacon so that the ends of the bacon strips extend over the edges of the pan(s). Add the pâté mixture and lay the bay leaves on top. Fold the bacon ends over the pâté, cover the pan(s) with aluminum foil.

4. Preheat the oven to 325°. Partially fill a large roasting pan with boiling water and place the pâté(s) in the water bath. Bake for 3 hours (if you're making two small pâtés) or 3½ hours (if you're making one large loaf). Let the pâtés cool. Drain the liquid fat from the pâté pan(s).

5. In a small saucepan, combine the wine and beef broth. Sprinkle gelatin over the liquid and let it soften for 2 minutes. Bring the mixture to a simmer, stirring constantly to dissolve the gelatin.

6. Pour the hot gelatin/broth mixture into the pâté pan(s). Refrigerate the pâté(s) overnight.

7. To serve, remove the pâté from the pan(s) by dipping the pan(s) into warm water and then inverting onto a platter. Slice the pâté thinly and serve.

First Courses

I've always felt that the tone of a truly good meal is
determined by what's served before the main course. There
are many superb dishes which, although they can and often
do serve as main courses, are more thoroughly enjoyed in
smaller servings presented before the main dish. Each of
the recipes that follows offers distinctive tastes and can,
with imaginative menu planning, be featured as first
courses and blended into memorable dining experiences.

Stilton and Sun-Dried Tomato Tart

MAKES ONE 10-INCH OR FOUR 4½-INCH TARTS

Sarah Fortune and I developed this dish when we were experimenting with fillings for the quiches we sell at Pasta & Cheese. We stumbled upon the combination of Stilton cheese and sun-dried tomatoes that had been marinated in olive oil and then blotted dry and realized immediately that we had a hit on our hands.

1   recipe pot pie crust, p. 150

FOR THE BATTER:

3   extra large eggs   1½   tablespoons Port wine

1   cup heavy cream   ¼   teaspoon pepper

FOR THE FILLING:

1   cup crumbled Stilton cheese   8   sun-dried tomatoes (4 double),
                                                            dried with paper towels and
                                                            cut into julienne strips

1. On a lightly floured board, roll the dough out to a thickness of
   ⅛-inch. Gently lay an inverted tart pan (make sure you use pans
   with removable bottoms) on the dough and cut a circle that's one
   inch larger than the tart pan (this allows enough dough to fold
   up for the sides). If you're preparing 4½-inch tarts, repeat with
   the other pans. Line the pans with dough, gently pressing it
   against the edges and sides. Trim the excess dough and chill the
   pans for 15 minutes. Preheat the oven to 350°.

2. In a medium bowl, combine all the ingredients for the quiche batter
   and whisk well. Reserve.

3. Preheat the oven to 375°. Spread the crumbled Stilton over the
   baked pastry shell, then pour the batter into the shell and arrange
   the julienne tomato strips over the top in a decorative design.
   Bake the tart in the preheated oven for 20-30 minutes, until
   the custard is set.

4. Remove the tart, let it cool for 5 minutes, and serve.

Tart Pissaladière

MAKES ONE 9-INCH TART OR FOUR 4½-INCH TARTS

FOR THE PASTRY:

1   recipe pot pie crust, p. 150

FOR THE FILLING

8	tablespoons (1 stick) unsalted butter	2	anchovies, mashed
14-16	cups coarsely chopped yellow onions	1	teaspoon sugar
		½	cup chicken broth or water
1	cup dry white wine	Salt	
2	teaspoons balsamic vinegar	Pepper	

FOR THE TOPPING:

8   anchovies

8   black olives (preferably spicy, imported ones)

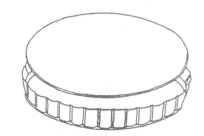

FOR THE PASTRY:

1. On a lightly floured board, roll the dough out to a thickness of ⅛-inch. Gently lay an inverted tart pan (make sure you use pans with removable bottoms) on the dough and cut a circle that's one inch larger than the tart pan (this allows enough dough to fold up for the sides). If you're preparing 4½-inch tarts, repeat with the other pans. Line the pans with dough, gently pressing it against the edges and sides. Trim the excess dough and chill the pans for 15 minutes. Fill the crusts with pie weights. Preheat the oven to 350°.

Be sure to use a tart pan with a removable bottom

2. Let the crust bake for 30 minutes while you prepare the filling.

FOR THE FILLING:

3. While the tart shells are baking, prepare two large, heavy pans for sautéing the onions. Divide the butter between the pans. Divide the onions between the pans and sauté them over medium-high heat until they are well browned (about 30 minutes). Stir the onions frequently and lower the heat as necessary to prevent burning. There is no short cut to properly browning onions—the longer they cook without burning, the sweeter they taste.

4. While the onions cook, combine the wine, vinegar, anchovies, sugar, and broth or water in a cup. When the onions are browned, add half this liquid to each pan all at once and let it reduce, stirring, until most of it is absorbed. Remove from the heat and season to taste with salt and pepper.

5. Remove the tart shells when done.

6. Add the filling to the tart shells, smoothing its surface. Place 2 anchovies across the top of each tart and top each with 2 olives. If you are using one 9-inch tart pan, arrange the anchovies and olives in a decorative pattern. Bake at 350° for 20-30 minutes, until the exposed edge of the crust is nicely browned. Remove from the oven, slip the sides off the pans, and serve.

NOTE:
Browning onions by stirring frequently over medium-high to high heat for 10 to 15 minutes reduces the original quantity by at least half. As onions cook down, they release a natural sugar that gives sweetness to a finished dish.

Rotolo al Burro Bruno

SERVES 4-6 AS A FIRST COURSE

FOR THE PASTA DOUGH:

½   recipe pasta dough, p. 20

FOR THE FILLING:

1 pound fresh spinach	8 tablespoons (1 stick) unsalted butter
½ cup ricotta cheese	Salt
¼ cup freshly grated Parmigiano cheese (Reggiano or Grana Padano)	Pepper
3 ounce prosciutto, thinly sliced	

1. Remove the stems from the spinach and wash the leaves well. In a large pot, combine 4 quarts of water and 3 tablespoons of salt, then bring to a boil over high heat. Add the spinach leaves and cook for approximately 3 minutes. Remove the pot from the heat, drain the spinach in a colander and submerge it in cold water until it is cool enough to handle. Use your hands to squeeze all of the water from the spinach.

2. In the bowl of a food processor fitted with the steel blade, combine the spinach, ricotta, Parmigiano, and ¼ teaspoon pepper. Pulse until the spinach is chopped and the mixture is well combined. Reserve.

3. On a lightly floured surface, roll out the pasta dough until it is as thin as it can be without breaking. Cut a 9 x 12 inch rectangle from the dough sheet and reserve the remaining dough for another use. Bring 4 quarts of water with 3 tablespoons of salt to a boil in a large pot, add the pasta sheet, and parboil for 1 minute. Then, using a pasta strainer or wok strainer, carefully remove the sheet from the water. Drain it and pat it dry with paper towels.

4. Spread the pasta sheet flat and cover it with thin prosciutto slices. Spread the spinach mixture over the prosciutto.

5. Roll the sheet tightly, using the 9-inch side as the leading edge. Wrap the pasta roll in kitchen wrap and chill for 30 minutes before cooking.

6. In an 8-10 inch heavy pan over medium heat, melt the butter until it just begins to brown. Turn off the heat and reserve in the pan.

7. Take the pasta roll out of the kitchen wrap and trim the uneven ends with a sharp knife. Then carefully slice the roll into ½-inch thick rounds. Return the butter in the heavy pan to medium heat and place the rounds in the pan, on their sides, for approximately 2-3 minutes until they are heated through. (Heat the pasta, do not burn it.)

8. To serve, divide the slices among individual plates and top with the warm brown butter. Serve immediately.

Crostini with Prosciutto, Tomato and Cheese

SERVES 4 AS A FIRST COURSE

These easy-to-make crostini, enhanced by the flavor of sun-dried tomatoes, are an excellent beginning to a meal. They can also be cut into bite-size pieces and served as hors d'oeuvres.

1 small loaf Italian bread, cut into 12 approximately ⅓-inch slices	½ pound mozzarella cheese, cubes
2 tablespoons (¼ stick) unsalted butter, softened	1 cup grated Parmigiano cheese (Reggiano or Grana Padano)
12 pieces sun-dried tomatoes	Salt
12 pieces prosciutto, thinly sliced	Pepper

1. Lightly butter each slice of bread on both sides. Sauté in a heavy pan until lightly browned on both sides. Lay the slices on a baking sheet.

2. Top each slice with tomatoes. Cut the prosciutto to fit and lay a slice on top of each tomato.

3. Add the cheeses to the bowl of a food processor fitted with the steel blade and process quickly, pulsing a few times. Add salt and pepper to taste and pulse until mixed. Cover the tops of the crostini with the cheese mixture.

4. This recipe may be prepared in advance up to this point. Just before serving, preheat the broiler, then place the crostini under the broiler for about 3-4 minutes, until the cheese is lightly browned and begins to melt.

Menu for a Light Summer Dinner

Crostini
Vitello Tonnato
Cold Asparagus Vinaigrette
Sorbet
Fruit

Scallops in Brandy Sauce

SERVES 4 AS A FIRST COURSE

This salad was inspired by scallops prepared by Jacques Rachou of La Côte Basque. Most people never taste cold scallops. When you simmer scallops quickly, as you will in this recipe, they retain their natural sweetness and delicacy. Here, an excellent brandy sauce highlights the taste.

½ egg yolk

1 tablespoon balsamic vinegar

2½ tablespoons finely chopped scallions

3 tablespoons finely chopped parsley (2 for dressing; 1 for garnish)

1 tablespoon brandy

3 tablespoons chili sauce (preferably Heinz)

¾ cup safflower oil

1½ cups dry white wine

1 pound bay scallops

Salt

Pepper

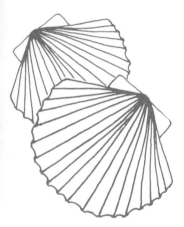

1. In a bowl, whisk the egg yolk, vinegar, scallions, parsley, brandy, chili sauce, ½ teaspoon salt, and ½ teaspoon pepper. Then whisk in the oil in a slow, steady stream. (This dressing can be made 1-5 hours in advance).

2. Bring the wine, 1½ cups of water, and ½ teaspoon of salt to simmer in a medium saucepan. Add the scallops and let them simmer for 1 minute, then turn off the heat and let the scallops rest in the hot liquid for 3 minutes more. Drain and transfer the scallops to a bowl. Let them cool.

3. When the scallops have reached room temperature, drain off any excess liquid and mix the scallops with the dressing. Cover with plastic wrap and refrigerate for at least 1 hour.

4. Let the dressed salad stand at room temperature for 10-15 minutes before serving. Serve on individual plates, with the scallops on lettuce leaves or accompanied by thin avocado slices, and sprinkled with parsley.

Eggplant and Spinach Rolls

SERVES 4 AS A FIRST COURSE

This recipe was inspired by a dish served to me by Luigi Fulvio Nanni in his superb New York restaurant, Nanni al Valetto.

1	large eggplant, cut lengthwise into slices, ¼-inch thick	Safflower oil
1	pound spinach	1 cup sauce (creamy tomato, p. 84, Pasta & Cheese Della Nonna Sauce, or tomato sauce)
¼	cup ricotta cheese	
⅓	cup grated Parmigiano cheese	Salt
	Flour for dusting the eggplant	Pepper

1. Rub the eggplant slices with 3 tablespoons of salt and place them in a colander to let the juices drain for 30 minutes.

2. Separate the spinach leaves from the stems and wash them thoroughly under cold water to remove all the sand and dirt. Bring 3 quarts of water and 1 tablespoon of salt to a boil. Add the spinach. Return to a boil and cook for 3 minutes, then drain in a colander. Rinse the spinach under cold water until it is cool enough to handle, then squeeze all the water out with your hands.

3. In the bowl of a food processor fitted with the steel blade, combine the spinach, the cheese, and ½ teaspoon of pepper. Process until the spinach is chopped and mixture is combined.

4. Rinse the eggplant slices under cold water to remove the salt and dry them with paper towels. Flour each slice and shake or pat off the excess. Heat the oil in a frying pan until it is hot. Fry the eggplant in batches, taking care that the slices don't get too brown. (If they cook too quickly, lower the heat.) Drain the eggplant on paper towels and pat dry to absorb all of the oil. Cool.

5. Spread the spinach mixture lightly and evenly over the eggplant slices. Roll the slices. (The rolls can be refrigerated at this point, if you don't plan to serve it immediately.)

6. Preheat oven to 375°. Spread a little sauce in the bottom of a baking dish and arrange the rolls on the sauce. Cover the slices with the remaining sauce. Bake the eggplant rolls for 15-20 minutes or until heated through. Transfer to plates and serve.

NOTE:
Eggplant, called aubergine in Europe, originated in China and India. When choosing eggplant, look for those that are firm, heavy, and uniformly dark purple. Avoid pale, soft, spotted or shriveled eggplant. Available year-round, it is abundant during the late summer.

Smoked Salmon Soufflé

SERVES 10

This dish, developed by Steven Philips, offers the best of two taste experiences — the distinct flavor of smoked salmon and the lightness and texture of a well-made soufflé. It is outstanding and memorable as a main course for brunch or lunch, or as a first course for dinner. You can prepare the soufflé base one day in advance and the egg whites may be whipped and folded in up to one hour before cooking. When tasting a soufflé base before the egg whites have been added, remember that the mixture will seem overseasoned. This strong flavor will be diluted with the egg whites, which have very little taste.

6 tablespoons (¾ stick) unsalted butter (2 tablespoons softened to grease the soufflé dish)	1 teaspoon Liquid Smoke, or to taste (optional)
4½ tablespoons flour	1 cup grated Parmigiano cheese (Reggiano or Grana Padano)
1⅔ cups milk	4 egg yolks
2 anchovies, mashed, or 1 teaspoon anchovy paste	¼ pound thinly sliced smoked salmon, coarsely chopped
	5 egg whites
	Salt
	Pepper

TO PREPARE THE BASE:

1. In a large saucepan, melt 4 tablespoons butter over medium heat and add the flour. Mix well with a whisk and cook, stirring frequently, for 3-5 minutes or until the mixture is very hot but not yet beginning to brown.

2. Remove the saucepan from the heat and gradually whisk in the milk until smooth. Return to medium heat and cook, stirring constantly, until the mixture is very thick and begins to bubble when you stop whisking. Then lower the heat and cook for 5 minutes, stirring frequently. Remove the saucepan from the heat.

3. Mash the anchovies into a smooth paste (using a knife or spoon) and add to the saucepan. Add 1 teaspoon pepper, the Liquid Smoke, and ½ cup of Parmigiano cheese and stir until blended. Then whisk in the egg yolks.

4. Return the pan to the stove and cook over medium heat, stirring constantly, until the mixture thickens (about 3-5 minutes). Do not let it boil. Remove the sauce from the heat and stir in the smoked salmon. Season with salt to taste and add more mashed anchovies if needed. (You can also add more Liquid Smoke if a smokier taste is desired.)

TO PREPARE THE SOUFFLÉ

1. Preheat the oven to 450°. Generously grease an 8-inch soufflé dish with the 2 tablespoons softened butter, paying particular attention to the sides. Add ¼ cup of Parmigiano cheese and tilt the dish to coat the inside thoroughly with cheese. Reserve.

2. Whip the egg whites until they hold stiff peaks. Fold ⅓ of the whites into the soufflé base, then gently fold this mixture into the remaining egg whites until thoroughly mixed.

3. Pour the soufflé mixture into the prepared dish and sprinkle the top with the remaining ¼ cup of cheese. Bake the soufflé at 450° for 5 minutes. Lower the heat to 350° and continue baking the soufflé until it has risen and is well browned on the top (about 35-40 minutes).

4. Gently remove the soufflé from the oven, place the dish on a plate and gently bring it to the table at once. Spoon portions onto plates, serving each person a bit of the top crust as well as the inside.

Terrine of Salmon

SERVES 8 AS A FIRST COURSE

This is one of my favorite ways to enjoy salmon. I was first introduced to a version of this terrine by my father, who discovered it on one of his frequent visits to England. The salmon pâté layered with pimiento and scallops and served with a sauce for cold seafood is an excellent introduction to an outstanding meal.

2	tablespoons unsalted butter (plus as needed to grease the terrine)	1	egg white, chilled
4	ounces mushrooms caps, rinsed and dried	1½	cups heavy cream, well chilled
1	pound fresh salmon fillet, skinned and boned, well chilled	¼	cup coarsely chopped pimiento
1	egg, chilled	4	ounces sliced bay scallops
		1	recipe sauce for cold seafood, p. 65
		Salt	
		Pepper	

Menu
Terrine
of Salmon
Chicken Breasts
in Brandied Cream
Sauce
Brussels Sprouts
Green Salad
Raspberry Tart

TO MAKE THE TERRINE:

1. Line a 3½-inch x 8½-inch x 3½-inch deep terrine with waxed paper that has been lightly buttered on both sides.

2. Melt 2 tablespoons of butter in a heavy pan over medium heat. Add the mushrooms, increase the heat to medium-high, and sauté for 5 minutes. Drain the mushrooms through a strainer and place them on a paper towel. Pat them dry with another towel, transfer them to a bowl, and chill in the refrigerator for about 20 minutes.

3. Cut ¼ pound of the salmon into ¼-inch pieces. Reserve.

4. In a food processor fitted with the steel blade, purée the remaining ¾ pound of salmon for 10-15 seconds. Then add the egg, egg white, and salt and pepper to taste and pulse for 10 seconds. With the machine still running, add the heavy cream in a slow, steady stream, processing until it is completely absorbed. Transfer this mixture to a bowl and chill.

5. Add the chilled sautéed mushrooms, the pimiento, and salmon pieces to the bowl containing the puréed salmon mixture. Mix thoroughly.

6. Add ½ of the salmon mixture to the waxed paper lined terrine. Push the mixture carefully into the corners of the dish to prevent air pockets from forming. Transfer ½ cup of the remaining salmon mixture to a small mixing bowl, add the sliced scallops, and mix well. Then spread this mixture into the terrine in an even layer.

7. Add the remaining salmon mixture to the terrine and smooth its top. Then cover the terrine with its lid or aluminum foil. Place the terrine in a large baking pan.

TO BAKE THE TERRINE:

1. Preheat the oven to 350°. Bring 2 quarts of water to a boil in a pot or a tea kettle. Place the baking pan containing the terrine on an oven rack and pour water into the baking pan to a depth of 1½ inches. Bake for 45-50 minutes or until the terrine is firm throughout.

2. Remove the baking pan with the terrine from the oven. Then remove the terrine from the baking pan and, when it has cooled to room temperature, transfer it to the refrigerator and chill for 30 minutes. When the terrine is cold, drain it by placing a plate over the top and inverting the dish over the sink, allowing the liquid to drain. Then lift off the mold and peel the lining paper from the loaf. Cut thin slices and serve on individual plates with the sauce for cold seafood on the side.

Sauce for Cold Seafood

½   egg yolk

1   tablespoon balsamic vinegar

1   tablespoon chopped scallion

2   tablespoons chopped parsley

1   tablespoon brandy

3   tablespoons chili sauce (Heinz preferred)

¾   cup safflower oil

Salt

Pepper

In a mixing bowl, combine the egg yolk, vinegar, scallions, brandy, chili sauce, ½ teaspoon of salt, and ½ teaspoon of pepper. Then, whisking constantly, pour the oil into the mixture and blend thoroughly. Serve.

Mussel and Clam Salad

SERVES 6-8 AS A FIRST COURSE

I first sampled this dish when I was visiting William Court Cohen's home on the east end of Long Island. The vinaigrette and chopped red onion provide the perfect accent to the seafood's flavor.

24 mussels	2 cups medium coarsely chopped red onion
½ cup dry white wine	2 cups basic vinaigrette, p. 170
6 peppercorns	½ cup finely chopped fresh parsley
3 shallots, chopped	
24 cherrystone clams	

1. Check the mussels to look for the tiny crabs that they may house, especially in the late summer. Do not use any mussels or clams that are open before cooking — these are dead and not fit to eat. Wash the shellfish well and remove the beards from the mussels.

2. In a large pot, bring the wine with the peppercorns and the shallots to a boil. Add the clams, cover, and steam for 3 minutes. Add the mussels, cover again, and continue to steam until both the clams and the mussels have opened (about 3-4 minutes).

3. Remove the shellfish from the pot with a slotted spoon and rest them on a baking pan until the shells are cool enough to handle. Remove the mussels and clams from their shells, transfer to a large bowl, and cool.

4. In a large bowl, mix the seafood, chopped onion, and the vinaigrette and toss well. Sprinkle with chopped parsley and serve. I like to present this dish in a large wooden bowl.

NOTE: *Harvested year-round along the Atlantic coast from Nova Scotia to North Carolina, mussels are especially abundant off the coast of New England.*

Crab Casablanca

SERVES 4 AS A FIRST COURSE

A unique blend of ingredients makes this crab salad far more interesting
and appealing than traditional versions.

¾ cup fresh mayonnaise, p. 168

2 teaspoons cognac

3 tablespoons chili sauce (Heinz preferred)

2 tablespoons finely chopped parsley

½ teaspoon freshly ground pepper

3 tablespoons finely chopped chives

1 pound fresh Maryland lump crabmeat

1. In a large bowl, combine all the ingredients except the crabmeat
   and blend well. Add the crabmeat and toss until it is well coated
   with dressing.

2. If you do not plan to serve the salad immediately, cover it with
   plastic wrap and refrigerate. Let it stand at room temperature for
   15 minutes before serving.

3. Line a serving platter or individual plates with lettuce leaves and
   spoon the crabmeat into the center.

*Garnish with tomato wedges and thinly sliced cucumbers or thinly
sliced avocados and vinaigrette.*

Crab Crepes Allison

SERVES 6 AS A FIRST COURSE

A good friend, Allison Brantley, worked with me in developing this recipe. I'm certain that you'll find that the taste of the crabmeat, complemented by this well-accented sauce and wrapped in the envelope of a crepe (p. 69) covered by soft cheese sauce, is an exceptional addition to a meal.

¾	pound fresh lump crabmeat	1	bay leaf
2½	tablespoons unsalted butter (2 for the batter; ½ melted to grease the crepe pan)	1	egg yolk
		¾	cup grated Gruyère cheese
3	tablespoons flour	½	cup grated Parmigiano cheese (Reggiano or Grana Padano)
2½	cups milk	½	cup heavy cream
1	cup chopped onion		Salt
			Cayenne pepper

1. Prepare the crepes.

2. Carefully pick through the crabmeat to remove all pieces of cartilage or shell. Then cover the crabmeat tightly with plastic wrap and reserve in the refrigerator.

3. In a medium saucepan, melt the butter over medium heat. Remove it from the heat and stir in the flour. This is a roux (see p. 41). Return the saucepan with the roux to a medium heat and cook the mixture, whisking constantly, for 5 minutes or until the mixture is hot and bubbling but not browned. (The whisking breaks up the starch granules that would otherwise form lumps when liquid is added.) Remove the pan from the heat.

4. In another medium saucepan, combine the milk, onion, and bay leaf. Bring the liquid to a boil over medium heat. Then remove it from the heat and strain the hot milk mixture into the roux, whisking constantly. Return the pan with the sauce to a boil over medium heat, stirring constantly. Then lower the heat to a slow simmer, letting the sauce thicken, for 5 minutes. Stir occasionally so that the bottom does not burn. Add the egg yolk and mix well. Remove the sauce from the heat and cool 2-3 minutes, then blend the cheeses into the sauce and add salt and pepper to taste.

5. Whip the cream in a bowl until it holds stiff peaks. Using a spatula, gently fold it into the cheese sauce until it is thoroughly blended. Then spoon ¼ of the mixture back into the mixing bowl and gently fold in the crabmeat. Reserve the remaining cheese sauce.

6. Preheat the oven to 375°. Spread out the crepes and divide the crab mixture among them. The crepes are easiest to roll if you lay the filling evenly in a line slightly off center. Roll up the crepes,

starting at the edge that is nearest the filling. Bake them on individual ovenproof plates or lay them side by side in a large ovenproof baking dish.

7. Cover the crepes with the remaining sauce and bake at 375° for 10 minutes or until the crepes are warm throughout. Then place them under the broiler for 1 minute or less, until the sauce is lightly browned. Serve.

The Crepes

MAKES 8 CREPES

Like soufflés, crepes are easier to make than you might think. If you're making dessert crepes, you may want to add a little sugar to this recipe (no more than two tablespoons, though, because the filling will also be sweet). Beat the sugar in with the eggs before adding the flour. If you are not going to serve the crepes covered with sauce, brown them a little longer. The crepes will keep at room temperature for several hours if covered with a barely damp towel. They can also be covered and refrigerated for several days.

2	extra large eggs, beaten	2½	tablespoons unsalted butter (2 for the batter; ½ melted to grease the crepe pan)
¾	cup flour		
⅞	cup milk		
		Salt	

1. Mix the eggs and flour in a mixing bowl and whisk until the mixture is light yellow and forms ribbons when you lift the whisk. (This will take a few minutes.) Add the milk, ¼ cup at a time, mixing after each addition until smooth. Add salt to taste and stir. Melt 2 tablespoons butter in a small saucepan and whisk it into the batter.

2. For the best results, refrigerate the batter for about 30 minutes to allow the air bubbles to escape from the mixture. If the batter is to be used immediately, pour the milk and the melted butter into the batter very slowly and stir gently so that you don't incorporate too much air.

3. Heat a crepe pan over medium-high heat and swirl ½ teaspoon butter in it. When the butter is melted, pour out the excess. Add 3 tablespoons batter to the pan and swirl to spread evenly. Cook the crepe until it browns around the edges (about 30 seconds). Turn the crepe (you can use your fingers; the crepe will slide off easily) and cook 30 seconds on the second side. Remove the crepe from the pan and add another 3 tablespoons batter, adjusting the heat so that it takes 45 seconds to 1 minute to lightly brown a crepe on both sides. Cook the remaining crepes at this pace. (Sometimes the first crepe will stick if the temperature of the pan is not just right. If it does, just scrape it out and clean the pan with a paper towel.)

4. Repeat until the remaining batter has been cooked. Stack the crepes on a plate and cover until ready to fill.

Soups

For years, whenever I tasted a well-made soup in a restaurant, I resolved to make soup more often at home. But it was only a few years ago, when I decided to add freshly prepared soups to the Pasta & Cheese stores, that I became serious about cooking soup in my own kitchen. I have realized that a wide range of tastes and textures can be developed in soup, a fact that most people overlook. I think that I was slow to become involved in preparing soups because I felt that assembling and preparing the ingredients was much more time-consuming than it actually is. When I began to devote time to experimenting with soup I was amazed at how simple it is to prepare and how difficult it is to go wrong if you begin with excellent ingredients. The soup recipes that follow offer a spectrum that ranges from light alternatives to first courses to soups that serve wonderfully as the main feature of a meal.

Lobster Bisque

SERVES 8

I've been testing and tasting lobster bisque recipes since the early '70s. This bisque is the happy result of experimentation both at home and in the Pasta & Cheese kitchens. The cooked lobster shells add greatly to its flavor, and the dish is further accented by the introduction of sherry and a light touch of Tabasco® sauce.

4	tablespoons safflower oil	2	cups tomato purée
4	cups chopped yellow onion	6	cups fish stock
3	garlic cloves, minced	1	teaspoon dried thyme
2	leeks, white part, well washed and chopped into ½-inch pieces	1	bay leaf
		⅛	teaspoon Tabasco® sauce, or to taste
1	carrot, chopped (about ½ cup)	4	tablespoons (½ stick) unsalted butter
1	stalk celery, chopped (about ½ cup)	¼	cup flour
2	lobsters, each 1¼-1½ pounds, cut into pieces (with sacs removed)	¾	cup heavy cream
			Salt
1	cup dry sherry		Pepper

1. Heat 2 tablespoons of safflower oil in a large, heavy pan. Sauté the onion, garlic, leeks, carrot, and celery over medium heat for 15 minutes or until the vegetables begin to brown. Transfer to a large soup pot.

2. While the vegetables are sautéing, heat the remaining 2 tablespoons of oil in another large, heavy pan over medium-high heat. When the oil is hot, add the lobster pieces and sauté, turning frequently, until some of the shells turn bright red and are cooked (about 10 minutes). Add the sherry and let the liquid reduce by half, about 4-5 minutes. Transfer the lobster pieces to a large plate and reserve. Pour the liquid into the soup pot, scraping the sides of the pan with a rubber spatula to get every drop.

3. Add the tomato purée, fish stock, thyme, bay leaf, Tabasco®, 1 teaspoon salt and ½ teaspoon pepper to the soup pot. When the lobster pieces are cool enough to handle, remove the meat and reserve. Add the shells to the soup pot. Let the liquid come to a boil, lower the heat and simmer for 1½ hours. Skim the soup several times while cooking.

4. While the soup is cooking, dice the lobster meat into bite-size pieces and reserve in the refrigerator.

5. Melt the butter in a small saucepan, stir in the flour and, whisking constantly, cook this roux over low heat for 5 minutes. The roux should not brown. Reserve.

6. When the soup has finished cooking, pour it through a strainer set over a large bowl. Mash the vegetables well with the back of a wooden spoon to extract all the liquid, then discard them. Shake the liquid from the shells through a strainer into the soup and discard them. Pour the soup back into the pot and let it return to a boil.

7. To thicken, gradually whisk the roux into the boiling soup. Allow the soup to simmer for 10 minutes after the roux has been added, skimming the liquid several times. Season to taste with salt and pepper. Add the proportionate amount of cream to the portion of the soup that is to be served immediately. (Without the cream added, this soup will keep in the refrigerator for several days or frozen for several months.) To serve, garnish each cup or bowl with the diced lobster meat.

Cheese Soup

SERVES 4-6

This was inspired by a soup that I tasted at the St. Francis Hotel in San Francisco. When I returned home I tried to match what I thought were the ingredients in that soup's rich blend of tastes and textures. I was delighted with the results. I prefer to use a Vermont or Canadian Cheddar in combination with the Roquefort in this soup to create a subtle, pleasantly full-bodied taste.

3	tablespoons unsalted butter	½	cup heavy cream
2	cups finely chopped onions	½	pound Roquefort cheese, crumbled
2	teaspoons finely minced garlic	½	pound Cheddar cheese, crumbled
⅓	cup flour	6	sprigs parsley, chopped (1 tablespoon tightly packed)
⅓	cup white wine		Salt
3	cups chicken broth		Pepper
1	bay leaf		

1. Melt the butter in a heavy pan. Add the onion and sauté over medium-high heat (lowering the heat as necessary to prevent burning), for 10 minutes.

2. Add the minced garlic to the pan with the onions and sauté over medium heat for 5 minutes more.

3. Add the flour to the mixture and cook, still at medium-high heat, for 2 minutes. Transfer the mixture to a medium saucepan.

4. Combine the wine and the chicken broth in a bowl, then whisk the liquid into the saucepan in a steady stream. Bring the mixture to a boil, add the bay leaf, and reduce the heat slightly. Simmer the mixture for 3-5 minutes.

5. Remove the saucepan from the heat. (The mixture can be made in advance up to this point, covered, and stored in the refrigerator for up to 2 days. Reheat it when you're ready to serve.) Whisk in the cream, the crumbled cheeses, pepper to taste, and parsley. Then return the soup to a slow simmer, stirring constantly, until the cheese is blended throughout (1-2 minutes). Season to taste with salt and serve in a tureen or in individual soup bowls.

Minestrone

SERVES 8-10

We added soup to the Pasta & Cheese menu in 1982. We began with the pea soup, p.78, and then added the lentil soup, p. 77. We were delighted that they were so well received and soon decided to add this minestrone. Within weeks, the sales of this soup overwhelmed the others. Ministrone offers so many ingredients that it can be a meal in itself. The celery, cabbage, potatoes, zucchini, white beans, and spinach, accented by both beef and chicken broth and Parmigiano cheese, add up to an almost unbelievable variety of flavors in a single soup.

2	tablespoons (¼ stick) unsalted butter	1	cup small tubular pasta, or any dried pasta, broken into small pieces
1	tablespoon olive oil	1	small zucchini, finely chopped
2	cups chopped yellow onion	1	cup well-packed fresh spinach leaves, well washed and chopped
2	carrots, finely chopped (about 1½ cups)		
3	stalks celery, chopped (about 1½ cups)	2	10-ounce cans white beans (cannelini)
1	cup shredded cabbage	½	cup grated Parmigiano cheese (Reggiano or Grana Padano)
7	cups College Inn beef broth		
3½	cups College Inn chicken broth	2-3	tablespoons pesto, p. 86
			Salt
1	medium baking potato, peeled and diced		Pepper

1. In a heavy pan, melt the butter with the oil and sauté the onion over medium-high heat for 5 minutes. Add the carrots and celery and sauté 5 minutes longer. Add the cabbage and continue to sauté 3 minutes. Transfer the mixture to a large soup pot.

2. To the soup pot, add the broth and potatoes and bring the liquid to a boil over high heat. Lower the heat and let the soup simmer for 3 minutes. Add the pasta, return the liquid to a simmer, and cook another 2 minutes. Then add the zucchini, spinach, and beans and simmer 5 minutes longer, or until the pasta and potatoes are tender.

3. Add the cheese, pesto, and ½ teaspoon pepper and mix well. Season to taste with salt. Serve immediately, or let the soup cool and reheat later. (If you want to keep this soup overnight, you may want to add additional beef broth before heating to thin it.

Carrot Soup

The natural sweetness of the vegetables in this cold soup — carrots and onions — accented by the apple, the cloves, and the curry powder makes it a perfect first course before the roast chicken, p. 102. It can be made in advance and stored in the refrigerator, covered tightly, for two or three days. When you're ready to serve, just add cream.

2	tablespoons (¼ stick) unsalted butter	2	whole cloves, tied in a cheesecloth bag
2	cups coarsely chopped yellow onion	½	teaspoon sugar
4	cups carrots, peeled and chopped (8-10 carrots)	1	cup heavy cream, or to taste
2	cups apple, cored, peeled, and chopped (any type)	1½	tablespoons chopped chives or parsley
1	tablespoon Madras-Sun Brand curry powder, or to taste		Salt
2½	cups chicken broth		White pepper

1. Melt the butter in a large, heavy pan. Add the onions and sauté over medium-high heat, stirring frequently, for 5 minutes. Then add the carrots and apple, and sauté 15 minutes more. Lower the heat if the mixture begins to brown. Add curry and sauté briefly.

2. Add the chicken broth and cloves (tied in a cheesecloth). Return the liquid to a boil. Then lower the heat and simmer the soup for 30 minutes or until the carrots are very tender. Remove the cloves and pour ½ of the soup into the bowl of a food processor fitted with the steel blade. Purée the soup until smooth, for about 1 minute, and transfer to a large bowl. Add the remaining soup to the bowl of the processor and purée. Transfer to the large bowl.

3. Let the soup cool at room temperature and then refrigerate for several hours or overnight. When ready to serve, stir in the heavy cream to taste and season with salt and pepper. Ladle the soup into individual chilled bowls and garnish with chopped parsley or chives.

Eggplant Soup

SERVES 6-8

I am always amazed at the variety of uses for eggplant. I find that making it the dominant ingredient in a soup brings out its flavor completely. If you like the taste of eggplant, you will thoroughly enjoy this soup.

4	tablespoons safflower oil (or as much as is required for frying)	10-15	garlic cloves, finely chopped (about 3 tablespoons)
2	medium (10-12 ounce) eggplants, peeled and cut into 1-inch slices	1	large boiling potato, peeled and cut into ½ inch slices
4	tablespoons (½ stick) unsalted butter	4½	cups chicken broth
3	cups coarsely chopped yellow onion		Salt
			White pepper

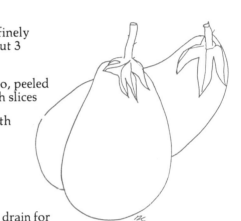

1. Salt the eggplant slices, place in a colander, and let them drain for ½ hour. Then rinse and pat dry.

2. Heat a heavy pan over medium-high and add 2 tablespoons of oil. When the oil is hot, fill the pan with a single layer of eggplant slices and cook, turning frequently, until well-browned, lowering the heat if necessary to prevent burning. As the pieces are done, transfer them to a large soup pot and add more eggplant slices to the frying pan. Add more oil and adjust the heat as necessary. If the oil becomes dark, pour it off and add new oil.

3. In another frying pan, melt the butter, add onions, and sauté over medium-high heat for 10 minutes, stirring frequently and lowering the heat if necessary to prevent burning. Add the garlic and continue sautéing for 5 minutes more. Then add the onion-garlic mixture, the chicken broth, and the potato to the soup pot.

4. Bring the liquid to a boil, lower the heat and simmer for 25 minutes or until the potato is soft all the way through. Pass the soup through a food mill or transfer it to the bowl of a food processor fitted with the steel blade and purée. Then strain to remove any seeds. Taste and season with salt and pepper.

5. Serve immediately, or keep it warm in the top of a double boiler over simmering water until you're ready to serve in a tureen or in individual bowls.

Fresh Fennel Soup

SERVES 6

This soup has an unusual, gentle flavor. Like celery root, fennel is a winter vegetable that is quickly gaining popularity in this country. It has a delicate anise flavor and goes well with a variety of dishes. Raw fennel is used in salad, and fennel braised in a little butter makes an excellent side dish. This soup can be served either warm or cold and will keep in the refrigerator for two or three days.

2	large bulbs fennel	1	small potato, peeled and sliced (2-3 ounces)
2	tablespoons (¼ stick) unsalted butter	4	cups chicken broth
2	cups chopped yellow onions	2	cups heavy cream (optional)
5-6	garlic cloves, minced (1½ tablespoons)		Salt
			Pepper

Fennel

1. Trim the fennel. Remove and discard the stalks, and separate the bulbs into leaves. Discard the core.

2. Melt the butter in a large saucepan over medium-high heat, add the onions and sauté, stirring frequently, for 10 minutes. Add the garlic and continue sautéing for 5 minutes or until the onions are golden brown. Lower the heat if the onions begin to burn.

3. Bring 2 quarts of water to a boil in a large pot and add the fennel leaves. Let the water return to a boil, blanch the fennel for 30 seconds, then drain immediately in a colander.

4. Add the fennel to the onion mixture along with the potato and the chicken broth. Bring the liquid to a boil, then reduce the heat and let it simmer for 30 minutes or until the potatoes and the fennel are tender.

5. Strain the soup through a colander placed over a large bowl. Transfer any solids that remain in the colander to the bowl of a food processor fitted with the steel blade. Purée, adding enough reserved liquid to give the liquid a smooth, thick texture. Stir this mixture into the remaining liquid and season with salt and pepper to taste. Serve the soup immediately, or keep it warm for up to 2 hours in the top of a double boiler set over simmering water. Stir the warm soup periodically. The soup may also be chilled and served cold or kept in the refrigerator for several days covered tightly with plastic wrap and then reheated. When serving the soup chilled, adjust the seasoning.

Lentil Soup

SERVES 8-10

This thick, rich soup is a taste delight. The wonderful consistency and flavor of lentils come alive with the addition of onion, garlic, and thyme. I often serve it as a first course followed by fillet of sole with cream sauce, p.114. I like to add crisp cooked bacon, frankfurter pieces, or bratwurst pieces just before serving as a tasty and attractive garnish to this hearty soup.

1   pound lentils, cleaned of extraneous material, soaked for 1 hour in cold water, drained, and well rinsed

1   large (4-5 ounce) potato, peeled and sliced

2   cups chopped yellow onions

3   garlic cloves, minced (2 teaspoons)

3   shallots, minced (¼ cup)

1   bay leaf

½   teaspoon thyme

⅛   teaspoon nutmeg

7½   cups chicken broth

2   cups heavy cream (optional)

Salt

Pepper

1. In a soup pot, combine the lentils, potato, onion, garlic, shallots, bay leaf, thyme, nutmeg, and chicken broth. Bring the mixture to a boil over high heat. Reduce the heat slightly and let the soup simmer, covered, for 1 hour or until the lentils are tender. Then remove the soup from the heat.

2. Use a slotted spoon to remove about one cup of lentils from the mixture, trying not to remove any potato. Reserve these lentils in a bowl. Strain the soup mixture through a colander into a large bowl. Reserve the liquid. Discard the bay leaf, and purée any solids that remain in the strainer in the bowl of a food processor fitted with the steel blade. Add enough of the reserved soup liquid to make a smooth, thick purée.

3. Return the purée, the remaining reserved liquid, and the reserved lentils to the soup pot. Stir in the cream, if desired. Then let the soup simmer gently for 5 minutes. Season with salt and pepper to taste. Serve in a tureen or in individual bowls. This soup can be prepared in advance and kept warm in the top of a double boiler set over simmering water for 2-3 hours.

NOTE:
When buying lentils, choose those that are uniform in size and color. Mixed sizes make cooking more difficult because the smaller lentils will be fully cooked before the large ones. Avoid lentils that appear cracked or have small holes that may have been caused by insects.

Potage St.-Germain

SERVES 6-8

If I had to choose but one soup to eat on a regular basis, this would be the one. Thickened with potato and accented with onion, garlic, and chicken broth, it is the best pea soup I have ever tasted. I serve this hearty soup as either a first course or a main course. It keeps well in the refrigerator for several days.

1 pound dried split green peas, rinsed, with extraneous material removed	2 cups chopped yellow onion
5½ cups chicken broth	2 cloves garlic, minced
1 medium potato, peeled and chopped	½ teaspoon thyme
	⅛ teaspoon nutmeg
¼ pound bacon, cut into ¼ inch pieces	1 cup heavy cream
	Salt

1. Combine the peas and chicken broth in a soup pot and bring to a boil. Add the potato and let the broth return to a simmer over medium heat. Let it continue to simmer while you prepare the remaining ingredients.

2. Cook the bacon in a heavy pan over medium heat until it is crisp. Then remove the bacon pieces from the pan and reserve, leaving the fat in the pan. Add the onions to the pan and sauté over medium heat for 10 minutes, stirring frequently. Add the garlic, lower the heat to medium and continue to cook for 5 minutes more. Add the thyme, nutmeg, and salt to taste; stir, and cook 1 minute longer. Then transfer this mixture to the soup pot.

3. Continue simmering the soup for 30-40 minutes, then check to see if the peas and potatoes are soft. It not, continue simmering until they are.

4. Pour the soup through a strainer into another pot or bowl. Transfer any solids that are retained by the strainer to the bowl of a food processor fitted with the steel blade. Purée, adding reserved soup liquid as needed. Then return the purée and the remaining liquid to the cooking pot. Add the bacon pieces to the pot and return to a boil. Stir in the cream and let the soup simmer until it is thoroughly heated, making sure that it doesn't boil. Serve in a tureen or individual bowls.

Pasta

Classic pastas — capelli d'angelo, linguine, fettucine, ravioli, manicotti, and lasagna — lend themselves beautifully to a diverse assortment of sauces and ingredient combinations. A smooth Gorgonzola sauce is an unlikely but delicious accompaniment to pasta, as are the barbeque, Cheddar, and broccoli sauces. Pasta is the basis of a nearly infinite variety of dishes. The unusual and innovative sauces and presentations included in the pages that follow should give you a good idea of pasta's wonderful possibilities.

Pasta with Broccoli Sauce

SERVES 6 AS A FIRST COURSE

Of the many vegetables that enhance pasta, broccoli is at the top of my list of favorites. Its taste, texture, and appearance (the bright green color against the white pasta) add up to a delightful dish.

1	large bunch of broccoli	1	pound fresh white linguine
3	tablespoons unsalted butter	1	cup (4 ounces) Parmigiano cheese (Reggiano or Grana Padano)
3	tablespoons olive oil		
8	medium cloves garlic, minced		Salt
¼	cup dry white wine		Pepper

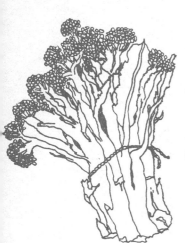

1. Trim the broccoli so that each floret has approximately 2 inches of stem remaining. Cut the florets into approximately ½-1-inch wide pieces.

2. In a large pot bring 3 quarts of water and 2 tablespoons of salt to a boil. Add the broccoli and cook until it just begins to get tender (about 3 minutes). Drain the broccoli in a colander and then rinse the pieces under cold running water until cooled. Reserve at room temperature.

3. In a medium sized pan, over medium-low heat, melt the butter with the oil and sauté the garlic and ½ teaspoon of black pepper. Stir the mixture constantly until it begins to turn a light brown color. Add the wine to the pan immediately to stop the cooking action. (If the garlic is allowed to brown too much it becomes bitter.) Then increase the heat under the pan to medium-high and bring the wine mixture to a boil. Reduce the temperature slightly and let the wine simmer for three minutes. Remove from heat and reserve it.

4. When ready to serve, add the broccoli to the pan with the garlic and wine mixture and reheat over medium heat until the broccoli is heated through (about 5 minutes).

5. Bring 4 quarts of water with 3 tablespoons of salt to a boil. Add the pasta and cook until al dente. Drain the pasta well. Transfer the broccoli mixture to a large mixing bowl. Add the pasta to the mixing bowl and add Parmigiano cheese on top. Mix gently and thoroughly. Serve on individual plates.

NOTE: *When buying broccoli, look for bunches with firm, compact clusters of small, dark green florets and fairly thin stems. Small bunches are usually the most tender. Available year-round, broccoli grows best and is most abundant in cool weather.*

Pasta Provencal

SERVES 6 AS A FIRST COURSE

This marvelous sauce flatters the pasta. It both seasons and grips it. The traditional provencal ingredients are garlic, white wine, parsley, and tomatoes. Here they are combined as a sauce for pasta and it works well.

2 tablespoons (¼ stick) unsalted butter	¾ cup white wine
2 tablespoons olive oil	1 cup chicken broth
6 cups yellow onion, cut into thin julienne strips	¼ cup finely chopped parsley
9 large garlic cloves, minced	1 pound fresh linguine or fettucine
6 large fresh tomatoes (or 6 cups canned tomatoes, peeled and drained	Salt
	Pepper

1. Place the butter and oil in a large heavy pan, add the onion, and sauté over medium-high heat for 5 minutes. Add the garlic and continue to sauté, stirring frequently, for 10 minutes or until the onions are lightly browned. Lower heat as necessary to prevent burning.

2. To peel the tomatoes, first plunge them into boiling water for 20-45 seconds. (Twenty seconds is sufficient for a fully ripe tomato, but longer blanching is necessary to loosen the skin of a less ripe tomato.) Remove the tomatoes from the boiling water and plunge them into cold water until they're cool enough to handle. Peel off the skins, core them, and cut them in half crosswise. Squeeze the seeds from the tomato halves and drain the natural liquids. Then cut the tomatoes into ½-inch pieces and reserve.

3. Add the wine to the onions in the heavy saucepan, bring the mixture to a boil and let the liquid reduce until it has almost completely evaporated. Add the chicken broth and the reserved tomato chunks to the saucepan. Return the sauce to a boil, then lower the heat and simmer the sauce until it is very thick. (This will take about 30 minutes.)

4. Add the parsley and salt and pepper to taste; let the sauce simmer for a few more minutes. (Transfer the prepared sauce to the top of a double boiler. Cover, and keep it warm over simmering water while you cook the pasta.)

5. Bring 4 quarts of water with 3 tablespoons of salt to a boil. Add the pasta and cook until al dente. Drain the pasta well. Transfer the sauce to a large mixing bowl. Add the pasta to the bowl and mix gently and thoroughly. Serve on individual plates.

NOTE:
A good way to peel a garlic clove, and to mellow the garlic flavor at the same time, is to place the separated cloves in a small saucepan. Add cold water to cover, bring to a boil, and drain. Allow the garlic to cool a bit, and the skins will slip off easily.

Pasta with Cheddar Cheese Sauce

SERVES 6 AS A FIRST COURSE

Cheddar, one of America's finest cheeses, is excellent for cooking. It melts well and blends wonderfully with heavy cream. In this sauce its taste softens and mellows slightly. The results are outstanding.

2 to 2½ cups creme fraîche or 3 cups of heavy cream reduced to 2½ cups

1¼ pounds Cheddar cheese, chopped or crumbled, Vermont preferred

1 pound fresh linguine or fettucine

1¼ cups (5 ounces) grated Parmigiano cheese (Reggiano or Grana Padano)

Salt

White pepper

1. In a medium saucepan, bring the crème fraîche to a simmer over medium heat. (If you're using heavy cream, reduce it over medium-high heat until it starts to thicken. This should represent a 20-25 percent reduction).

2. Add the chopped or crumbled Cheddar cheese and the grated Parmigiano cheese to the simmering cream. This will cause the cooking temperature of the cream to drop. Maintain the medium-high heat and stir the mixture constantly until it returns to a simmer. (Do not allow the mixture to boil or the cheese will separate.) When the mixture has returned to a simmer, remove the pan from the heat. Continue to stir until the cheese is thoroughly melted in. Then stir in 1 teaspoon of white pepper. (Transfer the prepared sauce to the top of a double boiler. Cover, and keep it warm over simmering water while you cook the pasta.)

3. Bring 4 quarts of water with 3 tablespoons of salt to a boil. Add the pasta and cook until al dente. Drain the pasta well.

4. Transfer the sauce to a large mixing bowl. Add the pasta to the bowl and mix gently and thoroughly. Serve on individual plates.

AGED Vermont CHEDDAR

To Make Crème Fraîche

MAKES 1 CUP

1 cup heavy cream

1 teaspoon plain yogurt

1 teaspoon buttermilk

1. In a saucepan, scald the cream. Remove the pan from the heat and let the cream cool to 100°, testing the temperature with a thermometer.

2. Stir in the yogurt and buttermilk until well blended. Then pour the mixture into a container, cover, and keep it in a warm place, about 80-90°, overnight or until it has thickened. Chill until ready to use.

NOTE:
Crème fraîche, a thickened heavy cream, will keep for 7-10 days in the refrigerator. Be sure to use a yogurt with active enzymes, such as Dannon or Columbo.

Pasta with Barbeque Sauce

SERVES 4 AS A FIRST COURSE

This remarkable dish came about because of a relatively empty refrigerator. We had been doing some research at Pasta & Cheese into the possibility of adding some barbeque dishes at one of our restaurants. One night, shortly after deciding against the idea, I had a friend over for dinner. All I had in the house was the sauce which we had made during our research on barbeque techniques, and some linguine from Pasta & Cheese. I put the two together and, as improbable as I thought the combination would be at the outset, I found this dish to be extraordinary.

1 cup heavy cream

1 recipe barbeque sauce, p. 134

¾ pound fresh linguine or
   fettucine

Bring the cream to a boil in a saucepan over medium-high heat. Reduce it by ⅓. Lower the heat to medium, add the barbeque sauce, and let the mixture simmer for 5 minutes, stirring frequently so that it doesn't burn. Remove the sauce from the heat, cover the pan, and let it rest while you cook the pasta. Reheat over low heat, stirring so the sauce doesn't burn before mixing with the pasta.

Pasta with Creamy Tomato Sauce

SERVES 6 AS A FIRST COURSE

This rich, delicious, creamy tomato sauce can be served on any pasta, with broiled chicken or broiled fish, or as the sauce for the veal parmigiano, p. 138. If fresh tomatoes are not of good quality, I prefer using Italian canned tomatoes.

3	pounds fresh plum tomatoes or 1 large (2 lbs., 3 oz.) can peeled tomatoes, drained	2½	cups chicken broth
3	tablespoons unsalted butter	1¼	cups heavy cream
1½	cups finely chopped yellow onions	1	pound fresh linguine or fettucine
1¼	cups dry white wine		Salt
			Pepper

NOTE: *For variety, try adding one of the following ingredients: 3 ounces dried porcini mushrooms which have been soaked until soft, washed well, dried, and chopped (add these to the onion mixture during step 4, with the tomatoes); or 2 ounces pâté de campagne, p. 52, crumbled (add during step 5, with the cream).*

1. In a medium saucepan, bring 2 quarts of water to a boil. Add the fresh tomatoes and submerge them for 20 seconds. (This blanches them and makes it possible for their skins to slide off easily.) Drain and rinse the tomatoes under cold water. When they are cool enough to handle, peel or slip their skins off. Then cut the peeled tomatoes in half crosswise and, using your hands, squeeze out the seeds and juice into a bowl. Reserve the tomato pieces, discarding the juice and seeds. (If you are using canned tomatoes, drain off any excess liquid.)

2. Melt the butter in a medium saucepan and, over medium heat, sauté the onions until they just begin to brown (about 10 minutes). Lower the heat if they start to burn.

3. Add the wine to the sautéed onions. Bring the mixture to a boil and reduce the liquid until approximately 3 tablespoons remain. Then add the chicken stock. Return the mixture to a boil and reduce the liquid until ½ cup remains.

4. In a food processor fitted with the steel blade, purée the tomatoes. Add the purée to the onion mixture and, over medium heat, bring the liquid to a boil. Then reduce to a slow simmer and cook for 30 minutes.

5. Add the cream and continue to cook at a slow simmer for 10 minutes, stirring frequently. Season with salt and pepper. (Transfer the prepared sauce to the top of a double boiler. Cover, and keep it warm over simmering water while you cook the pasta.)

6. Bring 4 quarts of water with 3 tablespoons of salt to a boil. Add the pasta and cook until it is al dente. Drain the pasta well. Transfer the sauce to a large mixing bowl. Then add the pasta to the bowl. Mix gently and thoroughly and serve on individual plates.

NOTE: *Only fully ripe tomatoes (rich red, slightly soft — not mushy) should be stored in the refrigerator — others should be kept at room temperature, away from direct sunlight, to ripen.*

NOTE:
A double boiler is simply a heatproof bowl suspended over a pot containing boiling water. It is used to cook foods that need to be protected from overheating, such as dishes containing eggs or cream.

Pasta with Pesto

SERVES 2-3 AS A FIRST COURSE

1½ cups basil, stems removed, washed and dried	2 cloves garlic
	1 cup olive oil
½ cup pignoli nuts (or walnuts if pignoli nuts are not available)	½ pound capelli d'angelo pasta
	Salt
½ cup (4 ounces) grated Parmigiano cheese (Reggiano or Grana Padano)	Pepper

1. Combine the basil leaves, nuts, cheese, garlic, ½ teaspoon of salt and ¼ teaspoon of pepper in the bowl of a food processor fitted with the steel blade. Begin to process and immediately start pouring in the oil in a slow steady stream, continuing until all the oil has been added. Stop the machine and scrape down any leaves that stick to the side of the bowl. When the pesto has been processed into a smooth purée (about 1 minute), stop the machine and transfer the mixture to a bowl. Cover with plastic wrap until ready to use.

2. Bring 4 quarts of water and 3 tablespoons of salt to a boil. Add the pasta and cook until it is al dente. Drain the pasta well.

3. Transfer the sauce to a large mixing bowl. Add the pasta to the bowl. Mix thoroughly and gently. Serve on individual plates.

Pasta with Roquefort Sauce

SERVES 6 AS A FIRST COURSE

There was a little restaurant, a few steps from the Post Centrale in Nice, that specialized in Italian food. I went there two years before I began Pasta & Cheese. I'm not sure that it still exists. It was there that I first had a Roquefort sauce over pasta. I've thought about that sauce often in the years since, but until writing this book I never attempted to recreate the spectacular taste. This recipe certainly matches my taste memory. I shouldn't have waited so long. The result of a carefully blended combination of cabbage, cauliflower, and Roquefort makes this, without question, one of the best pasta sauces that I have ever eaten. The last time I made this dish I served it as a first course before veal with eggplant, p. 140. It was a hit.

4 tablespoons (½ stick) unsalted butter	10-12 ounces Roquefort cheese, or to taste
1½ cups chopped onion	1 pound fresh green fettucine or linguine
2 cups chopped cabbage	Salt
2 cups chopped cauliflower	Pepper
2 cups chicken broth (or 1 14-oz can)	
1½ cups heavy cream	

1. In a medium saucepan, melt the butter and sauté the onions, stirring frequently, over medium-high heat for 7 minutes. Lower the heat if the onions start to burn. Add the cabbage and cauliflower, lower the heat to medium and cover the pan. Continue cooking, stirring frequently, until the vegetables are very tender, about 15 minutes.

2. Uncover the pan and add the chicken broth. Turn the heat up to medium-high and reduce the liquid until it has almost evaporated. This should take 10-15 minutes. Add the cream and reduce again over medium-high heat until it has reduced by about a third and the liquid is quite thick. (There will be about 2½ cups of sauce.)

3. Transfer the sauce to a food processor fitted with the steel blade and purée for about 10 seconds. Stop the machine. Add the cheese to the purée, crumbling it into small pieces as you do so. Process until very smooth. Taste and season with salt and pepper if needed. (Transfer the prepared sauce to the top of a double boiler, cover and keep warm over simmering water as you cook the pasta.)

4. Bring 4 quarts of water with 3 tablespoons of salt to a boil. Add the pasta and cook until al dente. Drain well.

5. Transfer the sauce to a large mixing bowl. Add the pasta to the bowl and mix gently and thoroughly. Serve on individual plates.

NOTE: *Cauliflower, available throughout the year, is most abundant from September through January. Buy cauliflower with white or cream colored curds that are clean and compact. Don't worry if the texture of the curds appears slightly grainy — it doesn't affect the taste or quality.*

Pasta Smothered with Onions

SERVES 6 AS A FIRST COURSE

When onions are cooked slowly, as they are in this remarkable sauce, their naturally sharp flavor attains a sweetness that's the result of the slow release of the onions' natural sugars. Here, the combination of sweet onions and Parmigiano cheese produces a spectacular flavor — you're well rewarded for the time it takes to cook the onions thoroughly. To me, this dish typifies everything I've ever liked about well-cooked smothered onions as well as everything I've ever liked about well-seasoned pasta.

4 tablespoons (½ stick) unsalted butter	1 cup (4 ounces) grated Parmigiano cheese (Reggiano or Grana Padano)
2 tablespoons olive oil	5 tablespoons fresh chopped parsley
8 cups chopped yellow onions	Salt
1 cup white wine	Pepper
2½ cups chicken broth	
1 pound fresh linguine or fettucine	

NOTE:
Shop for onions that are firm to the touch and have small necks. They should be covered with a thin, papery shell and be blemish-free. Avoid onions with wet or soft necks, and those that have begun to sprout. Onions are available throughout the year.

1. In a large saucepan, melt the butter with the oil over low heat. Add the onions, cover, and simmer over a low to medium heat for 45 minutes. Stir the onions occasionally so that they cook evenly. Then uncover the onions, increase the heat to medium-high and cook, stirring frequently, until almost all the moisture has evaporated and the onions are well-browned. (Lower the heat if the onions start to burn.)

2. Add the wine and reduce until it is almost evaporated. Then add the chicken broth and reduce until the onion mixture is thick. There should be only about ¾ of a cup of liquid remaining. (Transfer the prepared sauce to the top of a double boiler. Cover, and keep it warm over simmering water while you cook the pasta.)

3. Bring 4 quarts of water with 3 tablespoons of salt to a boil. Add the pasta and cook until it is al dente. Drain well.

4. Transfer the sauce to a large mixing bowl. Add the pasta to the bowl. Add the Parmigiano, parsley, and salt and pepper to taste. Mix gently and thoroughly. Serve on individual plates.

Pasta with Gorgonzola

SERVES 6 AS A FIRST COURSE

This is one of my favorites. If I could have only one cheese for the rest of my life, and I had to make the choice, the nod would go to Gorgonzola. Its creamy, soft consistency coupled with a memorable taste makes for a compelling sauce on a pasta.

1   pound fresh spinach linguine or fettucine

4   tablespoons unsalted butter (½ stick)

2   cups heavy cream

10 ounces creamy Dolcelatte Gorgonzola cheese

4   tablespoons grated Parmigiano cheese (Reggiano or Grana Padano)

Salt

Pepper

1. In a medium saucepan, reduce the cream over medium-high heat until 1½-1¾ cups remain and the cream has thickened. (This will take approximately 7-8 minutes.) Crumble the Gorgonzola into the cream and stir until it is completely melted in. (Do not boil once the cheese has been added or the sauce will separate.) Add the Parmigiano and ¾ teaspoon of pepper and stir until melted. Taste and add salt if needed. (Transfer the prepared sauce to the top of a double boiler. Cover, and keep it warm over simmering water while you cook the pasta.)

2. Bring 4 quarts of water and 3 tablespoons of salt to a boil. Add the pasta and cook until al dente. Drain the pasta well. Add the butter to the sauce and stir until it has melted. Transfer the sauce to a large mixing bowl. Add the pasta to the bowl. Mix well and serve on individual plates.

Menu
Pasta with
Gorgonzola Sauce
Roast Duck
Purée of Peas
Tarte Tatin

Pasta with Meat Sauce

SERVES 6 AS A FIRST COURSE, 4 AS A MAIN COURSE

4 ounces bacon (about 4 slices), cut into 1-inch pieces

4 cups chopped yellow onion

1 tablespoon finely minced garlic (about 5 cloves)

2 cups hearty red wine

4 tablespoons safflower or corn oil

½ pound lean ground beef, round or chuck

⅔ pound ground pork

1 14-ounce can beef broth

2 large (35-ounce) cans peeled tomatoes, drained and puréed

1 bay leaf

¼ teaspoon thyme

¼ teaspoon Maggi seasoning

Dash of Tabasco® sauce

1 pound fresh linguine or fettucine

Salt, pepper

1. In a heavy pan, cook the bacon over medium-high heat, separating the bacon pieces and turning them frequently until crisp. Remove the bacon with a slotted spoon, leaving the fat in the pan, and save the bacon for another use. Add the onion to the pan and sauté over medium-high heat for 15-20 minutes, stirring frequently until golden brown. (Lower the heat if necessary to prevent burning.) Add the garlic and sauté for 2 more minutes. To deglaze the pan, add the wine to the onions, scraping the pan well with a spatula.

2. Add the oil to a heavy pan set over high heat. Add the meat and brown, stirring frequently to break up any lumps. The meat should be thoroughly cooked (about 10 minutes). With a slotted spoon, transfer the meat into the pot with the onions and wine. Discard any oil remaining in the pan. Add the beef broth to the heavy frying pan and bring it to a boil over high heat. Then pour it into the meat mixture.

3. Let the liquid come to a boil and reduce until it has almost completely evaporated. Add the tomatoes, bay leaf, thyme, Maggi seasoning, and Tabasco® sauce. Return the sauce to a boil, lower the heat, and let the sauce simmer, stirring frequently, for 30 minutes or until it has thickened to the desired consistency. Remove the bay leaf. Season with salt and pepper. (Transfer the prepared sauce to the top of a double boiler. Cover, and keep it warm over simmering water while you cook the pasta.) This sauce will keep for several days in the refrigerator or for several weeks in the freezer.

4. Bring 4 quarts of water with 3 tablespoons of salt to a boil. Add the pasta and cook until al dente. Drain well.

5. Transfer the sauce to a large mixing bowl. Add the pasta to the bowl and mix gently and thoroughly. Serve on individual plates.

Pasta with Mussel Sauce

SERVES 6 AS A FIRST COURSE

The broth from the steamed mussels and wine produces a concentrated flavor that enhances the pasta. The broth is then reduced, further enriching its flavor and giving this dish great character. This recipe uses only about a third of the cooked mussels but, because mussels are inexpensive and versatile, and because you want a rich sauce, it's worth cooking six quarts. The remaining mussels may be served as a first course either mixed with mustard mayonnaise, p.168, or served with vinaigrette, p.170, and chopped red onion on a leaf of Boston or Bibb lettuce.

6	quarts mussels (about 10 pounds)	½	cup finely chopped parsley
2½	cups dry white wine	¼	cup dry sherry
5	shallots, minced	1	pound fresh linguine or fettucine
1	bay leaf	Salt	
3	cups heavy cream		

1. Rinse the mussels several times, pulling off the beards and discarding any mussels that are already open. In a large pot, place the wine with shallots, 1½ teaspoons pepper, and the bay leaf and bring to a boil. Then add the mussels, cover the pot, and let them steam at high heat until they open (about 2-3 minutes). Remove the pot from the heat to cool.

2. When the mussels are cool enough to handle, pour the mussel liquid into a mixing bowl, getting as much liquid as you can from the pot. Remove the mussel shells (in the summer, look out for tiny crabs that sometimes live in the shells).

3. Line a sieve or colander with 4 or more layers of dampened cheesecloth, set it over a saucepan, and strain the mussel liquid through it into the pan.

4. Over medium-high heat, bring the mussel broth in the saucepan to a boil and reduce it until ½ cup of liquid remains. Skim it if necessary. Stir in the cream and let it boil until it reduces to half its volume. (The sauce should be very thick.) Stir in the parsley and salt to taste. Then add the sherry and 35-40 of the shelled mussels. Cover the pan and keep it warm over a very low heat.

5. In a large pot bring 4 quarts of water and 3 tablespoons of salt to a boil. Add the pasta and cook until al dente. Drain the pasta well.

6. Transfer the sauce to a large mixing bowl. Add the pasta to the bowl. Mix gently and thoroughly. Sprinkle with the finely chopped parsley and serve on individual plates.

Pasta and Cream Sauce with Morels

SERVES 6-7 AS A FIRST COURSE, 4 AS A MAIN COURSE

The musky taste of morels, sponge-like wild mushrooms, makes this an outstanding sauce. Don't sprinkle it with cheese — you will only mask the sauce's unique flavor.

1	cup dried morels	¼	cup sherry, dry or medium-dry
4	shallots, peeled and finely chopped	1	pound fresh linguine
1½	cups dry white wine		Salt
3½	cups heavy cream		White pepper

1. Soak the morels in a bowl of water to soften them so they can be easily cut. When they are soaked they will puff up like a sponge. Slice them in half lengthwise and rinse the pieces well. Squeeze the excess moisture out of the mushrooms and drain on paper towels.

2. Add the shallots and wine to a medium sauce pan, bring to a boil over medium-high heat and reduce the liquid to ¼ cup. (This will take approximately 5 minutes.) Then add the cream and the morels. Return the mixture to a boil, still over medium-high heat, and reduce again, until ⅔ of the sauce remains or a desired consistency is reached. Season with the salt and white pepper to taste. Add the sherry. Continue to cook until the sauce has returned to a simmer. Then remove the pan from the heat. (Transfer the prepared sauce to the top of a double boiler. Cover, and keep it warm over simmering water while you cook the pasta.)

3. Bring 4 quarts of water and 3 tablespoons of salt to a boil. Add the pasta and cook until al dente. Drain well.

4. Transfer the sauce to a mixing bowl. Add the pasta, mix well, and serve on individual plates, garnished with chopped parsley.

It's important to rinse all of the sand and dirt from the morels

Fettucine Alfredo

SERVES 6 AS A FIRST COURSE

This dish is as basic to the Italian kitchen as quiche Lorraine is to the French kitchen. This fettucine Alfredo is special. The use of whipped cream results in a sauce that is thoroughly aerated and thus lighter than any I have ever tasted.

1	cup heavy cream	1	cup Parmigiano cheese (Reggiano or Grana Padano) freshly grated
12	tablespoons (1½ sticks) unsalted butter		Nutmeg, freshly grated
1	pound fresh fettucine		Salt
1	egg yolk, lightly beaten		Pepper, freshly ground

1. Whip the cream until it holds stiff peaks. Reserve.

2. In a large heavy pan, melt the butter over medium heat. Turn off the heat and reserve.

3. Bring 4 quarts of water with 3 tablespoons of salt to a boil. Add the pasta and cook until it is al dente. Drain the pasta well.

4. Add the fettucine to the pan with the melted butter. Turn the heat to medium and toss the butter and pasta thoroughly while the pan is on the heat.

5. Stir the cream gently into the fettucine. Then add the beaten egg yolk, Parmigiano, pepper, and nutmeg to taste. Toss well in the pan. Serve on individual plates.

Pasta with Salami

SERVES 6 AS A FIRST COURSE

8 medium slices Genoa salami	2 tablespoons chopped fresh parsley
2 cloves garlic, peeled	Grated Parmigiano cheese (Reggiano or Grana Padano) to taste
3 tablespoons olive oil	
4 tablespoons (½ stick) unsalted butter, cut into 4 pieces	Salt
1 pound fresh fettucine	Pepper

1. Cut the salami into julienne strips about ¼-inch wide. Bruise the garlic by pressing on it with the side of a large knife. (This allows the flavor to bleed out easily as it cooks.) Heat the oil in a heavy pan over a medium-high heat, add the salami, ½ teaspoon of pepper and the bruised garlic cloves and sauté until the salami is well browned. (This should take approximately 5 minutes.) Discard the garlic as soon as it browns. Turn off the heat, add the butter to the pan, and let it melt into the mixture while you cook the pasta. (Transfer the prepared sauce to the top of a double boiler. Cover, and keep it warm over simmering water.)

2. Bring 4 quarts of water with 3 tablespoons of salt to a boil. Add the pasta and cook until it is al dente. Drain the pasta well.

3. Transfer the salami mixture to a large mixing bowl. Mix the salami and the melted butter well and add salt to taste. Add the pasta, toss gently and thoroughly, and serve on individual plates. Sprinkle parsley over the top of each serving. Accent with a sprinkling of Parmigiano cheese to taste.

Canneloni

SERVES 4 AS A MAIN COURSE

¼ pound ground beef	1 egg yolk
¼ pound ground pork	¼ cup creamy tomato sauce (see p. 84)
1 bay leaf	3 tablespoons bread crumbs
¼ teaspoon rosemary	2 dashes Tabasco® sauce
¼ teaspoon thyme	1 recipe pasta, p. 20, or 1 pound prepared pasta sheets
2-3 cloves garlic, minced (½ tablespoon)	3 cups tomato sauce
¼ cup dry white wine	1 cup grated Parmigiano cheese (Reggiano or Grana Padano)
½ cup chicken broth	1 cup Mozzarella cheese, cut into ½-inch cubes
½ pound spinach, trimmed and washed (see note p.96)	Salt, pepper
¼ cup ricotta cheese	

(see note p.96)

NOTE:
Each pound of spinach, after cleaning and cooking, gives you about ½ cup of cooked and squeezed spinach. If there is a bit more or less on hand, don't worry; use what you have. Because of the work involved in washing, cooking, cooling, and squeezing spinach, I've always felt that creamed spinach is a bargain in good restaurants.

1. In a large mixing bowl, combine the ground beef, ground pork, bay leaf, rosemary, thyme, and garlic and mix well. Sauté this meat mixture in a large heavy pan over high heat, breaking the lumps into small pieces with a metal spatula. When the mixture is well cooked, about 5 minutes, transfer it to a strainer and drain off the fat. Transfer the mixture to a mixing bowl and remove the bay leaf. Reserve.

2. In a medium saucepan, over high heat, combine the wine and chicken broth and reduce it until only 2 tablespoons remain. Add this reduced mixture to the meat.

3. Bring 3 quarts of water and 2 tablespoons of salt to boil in a large pot. Add the trimmed and washed spinach and cook, stirring frequently, for 3 minutes. Then drain the spinach in a colander and rinse it under cold running water until it is cool. Squeeze all of the water out of the spinach with your hands. Then finely chop the spinach.

4. Add the chopped spinach, ricotta cheese, egg yolk, tomato sauce, and bread crumbs to the meat mixture and mix well. Taste and season with salt, pepper, and Tabasco® sauce.

5. Prepare and roll out the pasta dough according to the instructions on p. 20. Cut the pasta sheets into 5-inch squares. In a large pot bring 4 quarts of water and 3 tablespoons of salt to a boil and cook the pasta squares for 30 seconds. Drain the pasta in a colander and rinse under cold running water until it is cool.

6. Lay the pasta squares on a work table and dry off any excess water with a paper towel. Lightly spread about ¼ cup of the meat mixture over the bottom third of each of the pasta squares and roll the pasta up.

7. Preheat the oven to 350°. Spread a thin layer of creamy tomato sauce or Pasta & Cheese tomato sauce over the bottom of a large baking dish. Lay the canneloni on top of the sauce and cover with the remaining sauce. In the bowl of a food processor fitted with the steel blade, process the Mozzarella and Parmigiano cheeses until the Mozzarella is finely chopped. Sprinkle the cheese mixture over the canneloni. Bake in the preheated 350° oven for 25 minutes or until the canneloni is heated through. Serve.

Lasagna

SERVES 8-10 AS A MAIN COURSE

This rich, robust lasagna has three alternating layers of pasta, sauce, and cheese. The mild, sweet, full-bodied flavor of Fontina cheese gives this dish a spectacular taste. If Fontina is not available, grated Mozarella can be substituted but its mild flavor must be boosted with 1 cup of grated Parmigiano sprinkled evenly over each layer.

1   tablespoon unsalted butter, softened

⅔   pound lasagna noodles (approximately fifteen 2 ¼-inch pieces)

6   cups meat sauce, p. 90, or creamy tomato sauce with either the pâté or sausage, p. 84.

1¼   pounds Italian Fontina, grated

Salt

1. Preheat the oven to 350°. Butter a 9 x 12-inch baking dish with 1 tablespoon of softened butter.

2. Bring 4 quarts of water and 3 tablespoons of salt to a boil. Add the lasagna and cook until al dente. Drain the pasta in a colander and rinse with cold water until it is cool enough to handle.

3. Carefully remove enough pieces of lasagna to make a single layer in the bottom of the pan and dry these pieces on paper towels so there is no excess moisture. Cover the pan with the pieces. Spread 1½ cups of meat sauce over the pasta layer, then sprinkle approximately ⅓ of the grated Fontina over the sauce.

4. Place another layer of pasta over the cheese. Cover this layer with 1½ cups of the meat sauce and cover the sauce with half of the remaining cheese. Then make a third and final layer in the same order — pasta, meat sauce, and cheese.

5. Bake the lasagna, uncovered, in the preheated oven for 45 minutes. Remove it from the oven and let it rest for at least 10 minutes before serving. (This allows time for the flavors to settle.) You can cook this dish in advance — the day before is best. If you do make it in advance, reheat it covered with aluminum foil in a preheated 350° oven for 20 minutes, or until heated through.

Quadrettini

I was introduced to this very special dish in the late '70s by Mario Orlandi, who at the time was the captain at the San Marino Restaurant in New York City. The San Marino has since closed but Mario, who now owns the Rigoletto Restaurant on East 53rd Street in New York, still features this wonderful pasta specialty. He was kind enough to give me the recipe for "little pieces" when I first tried it. I've experimented with it over the years and what follows is my revision of a marvelous dish. In this dish, spinach is added separately to the small pieces of cooked pasta and blends with the flavors and textures of the prosciutto and the Parmigiano. The combination of these flavors together results in a truly unusual taste experience.

1   pound fresh spinach, washed, with the stems removed

1   cup beef broth

2   tablespoons (¼ stick) unsalted butter

2   medium slices prosciutto (3 ounces), cut into ¼-½ inch pieces

1   cup grated Parmigiano cheese (Reggiano or Grana Padano)

8   ounces fresh fettucine, broken or cut into approximately ¼-inch pieces

Salt

Pepper

1. Bring 4 quarts of water and 3 tablespoons of salt to a boil. Remove the stems from the spinach and discard. Add the spinach leaves to the water and return the water to a boil. Cook for 3 minutes in the boiling water, then drain the leaves in a colander. Rinse the spinach with cold water until it has cooled. Using your hands, squeeze the spinach tightly to remove all of the water. Then combine the spinach and the beef broth in the bowl of a food processor fitted with the steel blade. Purée and reserve.

2. In a large saucepan, melt the butter and sauté the prosciutto over medium heat for 5 minutes or until the fat is rendered out. Add the spinach mixture, the Parmigiano cheese, and salt and pepper to taste to the saucepan and mix well.

3. Bring 4 quarts of water and 3 tablespoons of salt to a boil. Add the pasta pieces and cook until they are al dente. Drain the pasta well and add to the saucepan with the spinach mixture.

4. Cook the mixture over medium heat, stirring constantly, until the mixture is heated through. Serve on individual plates.

Manicotti

SERVES 4 AS A LIGHT MAIN COURSE

1 pound fresh spinach, stemmed and washed (see note on p. 96)

1 cup ricotta cheese

1¾ cups grated Parmigiano cheese (Reggiano or Grana Padano)

1 recipe pasta dough, p. 20, or 1 pound prepared pasta sheets

3 cups creamy tomato sauce (see p. 84)

1 cup mozzarella cheese, cut into ½-inch squares

Salt

Pepper

1. In a large pot bring 4 quarts of water with 3 tablespoons of salt to a boil. Cook the spinach for 3 minutes. Drain in a colander and then rinse under cold running water until it is cool enough to handle. Using your hands, squeeze all of the water from the spinach. In the bowl of a food processor fitted with the steel blade, process the spinach until it is puréed.

2. In a mixing bowl, combine the spinach, ricotta, and ¾ cup of the Parmigiano and mix well. Taste and season with salt and pepper.

3. If you're using homemade fresh pasta, prepare and roll out the dough according to instructions on p. 20, then cut the dough into 5-inch squares. If you're using prepared pasta sheets, simply cut the sheet into 5-inch squares. Bring 4 quarts of water and 3 tablespoons of salt to a boil and blanch the pasta for 30 seconds. Drain the pasta in a colander and rinse it under cold running water until it is cool.

4. Dry the pasta squares carefully with paper towels. Place approximately ⅓ cup of the spinach and cheese mixture in a strip across a pasta square and roll up. Repeat with the remaining pasta squares and filling.

5. Preheat the oven to 350°. Spread a thin layer of tomato sauce over the bottom of an ovenproof casserole and arrange the manicotti in the dish. Spoon the remaining tomato sauce over the manicotti. In the bowl of a food processor fitted with the steel blade, process the mozzarella and 1 cup of Parmigiano cheese until the mozzarella is finely chopped. Sprinkle the cheese mixture over the manicotti and bake in the preheated oven for 25 minutes or until the manicotti is heated through. Serve.

Crabmeat Ravioli

SERVES 4 AS A FIRST COURSE

Here is a deliciously rich ravioli that is quite simple to prepare. It makes a welcome change from the more typical ravioli fillings. Be certain to pick through the crabmeat carefully to remove any bits of shell or cartilage.

1¼ cups heavy cream	½ pound crabmeat, fresh if available
½ cup Gruyère cheese	1 egg, beaten (for binding the pasta)
¼ cup grated Parmigiano cheese (Reggiano or Grana Padano)	1 recipe pasta dough, p. 20
1 egg yolk	Salt, white pepper

1. Bring 1 cup of heavy cream to a boil in a medium saucepan. Simmer for 5 minutes. Remove the pan from the flame and add the Gruyere cheese. Stir until the cheese melts. Add ¼ teaspoon of white pepper and the Parmigiano cheese and stir, blending thoroughly.

2. Let the sauce rest for 10 minutes. Then stir in the egg yolk.

3. Add ½ cup of the cooled sauce to a mixing bowl and stir in the crabmeat. This mixture is the filling for the ravioli. Reserve the remaining sauce to serve over the finished ravioli.

4. Roll out half the pasta with a machine or by hand until it is as thin as you can roll it without tearing the dough. Mark the pasta sheet lightly into 2-inch squares using a pastry cutter. Place a mound of crabmeat filling (about 1½ teaspoons) in the center of each of the squares. Dip a pastry brush into the beaten egg and brush the pasta in the spaces between the mounds of filling. (This will hold the layers of pasta together when they are cooking.) Roll the remaining dough out into a matching thin pasta sheet. Place this sheet lightly on top of the filled sheet. Press down gently between the mounds of filling. Then cut the ravioli squares apart with a pastry cutter or wheel, or a sharp knife. Press the edges of each individual ravioli piece together to seal.

5. Reheat the reserved cheese and cream sauce over low heat. Whip the remaining ¼ cup of heavy cream until it is stiff and holds peaks. Fold the whipped cream gently into the sauce. Preheat the broiler.

6. Bring 4 quarts of water and 3 tablespoons of salt to a boil. Gently add the ravioli to the boiling water and cook for 3 minutes. Drain the ravioli well and transfer it to a baking dish. Spoon the reserved sauce over the ravioli. Place the dish in the broiler until the top begins to just turn golden brown (about 2-3 minutes). Serve.

Mushroom Ravioli with Tomato Sauce

SERVES 4 AS A FIRST COURSE

1   recipe fresh pasta, p. 20

1   recipe mushroom filling, p. 190

1   egg, beaten (for binding the
    pasta)

1   recipe creamy tomato sauce,
    p. 84

Salt

1. Roll out half of the pasta dough with a machine or by hand until
    it is as thin as you can roll it without tearing the dough. Mark
    the pasta sheet lightly into 2-inch squares using a pastry cutter.
    Place 1 tablespoon of mushroom filling neatly in the center of each
    square. Dip a pastry brush into the beaten egg and brush the pasta
    in the spaces between the mounds of filling. (This will bind the
    layers of pasta together while they are cooking.)

2. Roll the remaining dough out into a matching thin pasta sheet.
    Place this sheet lightly on top of the filled sheet. Press down gently
    between the mounds of filling. Then cut the ravioli squares apart
    with a pastry cutter or wheel, or a sharp knife. Press the edges
    of each individual ravioli piece together to seal.

3. In a large pot, bring 4 quarts of water and 3 tablespoons of salt to
    a boil. Add the ravioli, let the water return to a boil and cook for
    3 minutes. Then drain the ravioli in a colander. Arrange the cooked
    ravioli on a large platter or in a large bowl or individual plates
    or bowls. Cover the ravioli with the tomato sauce and serve.

Chicken Tetrazzini

SERVES 4

2	whole chicken breasts (separated into 4 halves), skinned, boned, and well trimmed	2	tablespoons safflower oil
½	cup dry white wine	2	egg yolks
2	cups chicken broth	1	cup grated Gruyère cheese
3	tablespoons unsalted butter	½	cup grated Parmigiano cheese (Reggiano or Grana Padano)
3	tablespoons flour	½	cup heavy cream
1	pound dry fettucine		Salt
			Pepper

1. Preheat the oven to 350°. Rub the chicken breasts with 1 teaspoon of salt and set aside. Combine the wine and the chicken broth in a saucepan and bring the liquid to a simmer. Add the salted chicken, lower the heat to just below a simmer, and poach for 10-12 minutes, turning occasionally. Transfer the breasts to a plate and spread them out so they cool quickly. Leave the liquid in the pan.

2. In a medium saucepan over medium heat, melt the butter and add the flour. Cook the mixture, whisking constantly with a wooden spoon, for 3-4 minutes, until it is hot and bubbling but not browned. This is a roux.

3. Return the wine and broth mixture to a boil and pour it into the roux, whisking constantly. Lower the heat to a slow simmer and stir frequently for 10 minutes. Remove the sauce from the heat.

4. Bring 4 quarts of water with 3 tablespoons of salt to a boil over high heat. Add the pasta and cook until al dente. Drain the pasta in a colander, rinse with cold water, and transfer it to a bowl. Add oil and toss well. Reserve at room temperature.

5. Add the egg yolks to the sauce and whisk for one minute. Add the cheeses and salt and pepper to taste and mix well using a rubber spatula. Whip the heavy cream until it holds peaks, then fold it into the sauce. Pour all but ¾ cup of this mixture over the pasta and mix well.

6. Cut the cooled chicken breasts into julienne strips 1½-inches long and ¼-inch wide (about the size of a string bean).

7. Place ⅓ of the pasta in an 8-inch soufflé dish or large casserole. Add ½ of the chicken. Add another ⅓ of the pasta, then the remaining chicken. Finally, top the layers with the remaining pasta and smooth the top with a spatula. Spread the remaining sauce over the top.

8. Bake in the preheated oven for 10-15 minutes or until heated through. Transfer the dish to the broiler, and brown the top (2-3 minutes). Serve.

Fowl

I've always enjoyed roast duck and roast chicken in French restaurants, and when I started Pasta & Cheese I made up my mind that we would sell roast ducks and chickens cooked "the right way." We did sell them for a few months several years ago, but I found that it was impossible to maintain the freshness we aimed for unless we cooked them to order in each store. That experience, however, gave me an opportunity to learn a great deal about the cooking of both ducks and chickens. I'm certain that if you prepare chicken, duck, or goose using the techniques that are suggested in the following recipes, you'll become devoted to the methods and delighted with the results.

I've also gone into detail about how to prepare and poach chicken breasts. Chicken breasts simmered in a broth, rather than boiled in water, offer superb flavor and texture. This is very important at Pasta & Cheese because we feature chicken breasts in salads, pot pies, and sandwiches. I'm convinced that the care we take in preparing chicken is one of the reasons behind the success of the Pasta & Cheese stores.

The Ultimate Roast Chicken

SERVES 4-6

Most recipes for homemade chicken call for sticking the chicken in the oven and leaving it there for a specific length of time. The resulting roast chicken seldom if ever tastes as good as the ones found in fine restaurants, where it is basted constantly. By treating the chicken with a garlic, lemon, and salt mixture at the outset, cooking at a very high temperature, and basting frequently, you'll get chicken that is crisp and moist. The basting requires extra effort, but the results are worth it.

1   3-pound roasting chicken

3   cloves garlic, peeled (2 cloves whole; 1 clove mashed)

1½ tablespoons lemon juice

5   large sprigs parsley (3 sprigs whole; 2 sprigs chopped)

8   tablespoons (1 stick) unsalted butter

Salt

Pepper

1. Preheat the oven to 450°. Rinse the chicken and pat it dry with paper towels. Rinse all the innards except the liver and place them in a small saucepan with 2½ cups of water. Bring to a simmer over medium heat and cook for 15-20 minutes. Remove the innards with tongs. Increase the heat, let the liquid come to a boil, and reduce until only 1½ cups remain. Strain it into a bowl and reserve.

2. Sprinkle 1½ teaspoons of salt and 1½ teaspoons of pepper inside the chicken. Add 2 whole cloves of garlic and 3 sprigs of parsley to the cavity. Truss the chicken. Combine the lemon juice, mashed garlic, ½ teaspoon of salt, and ½ teaspoon of pepper in a bowl. Rub or brush this mixture all over the outside of the chicken.

3. Heat the butter in a large, heavy pan with an ovenproof handle over medium heat until it begins to bubble. Add the chicken and sauté it, turning the bird quickly until it is basted all over with butter. Then turn the chicken onto its side in the pan and place the pan in the middle level of the preheated oven.

Parsley
— freshen by trimming off the ends and placing the stalks in cold water.

4. After five minutes, open the oven and check that the skin is not sticking to the pan. (If it is stuck, use a knife to loosen it but be careful to avoid tearing the skin.) Baste the chicken thoroughly with the pan juices and close the oven.

A good sauté pan has a vertical wall that measures about 2½"

2½"

5. Continue to roast for 1 hour, basting every 5 minutes with pan juices. This will result in a beautiful, even brown color. The skin will be crisp and the moisture will be locked in. After 15 minutes in the oven (on the third basting), turn the bird onto its other side. After 15 minutes on the second side (the sixth basting), turn the bird breast up and continue roasting in this position for the final ½ hour. Each time you baste, nudge the chicken to prevent it from sticking to the pan.

6. Transfer the chicken to a warm platter, cover, and let it rest at room temperature for 15 minutes while you prepare the sauce.

7. Pour the dark roasting butter from the pan into a measuring cup and reserve. Add 1 cup of the reserved innard stock to the pan and bring the liquid to a boil over high heat, deglazing any chicken sediment that has stuck to the pan with a wooden spoon. Reduce by half.

Unlike the sloping skillet these straight sides prevent the oil from splattering while you're frying

8. Pour off all but ⅓ of a cup of the reserved roasting butter, being careful to retain the brown butter and drippings that have settled to the bottom. Add this to the reduced stock. When the sauce has thickened, remove from the burner and transfer it to a sauceboat.

9. Carve the chicken and arrange the pieces on a platter or individual serving dishes. If necessary, reheat the sauce, strain it into a sauceboat, and pour it over the chicken. Sprinkle with the chopped parsley and serve immediately.

Poached Chicken Breasts

FOR 2 CHICKEN BREASTS (4 HALVES)

This book features a number of recipes that call for poached chicken breasts. At Pasta & Cheese, our method for poaching breasts is to cook them relatively slowly in a rich, simmering (not boiling) broth. Our chicken salad and curried chicken salad, p. 78, have been tremendous successes. Without question, the care that we take in poaching chicken is one of the major reasons behind this success.

1 quart chicken broth (College Inn brand preferred)	6-8 black peppercorns
1 cup chopped yellow onion	2 whole chicken breasts (separated into 4 halves), skinned, boned, and well trimmed
½ cup chopped carrot	
½ cup chopped celery	Salt
1 bay leaf	

1. In a large saucepan, combine the chicken broth, onion, carrot, celery, bay leaf, peppercorns, and salt. Bring the liquid to a boil and reduce the heat until the liquid is barely simmering. Add the breasts and poach them 10-12 minutes, depending on their size, taking care that the liquid never goes above a simmer. (If it boils, the chicken will lose flavor and be tough.)

2. Transfer the breasts to a plate to cool. If they are not going to be used immediately, you can store them in a little poaching liquid, covered tightly with plastic wrap, in the refrigerator. They can be kept for 3-4 days.

Sautéed Chicken Breasts in Brandied Cream Sauce

SERVES 4 AS A MAIN COURSE

4   whole chicken breasts (separated into 8 halves) skinned, boned, and well trimmed

1½   teaspoons thyme

½   cup flour

8   tablespoons (1 stick) unsalted butter

⅔   cup brandy

2   cups heavy cream

Salt

Pepper

1. Rinse the breasts well with cold water and dry them with paper towels. Mix 1 tablespoon of salt, 2 teaspoons of pepper, the thyme, and flour together in a small bowl. Rub each breast with the mixture and shake off the excess.

2. Melt the butter in a heavy sauté pan over medium heat and add the breasts. Sauté each for about 3-4 minutes or until the meat just turns white, searing the breasts and sealing in the juices. Do not let them brown. Transfer the breasts to a platter, cover, and reserve.

3. Pour the brandy into the pan, increase the heat to high, and let it reduce by half (3-4 minutes). Don't worry if the brandy flames—it will burn out within a few seconds. Add the cream and let it reduce, still over high heat, for 6-8 minutes until the cream begins to thicken. Lower the heat, if necessary, to prevent the cream from boiling over.

4. Add the breasts to the pan. Move and turn them until the butter, brandy, and cream are reduced to a thick sauce.

5. Transfer the breasts to heated plates or a platter. Spoon the sauce over the breasts and serve immediately.

Lemon Chicken with Glazed Orange Peel

SERVES 4

A subtle lemon taste mixed with rich brown sauce gives this chicken a superb flavor.

2	tablespoons + 1 teaspoon unsalted butter	½	cup brown sauce, p. 42 , or easy brown sauce, p. 44 (if brown sauce is unavailable, use 1 tablespoon arrowroot whisked into 2 tablespoons boiling water)
2	tablespoons safflower oil		
1	frying chicken (2-2½ pounds), quartered		Peel from 1 orange, cut into very fine julienne strips
3	medium shallots, chopped		Peel from 1 lemon, cut into very fine julienne strips

Juice from 1 lemon

1 cup chicken broth (if brown sauce is not available, increase to 1½ cups)

1 tablespoon sugar

Salt, pepper

1. Heat a 10-inch heavy sauté pan over medium-high heat and add 2 tablespoons butter and 2 tablespoons safflower oil. Add the chicken pieces skin side down, and increase heat to high. Cook until well browned on the bottom (about 3-5 minutes). Turn and continue to sauté for 3-5 minutes longer until browned. Transfer chicken pieces to a plate and reserve.

2. Pour half the fat from the pan and let the pan cool a bit (until the fat stops smoking) to avoid burning. Add the shallots and sauté 30 seconds. Add the lemon juice, chicken broth, and brown sauce. Bring to a boil and add the reserved chicken. Return to a simmer, cover, and simmer 25 minutes or until the chicken is done.

3. While the chicken is simmering, bring 1 cup of water to a boil in a small saucepan over high heat and add the lemon and orange peel. Cook for 2 minutes and then drain in a strainer. Return the peel to the saucepan and add 1 tablespoon water, 1 tablespoon sugar, and 1 teaspoon butter.

4. Stir to mix and bring to a boil over medium-high heat. Lower heat to medium and cook, stirring, until all the moisture evaporates. Turn the heat to low and continue cooking until the mixture caramelizes (browns). Transfer to a plate and let cool, not touching the peel until it has cooled.

5. When chicken is ready, transfer pieces to a platter, cover, and keep warm. Let the sauce reduce over medium-high heat for 3 minutes or until thickened. If brown sauce was not used, whisk dissolved arrowroot into the sauce 1 teaspoon at a time, until the desired consistency is reached.

6. Taste the sauce and add salt and pepper to taste. Place the chicken on individual plates or a platter and spoon the sauce over it. Sprinkle glazed orange and lemon peel on top and serve.

Chicken Hash

SERVES 4 AS A MAIN COURSE

There are many chicken hashes, the most renowned perhaps being the version that is served at New York's 21 Club. That was the inspiration for this particular dish. If there is any trick to making an outstanding hash it is to use top quality, very well-trimmed chicken.

¾ cup white wine	4 tablespoons flour
2 cups chicken broth	¼ cup dry sherry
3 whole chicken breasts (separated into 6 halves), skinned, boned, and well trimmed	2 egg yolks
	½ cup heavy cream
1 bay leaf	¾ cup grated Parmigiano cheese (Reggiano or Grana Padano)
4 tablespoons (½ stick) unsalted butter	Salt, pepper

1. Bring the wine and the chicken broth to a boil in a large saucepan. Rub the chicken breasts with salt and pepper and add to the liquid. Add the bay leaf. Lower the heat to a simmer and poach the chicken at just below a simmer for 10-12 minutes, depending on the size of the breasts. Transfer the breasts to a plate and let cool. Reserve the liquid.

2. Melt the butter in a saucepan. Add the flour and cook over medium heat, whisking constantly, for 3-4 minutes, until this roux is hot and bubbling but not browned. Allow to cool for 3-5 minutes.

3. Return the wine and broth mixture to a boil over medium-high heat. Pour it into the roux in a steady stream, whisking constantly. Place the pot over medium-high heat and, while whisking, return the sauce to a boil. Lower the heat to a simmer and let the sauce cook, stirring frequently, for 10 minutes. Add the sherry and remove the sauce from the heat. Cool at room temperature for 3 minutes.

4. Whisk the egg yolks into the sauce. Add salt and pepper to taste. Whip the cream until it holds stiff peaks. Mix one half of the whipped cream into the sauce to lighten it. Fold in the remaining cream gently but thoroughly. Cut the chicken in ½-inch cubes and add to the sauce. Mix gently and thoroughly.

5. Preheat the oven to 375°. Transfer the hash to a large, ovenproof casserole dish or 4 individual casseroles, sprinkle Parmigiano cheese over the top and bake, uncovered, for 10-15 minutes. Then place the casserole under the broiler for 1-2 minutes to brown the top. Using a spoon or a pastry bag, garnish the edge of the hash with purée of peas, p.161, and serve.

Poached Chicken with Chicken Quenelles in a Chive Sauce

SERVES 6 AS A MAIN COURSE

FOR POACHING:

3½ cups chicken broth

1 cup white wine

1 cup coarsely chopped
yellow onion

½ cup chopped carrot (1 carrot)

½ cup chopped celery (1 stalk)

1 garlic clove, halved

1 bay leaf

6 whole peppercorns

2 whole cloves

2 whole chicken breasts
(4 halves) for poaching,
skinned, boned, and trimmed

FOR THE SAUCE:

¼ cup heavy cream

1 tablespoon chopped chives

FOR THE VELOUTE:

4 tablespoons (½ stick) unsalted
butter

4 tablespoons flour

2 cups of reserved
poaching liquid

FOR THE QUENELLES:

5 tablespoons chilled veloute

Pinch of nutmeg

Salt

Pepper

2 whole chicken breasts
(4 halves) for the quenelles,
skinned, boned, and trimmed

TO POACH THE CHICKEN:

1. In a saucepan, combine the chicken broth, wine, onions, carrots, celery, garlic, bay leaf, peppercorns, and cloves. Bring the liquid to a boil over high heat, reduce the heat slightly and let it simmer for 5 minutes. Then add 2 of the whole chicken breasts and poach for 10-12 minutes, depending on their size.

2. Transfer the breasts to a plate to cool. When they are cool enough to handle, cut the meat into 1-inch pieces and reserve. Add any liquid that drains from the chicken to the poaching liquid. Then strain the poaching liquid and reserve over low heat.

TO MAKE THE VELOUTE:

3. In a saucepan, melt the butter and add the flour, whisking well. Cook the mixture over medium heat, whisking constantly, for 3-4 minutes, until it is hot and bubbling but not brown. Remove this roux from the heat and pour 2 cups of hot poaching liquid into it, stirring until smooth. Reserve the remaining poaching liquid.

4. Return the saucepan to low heat and simmer for 3 minutes or until the sauce has thickened. (This is now a veloute.) Remove the sauce from the heat. Transfer 5 tablespoons of the sauce to a plate and chill in the refrigerator. Cover the remaining sauce and reserve.

TO MAKE THE QUENELLES:

5. Cut 2 uncooked whole chicken breasts (4 halves) into bite-size pieces. Add these chicken pieces, the chilled veloute, 2 teaspoons of salt, ¼ teaspoon pepper, and a pinch of nutmeg to the bowl of a food processor fitted with the steel blade. Purée the mixture quickly until smooth. Then start the machine and pour the cream into the chicken mixture.

6. Butter the bottom of a large casserole. Wet 2 soup spoons with water. With one, scoop up a heaping spoonful of the quenelle mixture. With the second spoon, smooth and shape the quenelle by passing it quickly but gently back and forth between the two spoons until it resembles a 1½-inch long football. Lay each quenelle on the bottom of the casserole. (If they don't all fit in as one layer, do this in batches.)

7. Gently pour the reserved poaching liquid over the quenelles. Bring the liquid just to a simmer over medium heat, then lower the heat and poach the quenelles for 5-7 minutes, until they are cooked through. Be careful that the liquid remains at a gentle simmer.

8. Using a slotted spoon, transfer the quenelles to a buttered baking dish. Poach a second batch of quenelles, if necessary, and transfer them to the dish, saving the liquid. Then transfer the reserved poached chicken breast to the baking dish. Add 3 tablespoons of the poaching liquid. Cover the dish with aluminum foil and reserve at room temperature. (At this point there should be almost 2 cups of poaching liquid remaining.)

TO MAKE THE CHIVE SAUCE:

9. Whisk 1 cup of the remaining poaching liquid into the reserved veloute. If the sauce is too thick, add more poaching liquid to bring it to the proper consistency. Then bring the sauce to a boil over medium heat, lower the heat and simmer for 5 minutes. (The entire dish can be prepared in advance up to this point and reserved for up to 1 hour until ready to complete and serve.)

10. Preheat the oven to 350°. When ready to serve, reheat the poached chicken and the quenelles for 10-15 minutes until they are heated through. At the same time, return the sauce to a simmer. Add ¼ cup of cream and the chives and continue to simmer until the sauce is thoroughly heated, taking care that it does not boil. To serve, arrange the chicken and the quenelles on individual plates, spoon sauce over the top, and serve.

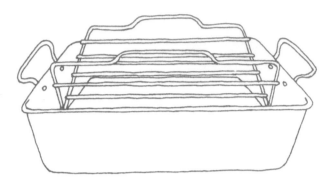

Roast Duck

SERVES 4

Everyone wants a roast duck that is crisp but not dry. After a great deal of experimentation at the Pasta & Cheese kitchens we discovered that by bringing the duck up to high heat at the beginning of the cooking process, and then dropping to a lower heat later, when the duck is really beginning to cook, you can have the best of both worlds: a duck that's crisp on the outside and still deliciously moist on the inside. Leaving the rendered fat in the pan throughout the cooking process tends to self-baste the duck.

1	duck (about 5 pounds)	1	tablespoon oil
5-6	sprigs parsley	Salt	
1	onion, peeled	Pepper	

NOTE: *The sautéed apples, p. 165, are my favorite complement to this dish.*

1. Preheat the oven to 450°. Rinse the bird under cold running water. Since ducks have so much fat, you should trim away any excess skin at the neck and tail as well as any clumps of fat inside the cavity. Prick the duck 10-12 times with a fork so that the fat drains from the meat during the cooking.

2. Dry the duck and sprinkle the cavity with 1 tablespoon each of salt and pepper. Add the parsley and onion to the cavity for flavor and rub the skin with salt. Rub the bottom of the bird with oil so that it doesn't stick, then place the duck on a rack in the pan.

3. Roast the duck at 450° for 20 minutes. Then lower heat to 325° and let the duck roast slowly for 2 hours and 15 minutes or until the leg moves easily. (This slow cooking insures that the meat stays tender). Move the duck on the rack several times to keep it from sticking.

4. Transfer the duck to a platter. Let it rest for 15 minutes so that the juices settle. Serve the duck with orange sauce (duck a l'orange), mustard cream sauce, p. 112, or currant sauce, p. 132.

Orange Sauce for Duck

MAKES 1½ CUPS SAUCE, FOR 2 DUCKS

This outstanding orange duck sauce is an example of how sweet and tart flavors can combine and create something even better.

The peel from 2 oranges, cut into very fine julienne strips

3 tablespoons sugar

½ cup white wine

1 tablespoon balsamic vinegar

2 cups orange juice

1½ cups brown sugar

Salt

Pepper

1. In a medium saucepan, combine the orange peel and 1 cup water. Bring the mixture to a boil, drain off the water, and rinse off the orange peel. Return the peel to the pan and re-boil with another cup of water, then drain. (This blanching process removes the bitterness from the peel.)

2. Return the orange peel to the saucepan, add the sugar and 1 tablespoon water and bring to a boil, stirring to dissolve the sugar. Once the mixture has begun to boil, reduce the heat and let it simmer, without stirring, until the liquid turns a caramel color. This will take about 4-5 minutes. (If the heat is too high, the sugar will burn.)

3. Once the sugar has caramelized, immediately pour in the wine and increase the heat to high. Add the vinegar and let the liquid reduce to about 3 tablespoons. Add the orange juice and reduce until ¼ cup of liquid remains.

4. Add the brown sugar and return to a boil. Then, lower the heat and let the sauce simmer for 5-10 minutes so that the flavors blend together and the duck sauce has thickened to a mildly gelatinous consistency. Add salt and pepper to taste and serve immediately or store in the refrigerator. This sauce will keep in the refrigerator for 1 week.

Mustard Cream Sauce

SERVES 4 (SUFFICIENT FOR 2 DUCKS)

This sauce is excellent with roast veal, veal scallops, roast or poached chicken, and poached salmon. It can be refrigerated for several days.

2   tablespoons minced shallots

½   cup white wine

1   cup heavy cream

2   tablespoons whole grain mustard

Salt

Pepper

1. Combine the shallots, ¼ teaspoon pepper, ¼ teaspoon salt, and wine in a saucepan and bring to a boil. Reduce until about 1 tablespoon of liquid remains. Add the cream and reduce again, until about ¾ cup remains and the sauce has started to thicken.

2. Pour the sauce through a strainer and return it to the pan. (If you prefer a chunky sauce, omit this step.)

3. Add the mustard, mix well, and return the sauce to a boil. Remove from heat and serve immediately with roast fowl, veal, or fish.

Seafood

I think that the fish and shellfish recipes in the pages that follow are both interesting to prepare and exciting to serve. The incredible range of tastes and textures that result from innovative preparation of sole, shrimp, salmon, lobster, and other seafood should appeal to even the most jaded palate. I'm especially pleased to be able to include my favorite poaching techniques for shrimp and salmon. They are proven methods of getting the most in terms of taste and, equally important, nutrition, from these two remarkable foods.

Fillet of Sole with Shallot Cream

SERVES 4

If you enjoy fillet of sole, I'm certain that you'll find that this white wine and cream-based sauce, accented with shallots, adds up to a spectacular experience.

The sole should be thoroughly coated with flour, eggs, and bread crumbs to seal in the juices and prevent the fish from absorbing the cooking fat. The breading method used in this recipe also works well with other fish, meats, and vegetables that are to be fried.

4	fillets of sole (2-2 ½ pounds), boned	2	eggs, lightly beaten
1½	cups sifted bread crumbs	4	tablespoons (½ stick) unsalted butter
½	cup flour		Salt, pepper

FOR THE SAUCE:

2	large shallots, minced	2	tablespoons chopped parsley
⅔	cup dry white wine		Salt
1	cup cream		Pepper

NOTE:
The shallot, a member of the lily family, has a flavor that is similar to but less pungent than onions and garlic. Although some are grown domestically, most are imported from France. Available throughout the year, they are most abundant from late June through October. Look for firm shallots with bulbs slightly less than an inch in diameter and smooth, dry skin. Avoid shallots that are shriveled or sprouting.

1. Remove the thin section of tiny bones that divide each fillet in half by first cutting each fillet along the seam. Then remove the tiny bones from the edges. Rinse the fillets well and dry them on paper towels. Sift the bread crumbs into a bowl, discarding any crumbs that remain in the sieve.

2. Arrange the coating ingredients on 3 dinner plates or in 3 mixing bowls as follows: in the first, mix the flour, 1½ teaspoons of salt, and 1 teaspoon of pepper; in the second, the beaten eggs; and in the third, the bread crumbs.

3. To bread the fillets, first coat each piece in the flour, gently shaking off the excess. Then dip it into the eggs, turning to wet it on each side. Finally, coat the fillets with bread crumbs, again shaking off the excess. Lay the breaded pieces on a baking sheet or platter, then chill the breaded fillets in the refrigerator for 5 minutes before cooking. Preheat the oven to 200°.

4. In a large heavy pan over medium heat, melt the butter. When the foam has begun to subside but the butter has not yet browned, use a soup spoon to remove most of the foam from its surface. Don't worry if some remains. Add the fillets to the pan and increase the heat to high. Cook the fillets quickly until browned on the bottom (about 45-60 seconds). Turn the fish over gently with a spatula and brown the second side. Then transfer the fish to a metal tray lined with paper towels and place the fillets in the warm oven while you prepare the sauce.

FOR THE SAUCE:

5. There should be about 1½ tablespoons of butter remaining in the pan. If there is more, pour off the excess; if less, add and melt a little more butter. Add the shallots to the heavy pan. Sauté the shallots over a medium heat, stirring frequently, until they begin to brown (about 1 minute). Add the wine to the pan and reduce until the liquid has almost completely evaporated. Then stir in the cream and let it reduce over medium heat until the sauce thickens.

6. Season the sauce with 1 teaspoon of salt and ½ teaspoon of pepper, or to taste. Spoon some sauce onto each plate, lay the sole on top, sprinkle with a little chopped parsley, and serve.

Poached Shrimp

SERVES 4

In developing dishes for Pasta & Cheese we've found that slowly poaching shrimp in this delicious broth guarantees exceptionally tender and flavorful shrimp. Virtually all pre-cooked shrimp available at fish markets and from the seafood departments in food stores is boiled in salted water, which makes it salty tasting and tough. Shrimp poached in this broth should be peeled soon after cooking and cooling because poached shrimp that are left in their shells for more than 20-30 minutes take on a strong flavor.

1	pound shrimp	1	bay leaf
	Juice of ½ lemon	1	whole clove
1	cup chopped yellow onion	3	whole peppercorns
1	carrot, chopped		Salt
1	stalk celery, chopped		

1. Rinse the shrimp well and drain. Combine the lemon juice, onion, carrot, celery, bay leaf, clove, 3 whole peppercorns and 1 teaspoon of salt with 4 cups of water in a large saucepan. Bring the mixture to a boil, lower the heat, and let it simmer for 10 minutes.

2. Add the shrimp to the mixture then lower the heat and cook, barely simmering, for 5-7 minutes depending on the size of the shrimp. (To test, remove a shrimp, run it under cold water to cool, and taste to make sure it is cooked in the middle but not overcooked.) When they have cooked, remove the shrimp from the liquid and let them cool. Then peel off the shells and devein the shrimp. Cover and chill in the refrigerator until ready to use.

NOTE:
Fresh shrimp are assigned size designations according to the number of headless shrimp that will make up a pound. "Jumbo" means that there are fewer than 15 shrimp to a pound; "Extra large" shrimp are 16 to 20 to the pound; "large" are 21 to 30 to the pound; and "medium" are 31 to 40 to the pound. If more than 40 shrimp are needed to make up a pound, they're classified as "small."

Shrimp with Saffron Cream

SERVES 4 AS A MAIN COURSE

I was on the Quai St. Pierre in Cannes one cloudy September day and wandered into the Vol au Vent, a small restaurant that overlooks the yacht basin. It was there that I tasted the marvelous shrimp dish that inspired this recipe. The amount of saffron used in this cream-based sauce should be determined by the desired strength and flavor. Saffron is expensive, but a small amount produces excellent results.

FOR THE SHRIMP:

4 tablespoons (½ stick) unsalted butter	2¼ cups white wine
6 medium shallots, minced	3 cups heavy cream
36 large shrimp, uncooked (1½-2 pounds)	Salt
1½-2½ teaspoons saffron threads	Pepper

FOR THE PASTA:

¾ pound fresh linguine or fettucine

Salt

Garnish with finely chopped parsley

1. Peel and devein the shrimp, reserving the shells. Place the shells in a colander, rinse, and drain well, pressing out the excess water.

2. In a large heavy pan, melt the butter and add the shallots, the shrimp, reserved shells, saffron, 2 teaspoons salt, and 1½ teaspoons pepper and increase the heat to high. Sauté the mixture for 3 minutes, turning the shrimp at least once. Add the wine to the pan, let the liquid come to a boil, and then immediately remove the shrimp with tongs or a slotted spoon. Reserve the shrimp at room temperature.

3. Let the liquid boil and reduce until about 2-3 tablespoons remain (approximately 10 minutes). Add the cream, return to a boil and reduce for about 3 minutes. The sauce will start to thicken. Strain the sauce into another frying pan or saucepan, using a wooden spoon to press all the liquid out of the shells. Discard the shells.

4. Return the strained sauce to a boil over high heat and reduce until it becomes thick. Add the reserved shrimp to the pan and return the sauce to a simmer. Taste and season with salt and pepper, if necessary. Cover the pan tightly and reserve over very low heat until the pasta is prepared.

5. In a large pot, bring 3 quarts of water with 2 tablespoons of salt to boil. Add the pasta and cook until al dente. Drain well and transfer it to a mixing bowl with 2 tablespoons of melted butter. Mix gently and thoroughly.

6. To serve, divide the pasta into portions and place each portion in a mound in the center of an individual plate. Remove the shrimp from the pan with a slotted spoon, divide them into portions, and arrange them around the pasta. Spoon the sauce generously over the shrimp and garnish with freshly chopped parsley.

NOTE: *Saffron, derived from crocus blossoms, is one of the world's most expensive legal crops, costing approximately $500 per pound. Fortunately, you need use only a tiny amount to lend flavor and color to a dish.*

Shrimp with Cabbage and Vegetables

SERVES 4 AS A MAIN COURSE

I was first introduced to the tastes that I've incorporated into this dish during a lunch at the Seventh Street Bistro in Los Angeles. The sauce in this recipe has a delicate flavor that complements the lightly cooked vegetables and shrimp, which are essentially sautéed in cabbage leaves. All of the ingredients should be prepared in advance so that they can be cooked together at the last minute, oriental style.

FOR THE SHRIMP:

1   pound large (16-20 to the pound size) shrimp, raw and unpeeled

½   cup dry white wine

1   medium cabbage, leaves separated (save as many leaves as there are shrimp and reserve the rest for another use)

FOR THE VEGETABLES:

2   carrots, cut into 2-inch long julienne strips

½   cup thin green beans (Haricot verts if available. If not, slice larger beans in ½ lengthwise)

1   leek, cut into 1½-inch long julienne strips

4   scallions, julienned into 1½-inch long strips

4½   tablespoons unsalted butter (3 for sautéing the cabbage, 1½ for sautéing the vegetables)

FOR THE SAUCE:

1   tablespoon unsalted butter

2   teaspoons minced fresh ginger

1   clove garlic, minced

1   tablespoon minced scallion

2   teaspoons arrowroot

2   tablespoons dry white wine

Reserved cooking liquid from shrimp

1   tablespoon soy sauce

FOR THE SHRIMP:

1. Peel and devein the shrimp and reserve them in a bowl. Rinse the shells well, drain, and reserve. In a medium saucepan, combine the wine, one cup of water, and the shrimp shells. Bring the liquid to a boil over medium-high heat and reduce until ¾ cup of liquid remains (about 10 minutes). Then strain the liquid into a bowl and reserve at room temperature. Discard the shells.

FOR THE CABBAGE:

NOTE:
To flatten the cabbage leaf, remove the hard spined end with a knife.

2. In a large pot, bring 4 quarts of water with 3 tablespoons of salt to a boil. Gently add the cabbage leaves, taking care not to break them, and return the water to a boil. Cook for 1 minute, then drain and rinse the leaves under cold running water to cool. Drain them on paper towels. Trim the cabbage leaves and use to towel wrap each individual shrimp. Reserve the wrapped shrimp at room temperature.

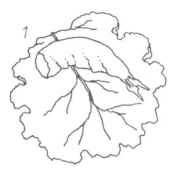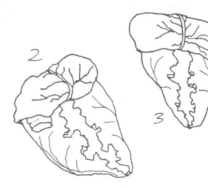

FOR THE VEGETABLES:

3. In a medium saucepan, bring 2 quarts of water and 1 tablespoon of salt to a boil. Add the carrots and return the water to boil. Add the green beans and gently boil for 2-3 minutes. Add the leeks and once more return the water to a boil. Then drain all the vegetables and rinse under cold water to cool. Transfer the vegetables to a bowl and add the julienned scallions. Reserve. (This can be held covered in the refrigerator for several hours or overnight.)

TO COOK THE DISH:

4. Preheat the oven to 200°. Melt 3 tablespoons of butter in a large, heavy pan over medium heat. Sauté the shrimp-cabbage rolls, turning them frequently until the cabbage has browned and the shrimp is cooked (about 8-10 minutes). In another heavy pan, melt 1½ tablespoons of butter over medium heat and sauté the reserved vegetables until they are heated through (about 5 minutes).

5. Remove the shrimp-cabbage rolls from the pan. Set the pan aside without cleaning it. Arrange the shrimp-cabbage rolls and the vegetables on a platter and place in a 200° oven. Add 1 tablespoon of butter to the shrimp pan, let it melt over low heat, then add the ginger, garlic, and 1 tablespoon chopped scallions to the pan. Increase the heat to high and sauté, stirring constantly, for 30 seconds.

6. In a cup, dissolve the arrowroot in the wine. Add the reserved shrimp stock and the soy sauce to the ginger-scallion mixture. The liquid should boil immediately. Remove the pan from the heat and, whisking vigorously, slowly drizzle in the dissolved arrowroot until the boiling sauce has thickened.

7. Divide the shrimp-cabbage rolls and the vegetables among individual plates, spoon the sauce over the shrimp and vegetables, and serve.

Poached Salmon

SERVES 3-4 AS A MAIN COURSE

Fresh salmon reaches it zenith when it is simmered slowly in court bouillon. You can, of course, poach a whole salmon with this technique — just be sure to make enough court bouillon to cover the fish.

3   pounds salmon fillet, skinned
    and boned

FOR THE COURT BOUILLON:

2	cups white wine	6	peppercorns
2	cups chopped yellow onion	1	clove garlic, halved
2½	cups chopped celery	1	sprig parsley
1	cup chopped carrot	1	whole clove
1	bay leaf	½	pound fish bones, heads or tails
1	pinch thyme	2	envelopes unflavored gelatin

1. Combine all the court bouillon ingredients except the gelatin in 6 cups of cold water in a large saucepan. Bring the liquid to a boil over medium-high heat, then lower the heat and let it simmer for 45 minutes. Skim off the scum that rises to the surface as it cooks. Then strain the liquid through a strainer or through cheesecloth into a poaching pan or pot large enough to hold the salmon.

2. Return the court bouillon to a boil and reduce it for 10 minutes. Sprinkle the gelatin into ½ cup of cold water and let it soften for 3 minutes. Add the gelatin to the court bouillon and return the bouillon to a boil.

3. Reduce the heat so that the liquid just simmers. Add the salmon and poach gently for 8 minutes per inch of thickness. Be sure that the liquid doesn't boil or the salmon will be tough.

4. Remove the pan from the heat and let the liquid and the fish cool. Cover the pan and refrigerate several hours until the salmon has chilled. (The salmon may be left in the liquid for up to 12 hours.)

5. To serve, remove the salmon and scrape off any remaining gelatin. (Reserve the court bouillon for another use. It can be stored in the refrigerator covered tightly for about 2 weeks.) Serve the salmon sliced or as a cold fillet with cold seafood sauce, p. 65, mayonnaise, p. 168, or apricot curry sauce, p. 112.

Salmon with Mustard Mousse

SERVES 6-8 AS A FIRST COURSE

This was inspired by an appetizer that I enjoyed immensely at Lutece. The few minutes under the broiler cooks the fresh salmon to perfection; and the flavor and texture of this distinctive mustard sauce heightens the pleasure offered by the salmon. In preparing this dish, I use ovenproof plates or any plates that can withstand three or four minutes under the broiler.

1   cup heavy cream

2   egg yolks

6   tablespoons whole grain mustard, such as Pommery, or to taste

½   teaspoon safflower oil

1   pound fresh salmon fillet, thinly sliced (⅛-inch or less)

Salt

White pepper

1. Whip the cream until it holds stiff peaks. In a small mixing bowl, combine the egg yolks and mustard, then fold this mixture into the cream. Season with ½ teaspoon salt and ¼ teaspoon white pepper, stirring to mix, and reserve. Oil 4 ovenproof dinner plates with 1-2 drops of oil per plate, spreading the oil with paper towels to absorb the excess.

2. Preheat the broiler. Divide the salmon slices and lay them in a single layer covering the plates. Season with a little salt and white pepper. Spread ¼ of the reserved mustard cream over the salmon and smooth the top. Place 2 of the plates on a rack set about 5 inches from the broiler and broil until the salmon is cooked and its surface is well browned, about 3-4 minutes. Repeat with the remaining 2 plates. To serve, place the salmon plates on under-plates with a doily in between, if necessary, to prevent slipping.

Cold Lobster with Apricot Sauce

SERVES 4 AS A MAIN COURSE

I usually spend a few weeks in the south of France each summer. As good as the restaurants are throughout the region, the food served on board Sir Walter and Lady Salomon's yacht rivals any on the Riviera. Lady Salomon was kind enough to give me her recipe for this exceptional presentation of cold lobster. I've also tried this wonderfully fresh-tasting dressing with cold poached chicken breasts, p. 104, and it provides the same excitement.

4   1-1½ lb. lobsters, cooked and chilled

FOR THE SAUCE:

½   cup finely chopped onion

1   tablespoon oil

2   teaspoons curry powder

¾   cup hearty red wine

1   bay leaf

1   teaspoon tomato paste

1   tablespoon lemon juice

Dash of Tabasco®

1½   cups mayonnaise, p. 168

2½   tablespoons apricot preserves

2   tablespoons heavy cream

Salt

TO STEAM THE LOBSTERS:

1. Place the rack on the bottom of a large pot, raised 2-3 inches above its floor. Add water to just below the rack. cover the pot and bring the water to a boil. When steam has formed and begins to escape from the pot, add the lobsters, placing them on the rack.

2. Cover the pot tightly and begin timing the cooking as soon as the steam has again begun to escape from the pot. Allow 10 minutes cooking time for the first pound and 4 minutes for each additional pound. (A 1½ pound chicken lobster would require 12 minutes cooking time.)

3. Remove the lobsters, transfer them to a platter and chill in the refrigerator for 15-20 minutes before preparing them for serving.

TO PREPARE THE SAUCE:

4. In a medium heavy pan, sauté the onion in oil over medium-high heat for 8-10 minutes or until it just begins to brown. Add the curry powder and sauté 1 minute longer. Then add the wine, bay leaf, tomato paste, lemon juice, and Tabasco®, increase the heat to high, and reduce the mixture until only ¾ cup remains (7-8 minutes). Remove the bay leaf. Transfer the mixture to a small bowl and allow it to chill for 5 minutes in the refrigerator.

5. Place the mayonnaise in the bowl of a food processor fitted with the steel blade. Add the wine and onion mixture and the apricot preserves to the bowl and purée until smooth (about 1 minute). Season with salt to taste.

6. Chill the sauce for at least ½ hour, then divide it among 4 individual plates, spreading it over the center of each plate. Remove the meat from each lobster tail, slice it down the center, and place it on the sauce. Remove the meat from the lobster claws and lay it on either side of the sliced tail. Serve.

NOTE: *Lobsters are graded according to weight: chicken lobsters range from ¾-1 pound; quarter lobsters from 1¼-1½ pound; large, from 1½-2½; jumbo, over 2½ pounds.*

Meat

The almost endless variety of preparation techniques, tastes, and presentations of meat has always fascinated me. The possibilities are endless. The recipes presented here cover a broad spectrum of those limitless possibilities and are divided into just two general categories which overlap each other by degrees. They include dishes that can be prepared almost entirely in advance to let you entertain six to eight people without difficulty as well as dishes that require time and concentration throughout their preparation, which I usually serve to no more than four people. The veal parmigiano, veal with eggplant, and saltimbocca are dishes that I usually cook only for two, and never for more than four, people. The oven barbeque dishes can, on the other hand, be prepared for a crowd well in advance and reheated just before serving without loss of flavors. That is also the case with the pork with currant sauce and vitello tonnato. Only the finishing touches will take you away from your guests.

Poached Filet Mignon with Chive Sauce

SERVES 4

This recipe was inspired by a marvelous dish I had at one of my favorite Parisian restaurants, La Ciboulette, at 141 Rue Saint-Martin. The outside of poached filet mignon looks very much like boiled beef, so I was amazed and delighted when I separated the pre-sliced pieces and discovered that it was still rare on the inside. Poaching makes for an incredibly tender piece of meat, and the superb chive sauce complements and maximizes the flavor.

MEAT

FOR THE SAUCE:

¼ cup balsamic vinegar	16 tablespoons (2 sticks) unsalted butter
4 teaspoons lemon juice	2 egg yolks
3 teaspoons finely chopped shallots	5 tablespoons (2 bunches) chives, finely chopped
¾ teaspoon tarragon	
⅛-¼ cup heavy cream	

FOR THE MEAT:

4 filets mignons, each about 5-8 ounces and 2 inches thick, trimmed.	5 cups beef broth

1. First make the sauce. In a medium saucepan, combine the vinegar, lemon juice, shallots, and tarragon, and reduce over high heat until about 1 tablespoon of liquid remains. Add the cream and reduce by half over medium-high heat until the sauce is quite thick. Strain into a small saucepan and reserve.

2. Melt the butter in a small saucepan and remove it from the heat. When it's lukewarm, use a soup spoon to skim most of the foam from its surface.

3. In the top of a double boiler, over simmering water, whisk together the egg yolks and two tablespoons of water. Cook, whisking constantly, until the mixture is thick and resembles zabaglione.

4. Slowly whisk the cooled butter into the yolk mixture. (If it separates, put 1 tablespoon of boiling water in a separate mixing bowl and mix in the separated mixture, then the remainder of the batter. Then whisk in the reserved cream mixture and 3 tablespoons of the chives. Cover and reserve in a warm place (off the heat on the back of the stove). The sauce should be served warm — it needn't be hot.

5. Trim the filets thoroughly, removing all fatty sinew. Add the beef broth to a 10-inch straight sided sauté pan or a large 10-inch wide saucepan. The broth should be sufficient to just cover the meat. Bring the beef broth to a boil over high heat. Add the filets and cook at a medium boil until rare (about 3-5 minutes) or medium-rare (about 5-6 minutes). Remove the meat to a cutting board, cover loosely with foil, and let rest 5 minutes.

6. To serve, divide and ladle the sauce over four dinner plates. Cut the filets into ⅓-inch vertical slices, leaving a bit intact at the bottom of each slice so the slices are not completely separated. Place one filet in the center of each plate and divide the remaining chives over the top of each.

Steak au Poivre

SERVES 2

If you're as fond of peppery flavor and good cuts of meat as I am, this steak presentation will become a standard at your table.

2   steaks, 8-10 ounces, each well trimmed (shell preferred)

3   tablespoons unsalted butter, softened (1 for rubbing steaks, 2 for sautéing).

3   shallots, minced

⅓   cup cognac

⅜   cup brown sauce, p. 42, or easy brown sauce, p. 44, or ½ cup beef broth

1   cup heavy cream

Salt

4-8   teaspoons crushed white or black peppercorns

Soften butter at room temperature — not over heat

1. Rub each steak lightly with 1 tablespoon of the softened butter. Then season each with ½ teaspoon of salt and 4 - 8 teaspoons of crushed peppercorns (to taste), pressing the pepper into the meat. Heat 1-2 tablespoons of butter in a heavy pan, and sauté the steaks over high heat until they are cooked to your taste. Add more butter if necessary to keep the steaks from sticking. Transfer the steaks to a platter and reserve.

2. Lower the heat to medium and add the shallots and 1 tablespoon of butter, if needed, to the pan. Sauté for 1 minute over medium heat, stirring frequently so the shallots don't burn. Add the cognac and reduce for 30 seconds. Stir in the brown sauce and let the liquid come to a boil. Add the cream and reduce for several minutes over high heat to create a thick sauce. Season with salt to taste.

3. Return the steaks to the sauce and let them simmer over medium heat for about 20 seconds, turning them to coat them with the sauce. Then transfer the steaks to individual plates or a platter and spoon the remaining sauce over them. Serve.

Steak with Shallot Sauce

SERVES 4

This recipe was inspired by a meal I enjoyed enormously at the
Tante Claire in London. The taste of shallots in butter, sprinkled
with a little parsley, is irresistible. I usually serve this following a
first course such as pasta with morels, p. 92, and accompanied
by green beans, p. 154.

7-8   tablespoons
       unsalted butter

2   medium shallots, minced

4   8-10 ounce steaks, well-
     trimmed, shell or fillet preferred

2   tablespoons finely chopped
     parsley

Salt

Pepper

1. In a small saucepan, melt 2 tablespoons of butter over medium
    heat. Add the shallots and ¾ teaspoon of pepper to the saucepan
    and sauté over medium heat, stirring frequently, until the shallots
    are lightly browned (about 5-7 minutes). Add 1 teaspoon of salt
    and 4 tablespoons of butter and cook, stirring frequently, until the
    butter melts and just begins to foam. Don't let the butter burn.
    Remove the pan from the heat, cover and reserve.

2. Melt 1 tablespoon of butter in a heavy pan. Add the steaks. When
    they are cooked to your taste, let them stand off the heat for 5-10
    minutes. If the sauce has cooled, reheat it over medium-high heat.
    I usually trim the steaks of all fat, slice them, and put them on a
    platter or indiviudal plates. Then I pour the sauce over the steaks
    and sprinkle them with finely chopped parsley.

    NOTE: *I prefer pan frying steaks to cooking in a standard home
    broiler. Most broilers don't get hot enough to truly grill
    meat — they bake it instead. When grilling meat, I always rub it
    with corn oil before placing it on the grill to prevent the meat from
    sticking and tearing.*

Beef Stroganoff

SERVES 4

In this dish, the combination of vinegar and dry white wine adds zest to top quality meat and enhances its taste. You can make the sauce up to half a day in advance, but the meat should be prepared at the last minute so that it's served when it is most tender.

4 cups coarsely chopped yellow onions	Safflower oil as needed
⅓ cup white wine	1 tablespoon paprika
1 cup red wine vinegar	½ cup cornichon pickles, chopped (optional)
1½ cups heavy cream	Salt
1½ pounds beef fillet, well trimmed of fat and sinew, cut into ¼ inch julienne strips	Pepper

NOTE:
Paprika, a spice, comes from a fairly mild variety of red pepper which has been seeded and then ground. Although it isn't as hot as many other spices, it adds both spicy flavor and an attractive color to dishes.

1. Combine onions, wine, and vinegar in a saucepan and boil over medium-high heat. Reduce until about 2 tablespoons of liquid remain. Add the cream and reduce by ⅓ until the sauce has thickened. Pour the thickened sauce through a heavy strainer into a bowl. Using a wooden spoon or spatula, press the onions to squeeze out any remaining sauce. Reserve.

2. In a mixing bowl, toss the meat with 2 teaspoons salt and 1 teaspoon pepper. Heat 2 tablespoons oil in a heavy pan and sauté a single layer of the beef, turning constantly until the meat is just browned (rare) or darker if you prefer more well-done meat. Transfer the beef to a bowl. Add more oil to the pan, if necessary, and sauté the remaining beef. Reserve the beef.

3. Pour off any oil that remains in the pan. Add the sauce to the pan (it will boil almost immediately because the pan is still hot). Add the beef to the sauce and, over medium-high heat, return the sauce to a boil. Turn off the heat and ladle the stroganoff into a serving dish. Sprinkle with paprika and garnish with chopped cornichons or chopped parsley.

Corned Beef Hash

SERVES 4-6

I usually see corned beef hash at convention breakfast meetings in hotels. There it sits, in a stainless steel tray over a can of flaming sterno. And I'm always suspicious of the origins of the ingredients. Some years ago, however, while having lunch at Perry's on Union Street in San Francisco, I had corned beef hash that was a memorable dish. It proved that good ingredients can make an old standby outstanding. I experimented with the ingredients that they have in their hash and came up with what I think is a spectacular dish.

2 large potatoes (1 pound)	1 pound lean corned beef, cooked and cut into ½-inch pieces
3-4 tablespoons unsalted butter	
2 cups coarsely chopped yellow onion	2 teaspoons finely chopped parsley
1 green pepper, chopped into ½-inch pieces	Salt
	Pepper, freshly ground

1. Bring 2 quarts of water and 1 tablespoon of salt to a boil in a saucepan over medium-high heat. Remove the knots from the potatoes. Scrub the potatoes well and add them to the pot. Let the liquid come to simmer and cook the potatoes until they are just tender (about 20-30 minutes depending on their size). Drain the potatoes and let them sit in cold water until they are cool to the touch. Peel them (their skins will slip off easily) and cube them into ½-inch pieces.

2. Melt the butter in a large frying pan. Sauté the onion over medium-high heat for 7-10 minutes, stirring frequently to prevent burning. Add the peppers and cook over medium-high heat for another 5 minutes or so until the onions are golden brown. Lower the heat if necessary to prevent burning. Add the potatoes and continue to sauté until the potatoes begin to brown. Add the corned beef and continue to cook just until the corned beef is heated completely. Add salt and pepper to taste. (You should not need to add much salt, as corned beef is quite salty). Serve garnished with a little freshly chopped parsley.

NOTE:
Corned beef is a cut of beef (usually brisket) treated with a brine solution of salt and hot water. Its name comes from the fact that it was originally cured using large chunks of salt the size of wheat kernels, which were also called "corns."

Boneless Rack of Lamb with Currant Sauce

SERVES 4

Rack of lamb, usually used for rib chops, is the finest cut of lamb and worth its slightly higher cost. Have the butcher remove the eye muscle from the bones and trim off most of the sinew attached to the meat. If you use beef broth instead of brown sauce in this dish, the sauce will not be as rich and will need to be thickened with a little arrowroot.

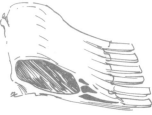

Rack of Lamb

Excess fat, sinews and bone removed

3	cups red wine	
2	cups chopped yellow onion	
¼	cup herbs de Provence	
1	bay leaf	
1	teaspoon thyme	
2	2-pound racks of lamb, boned, sinews mostly removed	
2	tablespoons chopped shallots	
5	tablespoons butter (2 for sautéing shallots, 3 for sautéing lamb)	

½   cup brandy

2   cups brown sauce, p. 42, or 3 cups beef broth

⅓   cup currant jelly, or to taste

2   teaspoons arrowroot mixed with 2 teaspoons water (optional)

¼   cup finely chopped parsley

Salt

Pepper

1. In a large bowl, mix the wine, onion, 1 tablespoon salt, 2 teaspoons pepper, herbs de Provence, bay leaf, and thyme with the lamb. Cover and marinate at room temperature for 6-8 hours; in the refrigerator for at least 10 hours; or overnight.

2. In a saucepan, melt 2 tablespoons of butter over medium heat and sauté the shallots until they are transparent (about 2-3 minutes). Add the brandy and don't worry if it flames — just be careful not to burn yourself or start a fire in the exhaust. Let the brandy boil and reduce until it has almost completely evaporated. Add the brown sauce or beef broth and let the liquid return to a boil. Reduce it by ⅓, stir in the currant jelly, and blend until the jelly has dissolved. The sauce should be fairly thick.

3. If the sauce still needs thickening, bring it to a boil and whisk in the arrowroot mixture a few drops at a time until the desired consistency is reached.

4. Let the sauce simmer for 5 minutes while you are cooking the lamb, then strain the sauce. Add salt and pepper to taste.

5. Remove the lamb from the marinade and dry it with paper towels. Melt 3 tablespoons of butter in a large heavy pan over medium-high heat. Add the lamb and cook it for about 3-6 minutes on each side, depending upon how rare you like it. Transfer the lamb to a platter and let it rest 5 minutes before carving.

6. To serve, spoon onto 4 plates, thinly slice the lamb on the bias, and divide it equally among the plates. Sprinkle finely chopped parsley over the top of the meat and serve.

Outdoor Charcoal Grilled Leg of Lamb
SERVES 6

1	4-5 pound leg of lamb, boned, butterflied, and well trimmed, with most of the sinew removed
1½	cups olive oil
2-3	cloves garlic, minced
25	basil leaves (20 whole; 5 chopped for garnish) or 2½ tablespoons dried basil
½	cup whole grain mustard (Pommery)
⅓	tablespoon freshly chopped parsley
	Salt
	Pepper

1. In a large bowl, combine the olive oil, garlic, basil, mustard, parsley, and salt and pepper to taste and mix with a fork. Add the lamb and turn to coat it well with the marinade. Cover the bowl with plastic wrap and marinate at room temperature for 6 hours or in the refrigerator overnight.

2. Light the coals in a barbeque and let them burn until they are white (30-40 minutes). Set the rack 6 inches above the coals and cook the lamb about 5-7 minutes on each side, depending on how you like it cooked.

3. Let the lamb rest for 15 minutes before carving. This will give the juices a chance to set so they won't run out when the meat is cut.

4. Thinly slice the lamb and transfer it to a platter. Sprinkle with parsley and serve

Roast Pork with Currant Sauce

SERVES 4-6

1   5-pound pork loin roast, bone in

Salt

Pepper

FOR THE CURRANT SAUCE:

Menu
—
Risotto
Roast Pork with
Currant Sauce
—
Sautéed Apples
Fresh Berries
with Zabaglione

2 shallots, chopped	Few drops Tabasco® sauce
1½ cups red wine	¼ cup Port wine
1 tablespoon balsamic vinegar	Salt
2 cups brown sauce, p.44	Pepper
½ cup red currant jelly	

1. Preheat the oven to 450°. Rub the pork with 1 teaspoon of salt and ½ teaspoon of pepper. Insert a meat thermometer into the center of the thickest part of the roast. (Keep the thermometer away from the bone, which heats faster and can give a false temperature reading.) Place the pork on a rack set in a roasting pan. Roast for 20 minutes in the preheated oven. Then lower the heat to 325° and continue roasting for 1 hour and 45 minutes. The internal temperature of the meat should reach at least 160° for the roast to be fully cooked.

2. Remove the pork from the oven and transfer it to a platter. Let it rest at least 10-15 minutes before carving.

3. In a medium saucepan, combine the shallots, red wine, and vinegar. Reduce the liquid over medium-high heat until only about 2 tablespoons remain. Add the brown sauce and bring it to a boil. Lower the heat and simmer for 5 minutes. Add the currant jelly and stir until it melts. Then add the Tabasco® sauce and Port. Return the sauce to a simmer and immediately remove it from the heat. Taste and season with salt, if desired.

4. To serve, carve the pork into thin slices. Spoon the sauce onto warm plates or a platter and arrange the slices of meat on top of it. If there is extra sauce, serve it on the side.

Barbeque

When we were recently considering adding barbeque to the Pasta & Cheese food line, Steven Philips researched the best barbeque techniques and dishes. In the process, he and I developed some easy and unusual techniques that allow you to use your oven to create the tastes and textures you'd expect to get only from the most complex open-fire barbeque pits. The dishes that follow, as well as the pasta with barbeque sauce, p. 83, are the results of this enjoyable research.

Barbeque Marinade

MAKES 4 CUPS

¾ cup balsamic vinegar

¾ cup hearty red wine

6 cloves garlic, minced

3 tablespoons Liquid Smoke (optional)

2¼ teaspoons Worcestershire sauce

1½ cups safflower oil

Salt

Pepper

In a bowl, whisk together the vinegar, wine, garlic, Liquid Smoke, Worcestershire sauce, 2¼ teaspoons salt, and 1½ teaspoons pepper. Then slowly add the oil, whisking constantly. Use as called for in barbequed pork, p. 134, barbequed ribs, p. 135, or barbequed pasta, p. 83.

NOTE: *You can find Liquid Smoke in the condiment section of most grocery stores.*

Barbeque Sauce

MAKES 4 CUPS

2 tablespoons (¼ stick) unsalted butter	2 tablespoons honey
	1½ teaspoons sugar
1½ cups finely chopped yellow onion	1 teaspoon powdered ginger
2 cloves garlic, minced	1 teaspoon soy sauce
1 bottle chili sauce (preferably Heinz)	5-6 dashes Tabasco® sauce
	½-1 teaspoon Liquid Smoke, according to taste (optional)
2 tablespoons balsamic vinegar	
2 teaspoons Worcestershire sauce	Salt
1 tablespoon Dijon mustard	Pepper

1. Melt the butter in a medium saucepan over medium-high heat. Add the onions and garlic and sauté over medium heat until the onion is golden brown (about 10-12 minutes), stirring frequently so that they don't burn. Add the remaining ingredients and simmer for 5 minutes.

2. Transfer the sauce to a bowl and let it sit for at least an hour so that the flavors become thoroughly blended. Use as called for in barbequed pork, p. 133, barbequed ribs, p. 134, or barbequed pasta, p. 83.

Barbequed Pork Roast

SERVES 6-8

This is a simple and flavorful oven cooked version of pit-barbequed pork.

3-3½ pounds boneless pork loin	1 recipe barbeque sauce
1 recipe barbeque marinade, p. 133	¼ cup Liquid Smoke (optional)

1. In a covered bowl, let the meat sit in the marinade for at least 4 hours at room temperature or overnight in the refrigerator. Turn the pork several times while it is marinating.

2. Preheat the oven to 500°. Remove the pork from the marinade and lay it on a rack in a large roasting pan. Pour the marinade into the bottom of the pan and add the Liquid Smoke. Cover the pan tightly with aluminum foil and bake on the lowest oven rack for 10 minutes. Then lower the heat to 300° and continue cooking.

3. Test the pork after it has cooked for 2½ hours by inserting the tines of a fork into it and twisting. If the meat is tender enough to split apart easily, it's done. If not, cook for another ½ hour or until the meat is tender.

4. When the meat is tender, transfer it to a platter, cover it loosely with aluminum foil, and allow it to cool for at least ½ hour. Reserve the pan juices, which may be used later to thin the barbeque sauce.

FOR SLICED BARBEQUE:

1. When you're ready to serve, reheat the meat in a 350° oven for 10-15 minutes. While the meat is reheating, heat the barbeque sauce in a saucepan over medium heat, using the reserved pan juices to thin the sauce if desired. Then remove the meat from the oven, transfer it to a platter, and cut into thin slices. Arrange the slices on individual plates or a serving platter. Spoon sauce over the meat; serve the remaining sauce on the side.

FOR CHOPPED BARBEQUE:

1. Dice the cooked pork into ½-inch pieces and add to a mixing bowl. Mix in the barbeque sauce, thinning with the reserved pan juices if desired. Toss the meat well in the sauce, then transfer it to a casserole, cover, and reheat in a 350° oven for 20-30 minutes.

Barbequed Ribs

SERVES 4

5 pounds spare ribs or baby back ribs	1 recipe barbeque sauce, p.134
	3-4 tablespoons Liquid Smoke
1 recipe barbeque marinade, p. 133	

1. If the ribs come in slabs, cut them into thirds so they will fit in a large bowl. Pour the marinade over the meat and turn to coat. Let the mixture stand, covered with plastic wrap, for at least 4 hours at room temperature or overnight in the refrigerator. Turn the ribs occasionally.

2. Preheat oven to 300°. Place the ribs on a rack in a roasting pan. Pour the marinade over the meat and add 3-4 tablespoons of Liquid Smoke to the bottom of the pan. Cover tightly with aluminum foil and bake on the lowest rack of the oven for 1½ hours or until the meat pulls away easily from the bones when tested with a fork. If the meat does not separate effortlessly from the bones, continue cooking, checking every 15 minutes until done.

3. Transfer the ribs to a baking sheet and let them stand until you're ready to serve, reserving the pan juices. When ready to serve, reheat the oven to 500°. Brush the ribs generously with barbeque sauce and bake until well browned. Pass the remaining sauce with the ribs. If you prefer a thinner sauce, use some of the pan juices to reach the desired consistency.

Saltimbocca

SERVES 2

Saltimbocca means "jump in the mouth." After tasting this elegant version of a traditional Italian dish, you'll understand why this remarkable combination of veal, prosciutto, and cheese received its name.

4 large scallops of veal, pounded thin	6 tablespoons (¾ stick) unsalted butter
2 thin slices prosciutto, halved	¼ cup Marsala wine
1 teaspoon fresh sage leaves (or ½ teaspoon dry sage)	¼ cup dry white wine
4 teaspoons grated Parmigiano cheese (Reggiano or Grana Padano)	½ cup brown sauce (or canned beef broth)
	Salt
1 egg	Pepper
1 cup flour	

NOTE:
Marsala, a sweet wine with a subtly acidic flavor, is imported from Italy. An excellent after-dinner drink, it is also used in sauces and is an essential ingredient of many desserts, including zabaglione.

1. Lay two scallops flat and place ½ slice prosciutto on each. Divide the cheese and sage evenly between the two. Place the remaining prosciutto on the cheese and sage, and top with the remaining scallops. Press these "packages" lightly to remove air pockets and refrigerate for 10 minutes.

2. In one bowl, beat the egg. In a separate bowl, combine the flour and 1 teaspoon of salt. Dip each veal package first into the egg, then into the flour and salt mixture to coat it.

3. Melt 2 tablespoons of butter in a large heavy pan over medium-high heat. Add the veal and sauté until browned on the bottom, then add another tablespoon of butter to the pan. Turn the veal and brown. Remove the veal and reserve on warm plates or a platter.

4. Add the Marsala and white wine to the pan and reduce over high heat until ⅛ cup remains. Add the remaining butter, lower the heat to medium, and whisk until the butter is melted into this sauce. Remove the pan from the heat and season the sauce with salt and pepper.

5. Spoon the sauce over the veal and serve immediately.

Vitello Tonnato

SERVES 6

This very special dish is as convenient as it is flavorful. It can be made well in advance and refrigerated as a cold main course for lunch or dinner. When I serve this vitello tonnato, I often hear "I never realized tuna fish could taste like this." I usually serve this with a green salad dressed with vinaigrette, p. 170.

2 tablespoons olive oil

1 cup chopped yellow onion

1 carrot, chopped (about ½ cup)

1 stalk celery, chopped (about ½ cup)

6 garlic cloves, minced

3–3½ pound boneless veal leg, well trimmed

1 7-ounce can tuna, packed in oil, drained

1 2-ounce can anchovies, drained

1 bay leaf

Pinch thyme

1½ cups dry white wine

Pepper

FOR THE SAUCE:

Reserved cooked vegetables

1 cup mayonnaise, p. 168

1 tablespoon fresh lemon juice

Salt

Pepper

Garnish with capers, small chunks of tuna, thin strips of pimiento, chopped parsley, lemon wedges

Celery

1. In a large, lidded casserole or Dutch oven, combine the olive oil, onion, carrot, celery, and garlic and sauté over medium-high heat for 5 minutes, stirring frequently. Add the veal, tuna, anchovies, bay leaf, thyme, ½ teaspoon pepper, and wine. Lower the heat and let the liquid come to a simmer. Cover the casserole and let it simmer gently for 1½ hours.

2. Transfer the veal from the casserole to a platter to cool. Turn the heat up to medium-high and let the liquid with the vegetables reduce until only ½ cup of liquid remains. Pour any juices from the veal into the pot. Remove the bay leaf and transfer the vegetable mixture to the bowl of a food processor fitted with the steel blade. Purée.

3. Transfer the purée to a bowl, cover, and chill in the refrigerator. Cover the veal and chill for several hours or overnight.

4. Before serving, add the mayonnaise and lemon juice to the purée. Mix thoroughly and season to taste with salt and pepper.

5. To serve, slice the veal across the grain into very thin slices. Arrange the meat on individual plates and cover with a thin layer of the sauce. Garnish to taste and serve.

Veal Parmigiano

SERVES 4

This is an easy and excellent parmigiano. Ask the butcher to pound the scallops or, if you're doing it yourself, place the meat between sheets of wax paper and pound it evenly with a flat-surfaced hand mallet.

FOR THE TOPPING:

6 ounces mozzarella cheese, cubed (1 cup tightly packed)

½ cup grated Parmigiano cheese (Reggiano or Grana Padano)

FOR THE SAUCE:

1 recipe creamy tomato sauce, p. 84

FOR THE BREADING:

1 cup bread crumbs

1 cup flour

1 heaping tablespoon salt

1 heaping tablespoon pepper

2 eggs, beaten

FOR THE VEAL:

8 2-ounce veal scallops, pounded very thin

4 tablespoons (½ stick) unsalted butter

3 tablespoons corn oil

Chopped parsley

1. Combine the cheeses in the bowl of a food processor fitted with the steel blade. Process them quickly, pulsing a few times until the mozzarella is cut into tiny pieces. Reserve while you prepare the veal.

2. Heat the tomato sauce in the top of a double boiler over simmering water. Keep the sauce warm until needed.

3. Sift the bread crumbs onto a plate, pressing and rubbing them with your fingers through a sieve or finely graded strainer. Discard any crumbs that remain in the sieve. Arrange the breading ingredients on 3 dinner plates or in 3 mixing bowls as follows: on the first, mix the flour, salt and pepper; on the second, the beaten eggs; and on the third, the bread crumbs.

4. To bread the veal, first coat each piece in the flour, gently shaking off the excess. Then dip it into the eggs, turning to wet it on each side. Finally coat the veal with the bread crumbs, again shaking off the excess. Lay the breaded pieces on a baking sheet or platter.

5. In a large heavy pan, melt the butter with the oil. Add the veal, one or two pieces at a time, in a single layer. Sauté over medium heat until each side is golden brown (about 30 seconds a side). Remove the veal from the pan, drain on paper towels and transfer to a large baking pan.

6. Preheat the broiler. Sprinkle the cheese over the scallops and place them under the broiler for 3-4 minutes or until the cheese has melted and is just beginning to brown.

7. Spoon the tomato sauce onto a serving platter or individual plates. Arrange the scallops on top of the sauce and garnish with a little chopped parsley.

Veal with Apples and Calvados

SERVES 2

3 tablespoons unsalted butter	½ cup peeled, diced apple
½ cup flour	¾ cup heavy cream
4 2-ounce veal scallops, pounded thin	Salt
¼ cup Calvados	Pepper

1. Season the flour with 1 tablespoon of salt and 1 teaspoon of pepper. Dredge the veal thoroughly and shake off the excess.

2. Heat the butter in a heavy pan, over high heat, until it starts to foam. Add the veal and sauté until it is lightly browned on both sides. Remove the veal from the pan.

3. Add the Calvados and the apples to the pan. It may flame momentarily; don't worry if it does. Cook 1 minute, then add the cream and reduce the mixture until it begins to thicken.

4. Return the veal to the pan and heat it thoroughly (approximately 20-30 seconds). Remove the pan from the heat.

5. Divide the veal on individual serving dishes, cover with the apple pieces and then with sauce, and serve.

Veal with Eggplant

SERVES 4

The eggplant just lights up this dish, a delicious combination of veal and eggplant parmigiano. The veal should be pounded thin, either by the butcher or at home. If you do it yourself, place the veal between sheets of wax paper to protect the meat and pound it evenly with the side of a meat cleaver or with a smooth-surfaced hand mallet.

FOR THE TOPPING:

6 ounces mozzarella cheese, cubed (1 cup tightly packed)

1 cup grated Parmigiano cheese (Reggiano or Grana Padano)

FOR THE VEAL:

1 large eggplant

Flour for dusting

4 tablespoons (½ stick) unsalted butter

2 tablespoons olive oil

FOR THE SAUCE:

1½ cups white wine

1½ cups brown sauce, p. 44

Salt

Pepper

2 tablespoons safflower oil

8 2-ounce veal scallops

Salt

Pepper

1. Peel the eggplant and cut it into thin slices. Choose 8 pieces that will best cover the veal and trim to size, reserving the rest for another use. Salt these pieces thoroughly, place them in a colander, and let them drain for ½ hour or longer. (This keeps the eggplant from absorbing all the oil.) Rinse off the salt and pat the eggplant dry.

2. Mix the flour, 1½ tablespoons of salt, and 1½ tablespoons of pepper in a large bowl. In a large, heavy pan, melt 2 tablespoons butter with 1 tablespoon each of olive and safflower oil. Dredge the eggplant, one piece at a time, in the flour mixture and sauté in a single layer over medium-high heat until golden brown, about 1 minute on each side. Drain the eggplant on paper towels while you cook the veal.

3. In the bowl of a food processor fitted with the steel blade, pulse the cheese a few times until the mozzarella is chopped into very fine pieces and the cheeses are mixed.

Menu
for an elegant
dinner:
Prepared in
advance

Lobster Bisque

Veal
with Eggplant

Asparagus
with
Mustard Sauce

Cold
Lemon Souffle

4. After all the eggplant has been sautéed, pour off the butter and oil and wipe the pan clean. Return the pan to the stove and heat the remaining butter with the remaining oil over medium-high heat. Dredge the veal in the flour mixture, shake off the excess, and sauté, one layer at a time, until well browned, about 1 minute on each side. Drain on paper towels.

5. Pour the excess butter and oil out of the pan. Add the wine and reduce it over medium-high heat as you deglaze the pan with a wooden spoon until about 2 tablespoons of liquid remain. Add the brown sauce, reduce the heat to low and let the sauce simmer while you prepare the veal.

6. Preheat the broiler and set the rack as close to the heat source as possible. Lightly oil the bottom of a large baking pan. Arrange the veal in a single layer in the pan and then top each piece of veal with a similarly sized slice of eggplant. Thoroughly sprinkle the top of each piece with the cheese mixture. Broil until the cheese melts and begins to brown, about 2-3 minutes.

7. Arrange the scallopini on individual plates or a platter and spoon the sauce around each or serve it on the side.

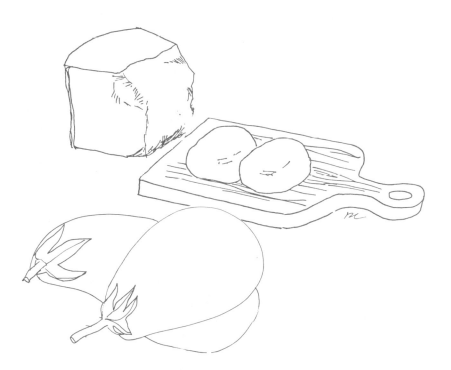

Veal Capriccio

SERVES 4

This recipe blends tastes and textures. The crunchiness of the fresh salad and the warm, smooth taste of the sautéed veal create an excellent light main course. Prepare the salad ingredients slightly in advance. When the veal, which takes only a couple of minutes to cook, is ready, just top it with the salad and serve.

FOR THE SALAD:

2   cups finely chopped iceberg lettuce

1   large tomato, seeded and chopped (1 cup)

1   small red onion, diced (¼ cup)

3   tablespoons balsamic vinegar

⅓   cup olive oil

Salt

Pepper

TO MAKE THE SALAD:

1. Combine the lettuce, tomato, onion, vinegar, and oil in a mixing bowl and toss. Add salt and pepper to taste and toss again. Reserve.

FOR THE VEAL:

1   cup flour

1   pound (4 large pieces) veal scallopini, pounded

4   tablespoons (½ stick) unsalted butter

Salt

Pepper

TO MAKE THE VEAL:

2. Combine the flour with 2 tablespoons of salt and 1 teaspoon pepper in a small mixing bowl.

3. Dredge ½ of the veal in flour mixture and pat off excess. Melt ½ of the butter in a large sauté pan over high heat. Add dredged pieces of veal and brown on both sides (about 1-1½ minutes on each side). Transfer the veal to a platter, cover with foil and reserve. Rinse pan or wipe it out with paper towels, and return it to the heat.

4. Dredge the remaining veal in the flour mixture. Melt the remaining 2 tablespoons of butter in the pan and brown the remaining veal over high heat. Arrange the veal on individual plates or on a platter and, using a serving spoon, arrange salad on top of the pieces of veal. Serve.

Stews

I've always been enthusiastic about stews and other dishes, such as pot pies, that are based on stew fillings. Something extraordinary happens when meat is slow-cooked in a combination of wine and brown sauce. And when you entertain, these dishes are unbeatable. One of the marvelous things about a stew is the fact that you can make it at a time that suits you and it will taste its best whenever you're ready to heat and serve it. I can think of no dish that is less demanding in the moments after your guests have arrived than a good stew. A few weeks before I finished this book, I invited friends over to play Saturday afternoon tennis. I made the stew, in this case the Beef Stew Henri, on Friday between 6:00 and 9:00 before going out for the evening. It was then just a matter of putting it in a Dutch oven, into the car, and out to Long Island on Saturday. Cooking for eight people didn't interrupt an afternoon and early evening of tennis. The only trick to reheating a stew on the top of the stove is that the temperature must be low enough to keep the bottom of the stew from burning. It takes only twenty to twenty-five minutes. If you reheat it in an oven, you need only preheat the oven to 350° and put the stew in for 30 minutes, or until thoroughly heated.

Beef Stew Henri

SERVES 6-8

This recipe was given to me by Peter Klaiser of Hilton Hotels
International, who was kind enough to name it after me. A few
years ago, Peter was involved with the Bull and Bear Restaurant
in New York's Waldorf Astoria. I thought that the best beef stew
I had ever tasted was the one that the Bull and Bear served every
Wednesday. Later, when we met, I seized the opportunity to ask
Peter how to make the Bull and Bear recipe. I'm not positive that
the recipe he gave me exactly matches the Bull and Bear; selfishly,
I think it's even better.

3	pounds beef chuck, cut into 1-inch cubes	1	tablespoon vinegar
Oil or shortening as needed to brown beef		1	quart brown sauce, p.42 (or Pasta & Cheese Brand or canned beef broth)
2	cups red wine	1	pound veal bones (optional)
4	ounces sliced bacon, cut into ½-inch pieces	3	cloves garlic
4	cups coarsely chopped yellow onions (2 medium onions)	¼	teaspoon thyme
2	carrots, peeled and chopped	1	bay leaf
2	stalks celery, chopped	Salt	
1	large leek, chopped	Pepper	
3	tablespoons flour		
3	tablespoons tomato paste		

*Garnish with vegetables according to taste. I like to use sautéed
quartered mushrooms and cooked and glazed vegetables (p.158) such
as carrots, pearl onions, and either turnips, parsnips, or potatoes.*

OPTION: *Brown sauce is an important element of this stew. You can
use beef broth, but the result will not be quite as flavorful. (If you do
use beef broth, increase the flour from 3 tablespoons to 5 tablespoons.)*

NOTE: *Chuck is the preferred cut of beef for stew because it is generously
marbled with fat and stays tender during the long cooking process.
Rump or round can also be used, but the meat will not be as moist.
Shin meat also tastes good in stew because it produces a rich,
gelatinous sauce, but it is also difficult to trim, not widely available,
and requires a longer cooking time.*

1. Preheat oven to 350°. In a large bowl, toss the beef with 2 teaspoons salt and one teaspoon pepper. Heat a little oil in a heavy skillet over high heat until it begins to smoke. Add the beef in batches so that it will fit in the pan in one layer and sauté over high heat until it is evenly browned. (This sears the meat to lock in the juices.) Transfer the meat to a colander and drain over a bowl to reserve all its juices.

2. Add the wine to the skillet and reduce over high heat until about 1 cup remains. Reserve.

3. In a flame-proof casserole or braising pan, sauté the bacon over medium-high heat until it is crisp. Remove the bacon with a slotted spoon and reserve. Add the onions to the bacon fat in the pan and sauté over medium-high heat, stirring frequently, for 5 minutes. Then add the carrots, celery, and leek and sauté the vegetables until they begin to soften (about 5 minutes). Finally, add the meat, sprinkle the mixture with flour, toss, and stir in the tomato paste.

4. Place the casserole in the preheated oven for 10 minutes. Then add the reduced wine, vinegar, brown sauce or broth, bacon, veal bones if available, garlic, thyme, and bay leaf. Skim the fat from the surface of the reserved juices, then add to the casserole. Return it to the oven and continue cooking for 2-3 hours until the meat is tender. Skim off fat that rises to the surface 2 or 3 times as it cooks.

5. While the stew is cooking, prepare the vegetable garnish. Wash the mushrooms and, if they're large, quarter them. Sauté them quickly in a little butter. Peel the carrots, turnips, or parsnips, and potatoes. Cut each into bite-size pieces and boil until barely tender. If you prefer, you can glaze the vegetables according to the recipe on p. 158.

6. When the stew meat is tender, remove the stew from the oven and let it rest for 10 minutes. Skim off the fat and remove the bay leaf. Taste and season with more salt and pepper if needed. Serve, using the vegetables as an accompaniment. This stew may be kept in the refrigerator for 4-5 days.

Beef Stew with Orange and Wine

SERVES 6-8

The orange peel gives this stew a compelling, bittersweet taste. As with beef stew Henri, brown sauce is an important part of its flavor, although you can substitute beef broth as long as you increase the flour from 1½ tablespoons to two.

½ pound bacon, medium slices	1½ cups brown sauce, p. 42, or canned beef broth
3 pounds beef chuck, cut into 1-inch cubes	Zest from one orange, removed with a vegetable peeler and chopped
1½ tablespoons flour	
2 tablespoons tomato paste	½ cup finely chopped parsley
4 cups coarsely chopped yellow onions	Salt
3 cups hearty red wine	Pepper

1. Preheat the oven to 350°. Cut the bacon into 1-inch pieces and sauté in a heavy pan until crisp. Remove the bacon with a slotted spoon and reserve for another use. Pour off and reserve all but 1 tablespoon of the fat. Place the beef in a bowl and toss with salt and pepper to season.

2. Over high heat, brown the beef quickly and evenly in the bacon fat, one layer at a time. (Add more bacon fat as needed.) Transfer each batch to a colander placed over a bowl to catch the juices that drain out. Reserve the drippings. After all the beef is browned and drained, transfer it to an ovenproof casserole or Dutch oven. Sprinkle the flour over the meat and stir in the tomato paste until well blended. Bake for 10 minutes.

3. Pour the remaining bacon fat into the frying pan and sauté the onions over high heat, stirring often, until they are well browned (about 15-20 minutes). Add 1 cup of wine, bring it to a boil and boil 1 minute, deglazing the bottom of the pan with a wooden spoon. Transfer to the casserole.

4. Add the remaining wine, the brown sauce (or beef broth), and orange peel to the casserole. Skim the fat from the surface of the reserved drippings and add them to the casserole. Partially cover the casserole (leaving the lid slightly ajar), return it to the oven and cook for 2½-3 hours, until the meat is tender, skimming the surface once or twice during cooking. Season with salt and pepper and serve.

Ragout of Lamb

SERVES 4

I've tasted many lamb stews in my life, but I consider this richly flavored ragout the best. The recipe was developed by Steven Heinzerling, an excellent chef who worked at Pasta & Cheese.

2 pound boneless lamb (well trimmed, with sinews removed), cut into 1-inch cubes	1 cup hearty red wine
3 tablespoons safflower oil	3 cups brown sauce, p. 42 (or beef broth)
3 tablespoons olive oil	⅜ cup tomato paste
4 cups chopped yellow onion	2 bay leaves
2 large cloves garlic, minced	Salt
	Freshly ground pepper

Garnish with glazed vegetables, p. 158 (use 2 carrots, 12 white onions, 2 white turnips, and peas or green beans)

1. Season the meat by tossing it with salt and pepper in a large bowl. Heat one tablespoon of each type of oil in a large, heavy pan and add just enough lamb to make a single layer. Over high heat, quickly and evenly brown the meat to sear in the juices. (This may be done in batches, adding more of the oils as necessary.) Let the meat drain in a colander over a bowl to reserve the juices.

2. In a large Dutch oven or ovenproof casserole, sauté the onion in 2 tablespoons of each kind of oil over medium-high heat until lightly browned (about 10-15 minutes), stirring frequently. Reduce the heat if the onions begin to burn. Add the garlic and sauté for 2 minutes more. (If you use beef broth instead of brown sauce, add 1 tablespoon flour to the onions and garlic, mix well, and cook for 1 minute more.)

3. Preheat the oven to 350°. Add the wine and the brown sauce (or beef broth) and bring the liquid to a boil, stirring frequently. Add the tomato paste, lamb, and bay leaves. Skim the fat from the reserved meat drippings and add the drippings to the stew, mix well, and return immediately to a simmer. Skim off any fat that rises to the surface. Cover the pot and cook in the preheated oven for 2-3 hours. Check the casserole a few times as it cooks, occasionally skimming the fat from its surface.

4. Remove the casserole. Serve immediately or let the casserole stand, covered, and reheat before serving. The stew will keep in the refrigerator for 4-5 days. To serve, arrange the vegetables around the ragout or place them atop each portion.

NOTE:
Pinto beans are usually the basis of Mexican refried beans. Like all legumes, dried pinto beans should be soaked overnight before they're cooked.

Chili

SERVES 6-8

This unique chili is made with small strips of chuck steak instead of the chopped meat that you expect to find in chili. The chuck is cooked until it is ready to fall apart, making it exceptionally tender. And I introduce the beans in the middle of the cooking process instead of at the end so that they break up and add to the chili's thick, hearty consistency. In this dish, the beans don't sit separately in the chili — instead, they permeate the blend.

3 tablespoons unsalted butter	2½ pounds beef chuck or round, cut into 1-inch cubes and then sliced across the grain into very thin strips
4 cups chopped yellow onion	
6 cloves garlic, minced	1½ tablespoons chili powder, or to taste
2 cups hearty red wine	1 tablespoon ground cumin
½ cup beef broth	1 teaspoon cayenne pepper
4 tablespoons tomato paste	2½ cups canned pinto or kidney beans, drained
1 38-ounce can tomatoes, drained and chopped	
4-6 tablespoons safflower oil for sautéing	

NOTE:
Cumin, a prime ingredient in curry, is a seed of a plant that grows in tropical climates. Whole cumin seeds are found in certain cheeses, breads, and sauerkraut; ground cumin is often used in Middle Eastern and Indian dishes.

1. In a heavy pot or ovenproof casserole, melt the butter and sauté the onions over medium-high heat for 10 minutes or until they are golden-brown. Stir in the garlic and sauté for 5 minutes more. Add the wine, broth, tomato paste, and chopped tomatoes. Bring the mixture to a boil, then lower the heat and let it simmer while you prepare the other ingredients.

2. In a large frying pan, heat 2 tablespoons oil over high heat and brown the beef in batches quickly and evenly, adding more oil as needed. Drain the meat in a colander placed over a bowl to catch the juices. Skim any fat that rises to the top of the drippings.

3. Add the beef, drippings, chili powder, cumin, and cayenne to the simmering broth mixture. Adjust the heat so the chili just simmers. Cover the pot and simmer for 3 hours, skimming the fat off the top several times as it cooks. Do not let the chili boil — it will toughen the meat.

4. Add the beans and let them simmer in the chili for another hour, stirring frequently to make the chili thick. Taste and adjust the seasonings — if you prefer spicier chili, add more chili powder, cumin, and cayenne.

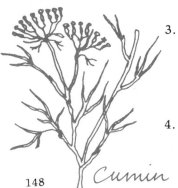

Cumin

Vegetarian Chili

SERVES 4-6

The same basic seasonings — chili powder and cumin — that are so important to traditional meat chili are, of course, present here. It is the use of an interesting combination of zucchini and mushrooms in addition to the traditional tomatoes, beans, and spices that add up to an authentic chili texture and taste.

NOTE:
The large, dark red kidney bean is extremely high in protein. Dried kidney beans should be soaked overnight prior to cooking.

8   large garlic cloves, unpeeled

4   tablespoons (½ stick) unsalted butter

12   cups chopped yellow onions

8-10   mushrooms, finely chopped

1   medium zucchini, finely chopped

1   38-ounce can peeled tomatoes, drained and chopped (reserve liquid)

1½   teaspoons chili powder

1½   teaspoons cumin

2   16-ounce cans of beans, drained (kidney, pinto, black, garbanzo or a combination to taste)

Salt

Cayenne pepper

GARNISH:

1   cup grated Leyden cheese

1   cup chopped yellow onion

1   cup sour cream

Chili Peppers

1. Place the garlic cloves in a small saucepan, cover them with cold water, and set the pan over high heat until the water comes to a boil. Immediately drain and cool the garlic for 5 minutes. Peel the cloves, chop them finely, and reserve.

2. Melt the butter in a large saucepan over medium heat. Add the onions and sauté, stirring frequently, for 10 minutes or until they are golden brown. Stir in the garlic and sauté for 5 minutes more. Then add the mushrooms and zucchini and sauté until they're just tender, about 5 minutes.

3. Add the chopped tomatoes, chili powder, cumin, and salt and cayenne to taste. Strain the reserved tomato liquid into the pan and bring it to a boil, then lower the heat until the mixture simmers. Cook at a slow simmer 40-50 minutes, then add the beans and simmer for another 20-30 minutes. Stir only occasionally at first, then more frequently as the chili thickens.

4. To serve, ladle the chili into bowls and pass the garnishes separately.

Pot Pies

Pot pies were an immediate success in the Pasta & Cheese stores. I've always enjoyed good pot pies, and I was especially pleased to discover that the Pasta & Cheese customers share my fondness for the dish. This pot pie recipe, developed in the Pasta & Cheese kitchens, was inspired by a dish I tasted at Laurent, an excellent New York restaurant. The pastry recipe can also be used with a number of fillings, including beef stew Henri, p.144, ragout of lamb, p.147, or any other stew filling you choose.

Pot Pie Dough

MAKES ENOUGH CRUST FOR FOUR 5-INCH POT PIES

FOR THE CRUST:

1½ cups flour	⅓ cup ice water
8 tablespoons (1 stick) cold unsalted butter, cut into pieces	1 egg, beaten
Pinch of sugar (optional)	Salt

TO PREPARE THE CRUST:

1. Place the flour and butter in the bowl of a food processor fitted with the steel blade. Add 1 teaspoon of salt and a pinch of sugar and process until the dough resembles coarse meal. Remove the bowl and chill in the freezer for 15 minutes.

2. Return the bowl to the processor, then start the machine and pour in ⅓ cup of ice water. Continue to process until the dough forms a ball. Remove the dough, pat it into a 1-inch thick disk, wrap it in waxed paper and refrigerate for at least one hour. (If you're in a hurry, chill it in the freezer for 15 minutes.)

3. Divide the chilled dough into four pieces and roll each into a ⅛-inch thick crust to fit over the pie pan or crock.

TO COMPLETE THE POT PIE:

1. Fill the pans or crocks with your choice of filling. Brush the outer edge of each crust with ¾ of the beaten egg, invert the crust over the filled crocks, and press the edges to seal. Use a paring knife to make several slits in the top of each crust to let steam escape.

2. Preheat the oven to 350°. Mix 1 tablespoon of water into the remaining beaten egg and brush this mixture over the top of each crust to glaze it. Bake the pies for 45 minutes or until the crust is well browned. Let the pies sit for 5-10 minutes to cool, then serve.

Chicken Pot Pie Filling

SERVES 4

Thyme

1¼ cups white wine	2 cups chopped yellow onion
2 cups chicken broth	4½ tablespoons unsalted butter
¼ teaspoon thyme	12 mushrooms
1 bay leaf	½ cup frozen peas, thawed and drained
2 whole chicken breasts (separated into 4 halves), well trimmed, boned, and skinned	2½ tablespoons flour
	¾ cup heavy cream
1 carrot, diced	Salt, pepper

1. In a saucepan, reduce the wine over high heat until only 2 tablespoons remain. Add the chicken broth, thyme, ½ teaspoon pepper, and the bay leaf. Let the liquid return to a boil, then lower the heat and simmer for 5 minutes. Add the chicken breasts and poach for 10-15 minutes, depending on their size. During poaching, the liquid should stay just below a simmer.

2. Remove the breasts and let them cool. Remove the bay leaf from the poaching liquid, add the carrot, and simmer until tender. Transfer the carrot pieces to a bowl, using a slotted spoon. Reserve the poaching liquid.

3. When the chicken is cool enough to handle, cut it into bite-size pieces and add it to the bowl with the carrots.

4. In a heavy pan, sauté the onion in 2 tablespoons of butter over medium-high heat until it just begins to brown. Add the mushrooms and sauté 5 minutes longer. Transfer the onions and mushrooms to the bowl with the chicken and carrots. Add the peas to the same bowl.

5. In a saucepan, melt the remaining 2½ tablespoons of butter. Add the flour and cook, whisking constantly, for two minutes to eliminate the flour's taste and prevent lumps. Take the pan off the heat and slowly whisk in the reserved poaching liquid. Return the pan to medium heat and cook, still whisking, until the sauce is thick.

6. Add the sauce to the chicken and vegetable mixture. Add cream and mix it in gently but thoroughly. Season to taste with salt and pepper. Divide the filling into 4 crocks and top with dough that has been rolled into four ⅛-inch thick crusts and complete the pie as directed on the previous page.

Menu
Potage
St. Germaine
Chicken Pot Pie
Green Salad
Peach or Pear
tart

Vegetables

My fascination with the preparation of vegetables began
when I realized that foods I had been told were "good for
you!" throughout my childhood could also taste good. The
variety of tastes and textures that can be achieved through
the use of relatively simple cooking techniques continues
to amaze me. Glazing, sautéing or puréeing adds
immeasurably both to the tastes that can be derived from
specific vegetables and to the presentation of a meal. In
the recipes that follow, I have chosen vegetables — such
as brussels sprouts, new potatoes, and peas — that are
very common and coupled them with the preparation
techniques that have both intrigued me and helped me
to enjoy cooking, serving, and eating vegetables.

Green Beans

SERVES 6

1½ pounds green beans

4   tablespoons (½ stick)
    unsalted butter

Salt

Pepper

OPTIONAL GARNISH: *½ cup sliced almonds or ½ cup sliced mushrooms*

1. Trim the ends off the beans by snapping them with your fingers or cutting them with a knife. Bring 4 quarts of water to a boil in a beans, and cover. Let the water return to a boil and uncover the pot. Meanwhile, fill a large bowl with cold water.

2. Cook the beans until they are tender but not overcooked, about 3-5 minutes depending upon their size and freshness. To check, remove a bean with a slotted spoon, cool it under cold running water, and taste. When the beans are done, drain and submerge them in cold water until they have cooled. Drain thoroughly and reserve.

3. To serve the beans plain, melt the butter in a sauté pan, add the beans and cook over medium heat until they are heated through. Season to taste with salt and pepper and serve immediately.

MUSHROOM GARNISH: *Sauté the mushrooms in the butter over medium-high heat for 3 minutes, stirring frequently. Add the prepared beans, toss to coat, and continue cooking until the beans are heated through.*

ALMOND GARNISH: *Sauté the almonds in the butter over medium-high heat until they have turned golden brown. Add the prepared beans, toss to coat, and continue cooking until the beans are heated through.*

NOTE:
When buying fresh green beans, look for those with bright, even color. Avoid beans that appear wilted, flabby, or fibrous — they're probably old and tough. Grown commercially in Mexico, Florida, and California, green beans are available year-round. Fresh beans can be stored in a plastic bag in the refrigerator for several days.

Brussels Sprouts with Onions

SERVES 6

6 cups coarsely chopped yellow onion	2 10-ounce packages brussels sprouts, trimmed
4 tablespoons (½ stick) unsalted butter	Salt
	Pepper

1. In a heavy pan, sauté the onions in ⅔ of the butter over medium-high heat for about 20 minutes, until well browned (lower the heat if the onions begin to burn). Add the remaining butter if the onions begin to stick. Remove the pan from the heat and set aside.

2. In a pot, bring 3 quarts of water with 2 tablespoons of salt to a boil. Add the brussels sprouts and cover. When the water returns to a boil, uncover the pot and let the sprouts boil 6-7 minutes, until they are tender but not overcooked. (They will lose some leaves when tender.) Drain the sprouts in a colander, return them to the pot, and submerge them in cold water for 5-10 minutes until they have cooled. Then, drain them again in a colander.

3. When ready to serve, reheat the onions over medium heat and add the brussels sprouts to the pan. (When the sprouts are larger than bite-size, I cut them in half before reheating them.) Cook over medium heat until they are heated through. Season with salt and pepper to taste and serve immediately.

NOTE: *When preparing brussels sprouts, remove the loose and dark leaves. Trim any uneven or discolored ends of the stems and make a cross-cut approximately ¼-inch deep in the stem. This hastens the cooking.*

Potato Cake

SERVES 4

This recipe is based upon a superb potato dish served at Christ Cella, one of my favorite New York restaurants. This potato cake should be sautéed in a generous amount of oil — if at any time the oil seems to have been completely absorbed, add more.

1¼	pounds new potatoes	Salt
4	or more tablespoons safflower oil, as needed	Pepper

1. Combine 3 quarts of water, 2 tablespoons of salt and the potatoes in a large pot. Bring to a boil over medium heat and then lower heat and simmer the potatoes until they are tender but slightly undercooked (20-25 minutes). Test by inserting a paring knife into the center of a potato. The center should be only slightly firm.

2. Drain the water from the potatoes and then, with the potatoes still in the pot, rinse them with cold water several times. Drain them in a colander. When they are cool enough to handle, peel off the skins and transfer the potatoes to a bowl. Mash them coarsely with a fork, leaving some small chunks. Add ½ teaspoon each of salt and pepper and mix gently.

3. In a 10-inch heavy sauté pan, over medium heat, heat the oil until it is hot but not smoking. Then add the coarsely mashed potato to the pan and press down with a wooden spoon to form a 1-inch thick pancake that fills the bottom of the pan. Sauté over medium heat until it is browned (6-8 minutes). Then, using a metal spatula, turn the potatoes very carefully, trying to keep the cake in one piece. (If it breaks, it's no real problem. Just turn the second piece and fit it into the pan.) Brown on the second side, still over medium heat, and turn again. Continue cooking until the bottom of the cake becomes dark brown (6-8 minutes), turn again and cook until both sides are equally brown. Transfer to a warm plate or platter and serve.

Yams, Peach & Calvados Casserole

SERVES 4

This is an excellent dish, rich with a spicy sweetness and the unexpected tastes of the peaches and currants. It goes well with many roasts, particularly the roast chicken on p.102, or a holiday turkey.

5	medium yams (2 pounds)	2	tablespoons (¼ stick) unsalted butter
1	1-pound can cling peaches		
¼	cup Calvados	¼	cup currants or raisins
½	cup brown sugar		Salt

1. Wash the yams, place them in a large saucepan and cover them with cold water. Bring the water to a boil, then lower the heat and let the yams simmer until they are tender (20-25 minutes). Test them with a paring knife to be certain that they are soft in the center.

2. Drain the yams in a colander and cool briefly under cold water. Peel the skins off with your fingers (they should slide off easily). Then cut the yams into 1-inch chunks and place them in a large mixing bowl. Reserve.

3. Drain the peaches and pat them dry on paper towels. Reserve the juice. Then cut the fruit into uniform ½-inch pieces.

4. In a saucepan, combine the Calvados, brown sugar, butter, peach syrup, and currants. Bring the mixture to a simmer and cook until the sugar is dissolved. Then strain the liquid and reserve the currants separately.

5. Add the yams and the Calvados-peach syrup mixture to the bowl of a food processor fitted with the steel blade. Purée quickly until the yams are just smooth. (Depending on the size of your food processor, you may want to do this in two batches.) Transfer the mixture to a casserole or soufflé dish, stir in the peaches and currants, and season to taste with salt.

6. Preheat the oven to 375°. Bake in the preheated oven until the yams are well heated (about 20 minutes). Let the casserole rest for 20 minutes before serving so that the peaches do not burn your mouth.

NOTE:
Available year-round, the yams (sweet potatoes) marketed in the United States are not members of the true yam species that grows in tropical climates. They're not members of the potato family either — they actually belong to the morning glory family. Choose yams (sweet potatoes) that are firm and have smooth, bright, uniformly colored skins. Avoid those with cuts, holes, or bruises in the skin.

Glazed Vegetables

SERVES UP TO 6

Root vegetables such as carrots, turnips, parsnips, rutabagas, or pearl onions are best for glazing. You can also cook the vegetables up to a day in advance and store them in a covered bowl in the refrigerator until you're ready to glaze and serve them.

Up to 6 cups vegetables,
cut into 1-inch pieces

1   cup sugar

¼   cup balsamic vinegar

1   tablespoon unsalted butter
     per cup of cooked vegetables

Salt

NOTE:
"Pearl" is simply the name given to a young white onion of any species that is less than one inch in diameter. Pearl onions tend to be sweeter and more tender than larger onions.

1. Cut the vegetables into desired shapes. I prefer "oriental cuts" on the diagonal.

2. Place each vegetable in a separate saucepan. Add cold water to cover and 1 tablespoon of salt per quart of water.

3. Bring the water to a boil over medium-high heat. Then lower the heat and simmer until the vegetables are tender but still crisp (al dente). Drain and submerge the vegetables in cold water until they are cool.

4. While the vegetables are cooking, combine the sugar and ¼ cup of water in a small saucepan and bring the liquid to a boil over medium-high heat. Lower the heat to medium and let the mixture continue to boil, occasionally swirling the pan gently until the syrup turns a medium brown color.

5. Remove the pan from the heat and immediately add the vinegar. Add ⅛ teaspoon salt and stir well to mix. If any of the sugar has hardened, continue to stir until it dissolves.

6. In a sauté pan, melt 1 tablespoon of butter for each cup of vegetables. Add the cooked vegetables (together) and sauté them over medium heat until they're heated through.

7. When the vegetables have heated through, add about 2 tablespoons of the caramel to the pan for each cup of vegetables. Toss to coat and serve immediately.

NOTE: *Turnips, available year-round, are especially plentiful during the fall and winter months. They are one of the most traditional of all American vegetables, having been introduced to New England from England in the 17th century. When selecting turnips, buy those that are smooth-skinned, firm, and fairly round. If the leaves haven't been removed, they should be a healthy, uniform green.*

Pureed Vegetables

The puréeing of vegetables is very much in vogue. A major reason for the increasing popularity of this technique is that, in certain vegetables (such as carrots, peas, parsnips, celery root, and turnips), the release of the natural sugars adds a delicacy to the palate. A puréed vegetable visually complements a well-presented main course.

Celery Root Purée

SERVES 8

1 pound boiling potatoes, peeled and cut into 2-inch pieces

2½ pounds celery root, peeled and cut into 2-inch pieces

8½ tablespoons unsalted butter (reserve ½ tablespoon to use in topping)

1 cup heavy cream

½ cup grated Parmigiano cheese (Reggiano or Grana Padano)

Salt

Pepper

1. Wash the peeled vegetables under cold running water. Bring 2 quarts of water with 1 tablespoon of salt to a boil in a large saucepan. Add the potatoes and simmer for 3 minutes. Then add the celery root and continue to simmer. Test the individual pieces with a fork during cooking. As they become tender, transfer them to a colander.

2. When all the vegetables are cooked, place ½ of them in the bowl of a food processor fitted with the steel blade. Add ½ of the remaining ingredients and purée. Transfer the mixture to the top of a double boiler, cover, and set over simmering water.

3. Purée the remaining vegetables with the rest of the ingredients and add to the double boiler. Taste, and season with additional salt and pepper if needed. Put the reserved ½ tablespoon of butter on top of the mixture and cover to keep warm until served. The butter will melt and prevent the surface of the purée from drying out.

NOTE: *Celery root (celeriac) is a variety of celery in which the root, rather than the top portion, is edible. The root is fairly round, light brown and about three inches in diameter. Look for firm, clean celeriac with fresh green tops. Avoid roots that have soft spots or have begun to sprout.*

Available year-round, it is most abundant in the fall and winter.

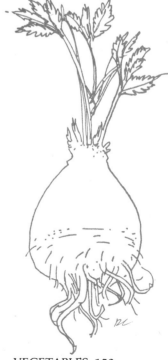

Parsnip Purée

SERVES 8

1	pound boiling potatoes, peeled and cut into 2-inch pieces	¼	cup heavy cream
2	pounds parsnips, peeled and cut into 2-inch pieces	¼	cup grated Parmigiano cheese (Reggiano or Grana Padano)
8	tablespoons (1 stick) unsalted butter, softened		Salt
			Pepper

1. In a large pot, bring 4 quarts of water and 3 tablespoons salt to a boil. Add the potatoes and simmer for 3 minutes. Add the parsnips and continue to simmer. Test the individual pieces with a fork during the cooking. As they become tender, transfer them to a colander.

2. Transfer ½ of the parsnips and ½ of the potatoes to the bowl of a food processor fitted with the steel blade. Add 4 tablespoons of the butter, 2 tablespoons cream, and 2 tablespoons Parmigiano and purée, stopping every 5-10 seconds to scrape down the sides of the bowl. Repeat this process, puréeing and seasoning the remaining ingredients.

3. Serve immediately or keep warm in the top of a double boiler set over simmering water for up to 30 minutes. You can set this dish aside for several hours in a tightly covered pan. When you're ready to serve, reheat over a low flame, stirring constantly so that the bottom doesn't burn. If the purée seems dry, add more butter. Serve on individual plates or in a serving dish.

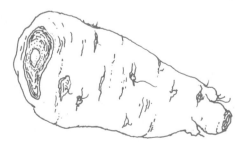

NOTE: *Parsnips, primarily a late winter vegetable, become more flavorful when harvested after exposure to temperatures under 40° F. Look for fairly small, firm, smooth-skinned parsnips. Avoid those with large, coarse, or wilted roots.*

Purée of Peas

SERVES 4

When puréed, the natural sweetness of peas is heightened and
the addition of butter and cream gives the vegetable a marvelous
consistency. Puréed peas are terrific for piping around a main dish
such as chicken hash, p.107, or pork in currant sauce, p. 132 . When
piping, I use a pastry bag with a star tip.

4 tablespoons (½ stick) unsalted butter	⅛ teaspoon nutmeg
	Salt
2 10-oz. packages frozen peas (or 2 cups fresh)	Pepper
2 tablespoons heavy cream	

1. Melt the butter in a saucepan over medium heat. Add the frozen
   peas and, stirring frequently to break up the frozen clumps, cook
   for about 10 minutes, until they are thawed and heated through.
   (If you are using fresh peas, steam or simmer them until they are
   barely tender—about 5-7 minutes—and then sauté them in the
   melted butter for 2-3 minutes.)

2. Transfer the peas to the bowl of a food processor fitted with the
   steel blade. Then add the cream and the nutmeg and purée quickly
   until smooth. Return the peas to the saucepan and add salt and
   pepper to taste. Serve, or keep the puréed vegetables warm in
   the top of a covered double boiler set over simmering water for
   up to 20 minutes. You can set this dish aside for several hours
   in a tightly covered pan. When you're ready to serve, reheat over
   a low flame, stirring constantly so that the bottom doesn't burn.
   Serve on individual plates or in a serving dish.

NOTE: *When selecting fresh peas, look for shiny green pods that
are smooth to the touch. Avoid excessively large pods or those that
seem "overstuffed"—both are signs that the peas inside are old and
tough. You can determine freshness by breaking the pod and tasting
the pea or by rubbing a few pods together—if they squeak, they're
fresh. Because they're grown year-round in Mexico as well as in
California, Texas, and Florida, fresh peas are nearly always available.*

Rice Pilaf

SERVES 4

Regardless of how tempting it is, don't uncover the pot during the 18-20 minutes while the rice is cooking. If you do, the steam will escape and the rice will be underdone.

3	tablespoons unsalted butter	1	cup Uncle Ben's long grain rice
2	cups finely chopped yellow onion	1	bay leaf
1¾	cups chicken broth		Pepper

1. Melt the 2 tablespoons of butter in a medium saucepan and sauté the onions over medium heat until they are golden brown (about 10 minutes). Lower the heat if necessary to keep the onion from burning. While the onion is sautéing, simmer the chicken broth in another saucepan, cover, and reserve.

2. Add the uncooked rice to the saucepan with the sautéed onions and stir to coat the grains well. Continue sautéing the rice-onion mixture over medium heat for 2-3 minutes more. Add the chicken broth, the bay leaf and ¼ teaspoon of pepper. Stir to mix. (The liquid should come to a boil almost immediatley.) Lower the heat to a slow simmer, cover the saucepan tightly, and let it simmer untouched for 18 minutes.

3. Transfer the rice to a casserole. Add the remaining 1 tablespoon of butter and keep the rice covered for up to 20 minutes until ready to serve. This rice may be held in a 200° oven for up to 1 hour.

New Potatoes with Rosemary

SERVES 6

When sautéing the potatoes, make sure you have the proper amount of butter in the pan. Too much butter will keep the potatoes from browning; too little will make them stick to the pan.

12	small new potatoes (about 2¼ pounds)	3-5	tablespoons unsalted butter, as needed
1	tablespoon chopped fresh rosemary, or 2 tablespoons if dried		Salt
			Pepper

Rosemary

1. Use a potato peeler to remove large knots or blemishes from the potatoes but don't peel them.

2. Place the potatoes in a pot and add enough cold water to cover them. Add 1-2 tablespoons of salt and bring the water to a boil. Cook the potatoes until they're tender, yet slightly undercooked (10-15 minutes.) Test by inserting a paring knife into the center of a potato, which should be only slightly firm.

3. Drain the potatoes in a colander. Rinse them under the cold water until they are cool enough to handle, then dry them and cut them into quarters. Transfer the potatoes to a bowl, add the rosemary, and salt and pepper to taste. Mix well.

4. In a large heavy pan, melt 3 tablespoons butter, add the potatoes, and sauté over medium-high heat. Add more butter if needed. Turn the potatoes so that the cut sides are nicely browned. Serve immediately.

NOTE: *New potatoes are most abundant in the late winter and early spring. When choosing any type of potato, look for reasonably smooth, well-shaped, firm, blemish-free potatoes. Avoid those with cuts or bruises (imperfections can be cut out before cooking but you're getting less for your money). Also avoid shriveled or sprouted potatoes and those with green discoloration, a sign of sunburn that can cause a bitter flavor.*

Cottage Fries

SERVES 6

1¼ pounds new potatoes	Salt
2 tablespoons vegetable or corn oil	Pepper

1. In a pot, combine the potatoes, 3 quarts of water and 2 tablespoons of salt. Bring to a boil over medium-high heat and then lower to a simmer. Cook the potatoes until they are tender but slightly undercooked (10-20 minutes). Test by inserting a paring knife into the center of a potato. The center should be only slightly firm.

2. Drain the water from the potatoes and then, with the potatoes still in the pot, rinse them with cold water several times. Then drain them in a colander. When they are cool enough to handle, peel the skins and slice the potatoes into slices approximately ⅓-inch thick.

3. In a large heavy pan, over medium-high heat, sauté the potato slices in the oil until they are nicely browned on both sides. (Arrange the slices in a single layer in the pan and turn them individually as they brown). Add more oil, if needed, as you add additional slices of potato.

4. Season with salt and pepper to taste and serve.

Risotto with Eggplant

SERVES 6

1   small eggplant, cut crosswise into ½-inch slices

4   tablespoons olive oil

3   tablespoons unsalted butter

2   cups coarsely chopped yellow onion

¾   cup white wine

2½   cups chicken broth

1   cup Italian Arborio rice

1   cup grated Parmigiano cheese (Reggiano or Grana Padano)

Salt

NOTE:
The unusual thickness of Arborio rice allows it to be cooked slowly in a small amount of liquid and retain its slightly firm texture and distinctive flavor. Although it isn't widely available in supermarkets, you can easily find it in specialty stores and gourmet shops across the country.

1. Place the eggplant in a colander and sprinkle slices with ¼ cup salt. Toss well and let drain for 15 minutes. Rinse the eggplant, drain, and dry on paper towels. In a heavy pan, sauté the eggplant in the olive oil over medium-high heat until it is very well browned. With a slotted spoon, transfer the eggplant from the pan to a plate lined with paper towels. Pat the eggplant to remove the excess oil and reserve.

2. In a saucepan, melt the butter and sauté the onion over medium-high heat for 15 minutes, stirring frequently, until it is well browned. Lower the heat if necessary to keep the onion from burning.

3. While the onion is sautéing, combine the wine and broth in a medium saucepan and bring to a boil. Cover the pan and lower the heat until the liquid barely simmers.

4. Add the rice to the onion and continue to sauté over medium-high heat for 2-3 minutes, stirring, until the rice is hot. Add more butter if necessary to keep the rice from sticking to the pan.

5. Add ½ cup of the simmering wine/broth mixture to the onion and rice, lower the heat to medium and cook, stirring constantly with a wooden spoon, until almost all of the liquid has been absorbed by the rice. Add another ½ cup of the simmering liquid and continue to cook as before until almost all the liquid is absorbed.

6. Continue this procedure until the last of the liquid has been added. After adding the last ½ cup of liquid, add the Parmigiano and continue cooking just until the liquid in the pot has been reduced to the consistency of a thick sauce. Add the reserved eggplant to the thick sauce. Add the reserved eggplant to the rice mixture and mix well. Remove the risotto from the heat and serve immediately.

Sautéed Apples

SERVES 4-6

Although sautéed apples are not a vegetable, I've included them here because they are a truly outstanding and unusual side dish. They go especially well with roast pork, p. 132. Although the recipe calls for lemon juice, you should also try this dish sprinkled with Calvados. I use Rome, Cortland, or Golden Delicious apples for sautéing.

4	large apples
2	tablespoons lemon juice
4-6	tablespoons (½-¾ stick) unsalted butter
1	teaspoon cinnamon (optional)

1. Peel and core the apples. Slice them into thin wedges (16 per apple). Pour lemon juice over them (if you're not going to be serving the apples immediately, the lemon juice will prevent discoloration in addition to enhancing the flavor).

2. In a large heavy pan over medium heat, melt the butter and sauté the apples in batches until they are tender. Turn them to lightly brown both sides of each slice. Sprinkle with cinnamon and serve.

NOTE: *When choosing any apple, remember that it must be fully mature to taste its best. A mature apple is firm, crisp, and has a glossy uniform color. Avoid apples that are shriveled or bruised.*

Salads

Salads are among the most versatile of all dishes. They serve well as first courses, side dishes, and main courses. Just a few years ago "salad" usually meant a combination of a variety of lettuces covered with a seasoned salad dressing. Happily, that's no longer the case. Today, the salads that get really rave reviews are the first course and meal salads that "hold the lettuce" and instead feature interesting ingredients, such as avocados, chick peas, asparagus, bacon, fish, meat, or fowl.

A thoughtful selection of dressing is, of course, critical in creating an outstanding salad. A vinaigrette works wonders, and I particularly like to use it with a salad served as an accompaniment to a main course. Other, more intensely flavored dressings, such as the lorenzo, remoulade, Gorgonzola, and curried mayonnaise work wonderfully with heartier salads served as first courses or main courses.

The Mayonnaise

MAKES APPROXIMATELY 1 CUP

Many recipes in this book call for mayonnaise. As with brown sauce and vinaigrette, mayonnaise should not be taken for granted; it is the key to the success of many dishes, particularly salads. It takes only about five minutes to prepare it, and the difference it makes, although subtle, is critically important.

If the mayonnaise becomes too thick, add a few drops of water and whisk to thin it out. If, on the other hand, it begins to separate as you're adding in the oil, heat a tablespoon of water to a boil and put it in a separate bowl. Slowly whisk in the separated mixture, then whisk in the remaining oil in a slow steady stream.

Fresh mayonnaise keeps well in a refrigerator for two or three days, It doesn't, of course, last as long as commercial products'to which preservatives and stabilizers have been added. The flavor, however, is very different. The finely chopped onion adds a zest to the dressing.

1 egg yolk	¼ cup olive oil
2 teaspoons tarragon vinegar	2 tablespoons finely chopped onion (optional)
¼ teaspoon lemon juice	Salt
½ teaspoon Dijon mustard	White pepper
¾ cup safflower oil	

1. In a large bowl, whisk the egg yolk. Then add the vinegar, lemon juice, Dijon mustard, ½ teaspoon of salt, and ⅛ teaspoon of white pepper. Whisk.
2. While whisking, add a few drops of the combined oils and blend well. Add a few more drops and repeat the process, whisking continuously, until the dressing begins to thicken. Then pour in the remaining oil in a slow, steady stream, whisking constantly. Stir in the onions, if using.
3. If the mayonnaise is not used immediately, cover it and keep refrigerated.

Curried Chutney Mayonnaise

MAKES 1¾ CUPS

Here is a mayonnaise with a difference. It was developed at Pasta & Cheese when we introduced the curried chicken salad, p.178, and the reaction from our customers has always been very positive. I also like it with the tuna and poached salmon, p. 120, and it is a nice touch in the deviled eggs, p. 49.

¾ cups mango chutney, preferably Major Grey's	2 teaspoons balsamic vinegar
1 cup mayonnaise, p. 168	Salt
2-2½ tablespoons curry powder, or to taste	

1. Place the chutney in a bowl. Remove any large pieces to a cutting board, coarsely chop them, and return them to the bowl.

2. Add the mayonnaise, the curry powder, vinegar, and ½ teaspoon salt. Mix well.

3. Serve immediately, or cover with kitchen wrap and keep refrigerated.

1000 Island Dressing

MAKES 1¾ CUPS

This is a superb dressing for any leaf lettuce salad. It is also outstanding with the cobb salad, p. 130 .

1 tablespoon finely chopped onion	¼ teaspoon chopped tarragon or parsley (⅛ teaspoon dried)
2 tablespoons sweet relish	1 cup mayonnaise, p. 168
½ cup chili sauce	Salt
1½ tablespoons tarragon vinegar	Pepper

Combine all the onion, relish, chili sauce, vinegar, tarragon (or parsley), mayonnaise, ½ teaspoon salt, and ¼ teaspoon pepper in a bowl and mix well.

Gorgonzola Dressing.

MAKES 1 CUP

If you like full-flavored cheese, you'll like this dressing. Here, the combination of the Gorgonzola mixed with Dijon mustard, balsamic vinegar, and safflower oil makes any salad come alive.

½ egg yolk	¾ cup safflower oil
2 tablespoons balsamic vinegar	3 ounces Gorgonzola cheese
1 teaspoon Dijon mustard	Salt , Pepper

1. Combine the egg yolk, vinegar, mustard, ¼ teaspoon salt, and ¼ teaspoon pepper in a bowl and mix well. Add the oil a few drops at a time, whisking constantly, until the dressing begins to thicken. Then pour in the oil in a slow, steady stream, still whisking constantly.

2. Trim the rind off the Gorgonzola, crumble it into very small pieces, and stir it into the dressing. Serve at room temperature.

Basic Vinaigrette

MAKES A SCANT CUP

NOTE:
The finest balsamic vinegar resembles wine in flavor and quality. Made in Modena, Italy, it is aged in balsamic wood casks for 30 years before it is sold.

This is one of the most important recipes in this book. A good vinaigrette, and this fits that description, can make the difference between winning and losing with many of the salads that you make. The type of mustard used greatly affects the taste of this dressing. Any Dijon mustard works well, but I especially like Cherchie's Champagne Mustard. I use safflower oil in combination with olive oil for this vinaigrette; however, feel free to change the ratio of oils to suit your taste. You can also flavor it with fresh herbs, minced shallots, or garlic.

You can keep this vinaigrette refrigerated for two or three days, but it's best when fresh. Add it, at room temperature, to salad just before serving. Salad greens may be served slightly chilled or at room temperature.

1 teaspoon egg yolk	¼ cup safflower oil
2 tablespoons balsamic vinegar	Salt
1 tablespoon Dijon mustard	Freshly ground black pepper
½ cup olive oil	

1. Combine the egg yolk, vinegar, mustard, ½ teaspoon of salt, and ½ teaspoon of freshly ground pepper in a mixing bowl. Whisk until well mixed.

2. Combine the olive and safflower oils and then add the oil in a slow, steady stream, whisking constantly until the dressing is well blended. Serve immediately or cover and keep in the refrigerator.

OPTION: *To make a creamy vinaigrette, substitute 2 tablespoons of heavy cream for 2 tablespoons of oil and whisk it in at the end.*

Avocado Vinaigrette

SERVES 2 AS A FIRST COURSE

This is a favorite of mine. The dressed avocado can be served as either a first course or as a side dish with broiled meat.

1 hard-cooked egg

½ cup basic vinaigrette

1 avocado, halved and pitted

Garnish with marinated tomatoes, p. 186, drizzled with 1 teaspoon olive oil or 2 tablespoons finely chopped parsley.

1. Cut the egg in half and mash the yolk in a bowl with a fork. Slowly whisk in the vinaigrette. Chop the egg whites and add to the mixture.

2. Cut a very thin slice off the bottom of each avocado half so that it will sit flat. Place each half on a salad plate and spoon the dressing into the center. Garnish with marinated tomatoes drizzled with 1 teaspoon of olive oil. Sprinkle parsley over the top and serve.

NOTE: *Available year-round, avocados are most abundant from November through May. A ripe avocado is slightly soft to the touch. Since most are picked before they are fully ripe, you'll probably find firm, slightly immature avocados at your produce shop. Two or three days in your kitchen at room temperature should ripen them and bring them to full flavor.*

Lorenzo Dressing

MAKES JUST OVER 1½ CUPS

I first tasted a version of this remarkable dressing at Christ Cella, an outstanding Manhattan restaurant. It was served with a marvelous salad of watercress and endive. I've used this dressing on a variety of dishes; it is excellent as a dressing for a green salad.

2	tablespoons balsamic vinegar	¼	cup olive oil
1	tablespoon Dijon mustard	¾	cup safflower oil
1	tablespoon minced shallot	Salt	
1	teaspoon egg yolk	Pepper	
⅓	cup chili sauce		

1. Combine the vinegar, mustard, minced shallot, egg yolk, chili sauce, ½ teaspoon salt, and ¼ teaspoon pepper in a mixing bowl and whisk together.

2. Begin adding the combined oils, one teaspoon at a time, to the mixing bowl, whisking constantly. When the mixture begins to thicken (after 2-3 tablespoons have been added), pour in the oil in a slow, steady stream while whisking constantly. Add salt and pepper to taste.

3. Serve immediately, or cover and keep refrigerated until used. It can be kept covered tightly in the refrigerator for several days.

Coleslaw

SERVES 4-6 AS A SIDE DISH

This coleslaw stands well on its own and is also an outstanding side dish with barbequed pork, p. 134. In fact, barbeque afficionados expect coleslaw to be an accompaniment to barbeque.

1   egg yolk

2   tablespoons balsamic vinegar

1   teaspoon lemon juice

1   tablespoon Dijon mustard

Pinch sugar, optional

1¼   cups safflower oil

1   small cabbage, cored and finely shredded

1   carrot, grated

2-3   scallions, finely chopped

Salt

Pepper

1. Combine the egg yolk, vinegar, lemon juice, mustard, 1½ teaspoons salt, 1½ teaspoons pepper, and sugar (if desired) in a bowl, whisking until smooth. Then, slowly whisk in the oil a few drops at a time. As the dressing begins to thicken, pour in the oil in a slow, steady stream, whisking constantly.

2. In a large bowl, combine the cabbage, carrot, and scallions. Add the dressing, mixing until it is well blended. Chill at least 1 hour before serving.

Cabbage

Carolina Coleslaw

SERVES 8-10

This wonderful coleslaw was originally created by Margaret Fortune of Greensboro, North Carolina. The recipe was given to me by her daughter, Sarah Fortune, who is one of the Pasta & Cheese chefs.

FOR THE DRESSING:

¾   cup safflower oil

¾   cup sugar

1   teaspoon dry mustard

¾   teaspoon celery seed

1   cup cider vinegar

1   teaspoon salt

FOR THE SALAD:

1   large head cabbage (approximately 3 pounds), cored

1   large yellow onion, finely chopped (3 cups)

1   large green pepper, finely chopped (1 cup)

1. Combine the dressing ingredients in a medium saucepan and mix well. Reserve.

2. Quarter the cabbage and cut it lengthwise into thin slices. In a large bowl, combine the cabbage, finely chopped onion, and green pepper.

3. Set the dressing in the saucepan over high heat. When it reaches a boil, remove it from the heat and pour it over the vegetables. Mix thoroughly, and refrigerate for 24 hours before serving.

Broccoli Salad

SERVES 4-6 AS A FIRST COURSE OR SIDE DISH

This is a wonderful dish to have as a side salad or as a first course salad-vegetable combination. It is an excellent accompaniment to veal parmigiano, p. 138, or veal with eggplant, p. 140.

1 bunch broccoli	¼ cup heavy cream
¼ teaspoon baking soda	3 tablespoons grated Parmigiano cheese (Reggiano or Grana Padano)
½ egg yolk	
1 tablespoon balsamic vinegar	Salt
1 teaspoon Dijon mustard	White pepper
3 tablespoons olive oil	

1. Trim 2 inches of the stem from the bottom of each stalk of broccoli. Slice the broccoli lengthwise into flat pieces ⅓-inch thick.

2. Bring 4 quarts of water with 2 tablespoons salt and ¼ teaspoon baking soda to a boil. Add the broccoli and cover until the water returns to a boil. Uncover and boil until the broccoli is al dente (about 4-5 minutes). Gently drain the broccoli in a colander and submerge the pieces in cold water until they are completely cooled. Drain well and reserve.

3. Whisk together the egg yolk, vinegar, mustard, 1½ teaspoons salt, and 1½ teaspoons white pepper in a small bowl. Whisk in the oil, a few drops at a time, until the sauce begins to thicken, then in a slow, steady stream. Reserve.

4. Whip the cream until it just begins to hold stiff peaks. Fold the cream together with the Parmigiano cheese into the dressing.

5. Dip the broccoli pieces into the dressing so they are well coated. Arrange the broccoli on a platter or on individual plates and serve.

Chicken Liver Salad

SERVES 4-5 AS A FIRST COURSE

At many of the leading nouvelle cuisine restaurants, it is considered very chic to serve salads made with warm duck livers. To my palate, chicken livers are every bit as good as duck livers. Crisp, warmed chicken livers, set atop lettuce and coated with vinaigrette, make a great first course. This salad goes well with main dishes such as veal tonnato, p. 137 or cold poached salmon, p. 120.

NOTE: *Clean the livers well and remove all the sinew. Once clean, rinse the livers under cold water and pat dry on paper towels.*

1	medium head Boston lettuce (about 1 pound)		Flour for dredging
1	recipe basic vinaigrette, p.170	3	tablespoons unsalted butter, softened
1	pound chicken livers, trimmed and cleaned		Salt
			Pepper, freshly ground

1. Clean and dry the lettuce leaves. Just before cooking the livers, toss the lettuce leaves in a bowl with ¾ of the vinaigrette, then arrange them on individual plates. Pour the remaining vinaigrette into the bowl and reserve.

2. Pat the livers dry, then toss them in the flour and shake off the excess. Heat a heavy pan over high heat until it is very hot. Add the butter and, as the last of it melts, add the livers, ½ teaspoon of salt, and ¼ teaspoon of pepper. Sauté the livers, turning frequently, until they are well browned, about 2-3 minutes. (They should be pink in the center.) Toss the livers in the remaining vinaigrette, divide them among the salads, and serve immediately.

Rice Salad with Bratwurst

SERVES 4

This is a delicious salad with a hearty flavor. No matter how tempted you are to check the rice as it's cooking, leave it alone. If you lift the cover before the rice has finished cooking, you will release the steam and the rice will be firmer than it should be.

1	cup Uncle Ben's long grain rice	½	cup finely chopped parsley
3	cooked bratwurst	2	recipes basic vinaigrette, p.170
2	tablespoons safflower oil		Salt
6-8	radishes, sliced or wedged thinly		

1. In a medium saucepan, bring 2 cups of water and 1 teaspoon of salt to a boil. Stir in the rice, lower the heat, cover, and simmer, untouched, for 20 minutes. Transfer the rice to a bowl and cool to room temperature.

2. Slice each bratwurst on the bias into ½-inch thick pieces. Heat the safflower oil in a heavy pan and, over medium-high heat, sauté the bratwurst slices until they are golden brown on both sides. Transfer the bratwurst slices to a plate to cool to room temperature.

3. Combine the rice, bratwurst, radishes, and parsley in a mixing bowl. Pour in the vinaigrette and mix well. Serve (I usually serve this salad on a platter alongside other dishes at a buffet), or cover until needed. If you refrigerate this salad, let it return to room temperature before serving.

NOTE: *Choose plump, firm radishes that are approximately 1 inch in diameter. Avoid large, flabby radishes. Available year-round, radishes are most abundant from May through July.*

Remoulade Sauce

MAKES 3½ CUPS

This is an excellent dressing for a chopped tomato salad, and it's terrific over hard-boiled eggs. It's also excellent for blanched, julienned celery root. And I enjoy it on julienned carrots and on zucchini that has been sautéed until tender and then cooled.

2	cups of mayonnaise, p. 168	2	tablespoons parsley
2	teaspoons Dijon mustard	1½	teaspoons tarragon
1	teaspoon balsamic vinegar	1	hard-cooked egg, finely chopped
5	tablespoons finely chopped gherkins		Salt
1	tablespoon capers		Pepper

Combine all the ingredients and mix well. Add salt and pepper to taste. Chill this dressing for at least one hour before serving.

NOTE: *Gherkins, made from very tiny cucumbers, are also called cornichon pickles.*

Egg Salad

SERVES 2

In this egg salad, the combination of curry powder, minced onion, and pickle relish gives a unique flavor to the dish. I've tasted quite a few egg salads, and I feel that this one is extraordinary.

6	eggs	2	tablespoons minced onion
1	tablespoon unsalted butter	4	tablespoons pickle relish
1	tablespoon curry powder	Salt	
¾	cup mayonnaise, p. 168		

1. Bring 2 quarts of water and 1 tablespoon salt to a boil. Pierce the broad end of each egg with a pin. Gently lower the eggs into the water, lower the heat, and let them simmer for 12-15 minutes, depending on their size.

2. Pour off the water and fill the pot with cold water. Gently crack the shell of each egg by tapping it against the pot or the sink and return it to the water. Replace the water with cold water as necessary to chill the eggs.

3. Melt the butter in a small pan over medium heat and add the curry powder. Stir and cook for a minute, then transfer the curry mixture to a mixing bowl and add the mayonnaise, onion, relish and ½ teaspoon of salt. Shell the eggs, dice them into ¼-inch pieces, and add them to the mixing bowl. Mix all the ingredients until well blended. Add more mayonnaise if you'd like, and salt to taste.

4. Cover the salad with plastic wrap and chill for at least an hour to let the flavors blend. Serve atop a lettuce leaf on individual plates.

NOTE:
Curry powder is a blend of flavorful herbs and spices that can be used to enhance nearly any dish. Although nearly all curry powders begin with coriander, cumin, fenugreek, cayenne, and tumeric, there isn't any one 'recipe' for curry powder. Commercial brands may be blends of a variety of ingredients, or you can blend spices to create your own.

Fettini

SERVES 4 AS A MAIN COURSE

In Italian, the word "fettini" means "strip". This dish, a salad of strips of ham, or mortadella, and cheese, was developed by Jean-Claude Nédélec of Glorious Foods for Pasta & Cheese. It's made with either mortadella or any good cooked ham, such as Prague. Although this is usually served as a luncheon salad, it blends marvelously when served as one of several salads in a buffet.

3 tablespoons finely chopped shallots	¾ pound Swiss cheese, preferably Emmenthaler, cut into ¼-inch julienne strips, 2 inches long
1½ tablespoons Dijon mustard	
1 clove garlic, minced	1¼ pounds good cooked ham or mortadella, cut into medium slices and then cut into julienne strips 2 inches long
¼ cup tarragon vinegar	
¼ cup olive oil	
¼ cup safflower oil	Salt
2 tablespoons finely chopped parsley	Pepper

1. In a mixing bowl, combine the shallots, mustard, garlic, vinegar, and salt and pepper to taste and mix well. While whisking constantly, slowly dribble in the oil.

2. Add the cheese and ham or mortadella and toss to moisten. Add salt and pepper to taste. Sprinkle parsley over the top. Garnish the salad on the side with fruit or sliced tomatoes and serve.

Chopped Tomato Salad with Roquefort

SERVES 4 AS FIRST COURSE OR SIDE DISH

I spend quite a bit of time in California on business and I've always marveled at the wonderful variety of salads served in Los Angeles. This salad was inspired by one that is on the menu at Chasens. Theirs is called Maude's Salad. This, although quite different, is equally compelling. I first made this several years ago and I've served it many times since with great success. Because the tomatoes are marinated, this is one tomato salad that can be made all year round.

NOTE:
When shopping, look for watercress with crisp, deep green leaves. Avoid bunches with yellow or wilted leaves. It's available year-round and is most abundant from May through July.

1 medium head Boston lettuce, washed, dried, and coarsely chopped	½ cup small chunks of Roquefort cheese
½ cup coarsely chopped watercress, with stems removed	1 recipe creamy vinaigrette, p.170, prepared without salt
1 recipe marinated tomatoes, p.186, drained and coarsely chopped	

Combine the lettuce, watercress, tomatoes, and cheese in a large bowl. Add the dressing and toss to coat the ingredients well. Divide the salad into four portions and serve immediately.

Mediterranean Salad

SERVES 4 AS A MAIN COURSE

This meal-salad, a unique cross between a salad nicoise and a traditional Greek salad, was developed at Pasta & Cheese in 1980. It's always been a favorite both of our customers and of mine.

Dill

2 large tomatoes, cored	2 tablespoons chopped fresh basil, or 1 teaspoon dried
1 green pepper, seeded and sliced into thin rings	½ teaspoon thyme
8 thin slices red onions	⅔ cup basic vinaigrette, p. 170
24 olives, preferably imported black olives	2 hard-cooked eggs, cut into quarters
8 ounces Feta cheese, cubed or crumbled	2 tablespoons finely chopped parsley
5 cups chopped lettuce	1 7-ounce can tuna, drained and coarsely flaked
2 tablespoons chopped fresh dill	
½ teaspoon oregano	

1. Cut one tomato into 8 wedges and reserve for garnish. Cut the other tomato in half crosswise. Squeeze out the seeds and cut into ¾-inch pieces.

2. In a large bowl, combine the tomatoes, green pepper, onion, olives, Feta cheese, lettuce, herbs, and vinaigrette. Toss until mixed.

3. Divide the salad among 4 plates and garnish with tomato wedges and eggs. Sprinkle finely chopped parsley and flaked tuna over the top and serve.

Curried Chicken Salad

SERVES 2-4 AS A MAIN COURSE

We first introduced salads at Pasta & Cheese in 1979 when we opened the store at 72nd Street and Madison Avenue. Lauren Kaye developed this sensational dish, and it was an immediate success. Since then I've seen this salad copied all over the city, and the enthusiasm for other curried chicken salads has only added to the success of ours. The trick here is to prepare and trim the chicken well and, as with all of the salads at Pasta & Cheese and in this book, use the finest ingredients.

1 cup broccoli florets, cut into bite-size pieces

2 poached whole chicken breasts (spearated into 4 halves), p.104

½ cup diced red pepper

1 cup curried chutney mayonnaise, p.168

Garnish with thin slices of fruit, such as apples, bananas, pears, grapes

1. Bring 1 quart of water with 1 tablespoon salt to a boil. Add the broccoli and cook until it is al dente (5-7 minutes). Drain, rinse with cold water until cool, then dry on paper towels. Transfer the broccoli to a large mixing bowl.

2. Cut the chicken into ¾-inch cubes and add them to the bowl with the broccoli. Add the red pepper. Toss with the mayonnaise, cover with plastic wrap and chill for one hour or more before serving to let the curry and chutney flavors blend.

3. To serve, arrange the salad on individual plates and place the garnishes around it.

Curried Tuna Salad

SERVES 2-3 AS A MAIN COURSE

Following the introduction of our curried chicken salad, I was delighted to discover that the unique curried chutney mayonnaise worked as well when combined with tuna. It's a great dish for a luncheon and it's also excellent as a sandwich. When I make a sandwich with this, or with curried chicken salad, I just chop the salad ingredients into slightly smaller pieces. I usually serve it on thin, lightly toasted rye bread.

2 7-ounce cans white tuna, drained

1¼ cups curried chutney mayonnaise, p.168

2 finely chopped scallions

1 tablespoon finely chopped fresh parsley

1. Add the tuna to a bowl and separate the meat with a fork, breaking up the large pieces. Add the remaining ingredients and blend well. Cover with plastic wrap and chill in the refrigerator for 15-30 minutes before serving.

2. Serve on individual plates, garnished with slices of fresh fruit.

Café Salad

This is an excellent, easy-to-prepare salad that makes a perfect summer meal. If you're poaching the chicken specifically for this salad, let it cool thoroughly first. I use canned, small shrimp in this dish, because it is both quicker and less expensive than poaching fresh shrimp. The canned shrimp should be rinsed well in cool water and drained on paper towels. After cutting the avocado, squeeze a lemon over it to keep it from turning brown.

1	tablespoon unsalted butter	¼	pound Gruyère cheese, diced into ½-inch cubes
1	cup mushrooms caps, sliced		
1	poached whole chicken breast (separated into 2 halves), p. 104, cooked and cut into ½-inch slices	1	avocado, peeled, pitted, and cut into ½-inch cubes
		2	tablespoons finely chopped parsley
¼	cup poached shrimp (small, canned, such as Pacific)	½	cup basic vinaigrette, p. 170

Garnish with fruit such as bananas or grapes

1. Melt the butter in a small, heavy pan and, over medium-high heat, sauté the mushrooms until they begin to release their moisture (about 2-3 minutes). Drain them on paper towels and let cool.

2. In a large bowl, mix the mushrooms with the chicken, shrimp, cheese, avocado, and parsley. Toss in the vinaigrette until all the ingredients are moistened. Serve garnished with fresh sliced fruit or a cluster of grapes.

Cobb Salad

SERVES 1

Chop all of the ingredients in this salad into small pieces, approximately ¼ inch x ¼ inch.

1	cup iceberg lettuce (about ⅙ of a large head) medium chopped	⅓	cup chopped tomato (seeded and juiced)
⅓	cup chopped ham (2 ounces) preferably Prague	1	hard-cooked egg, yolk and white separated, chopped
½	cup chopped Gruyère cheese (2 ounces)	2-3	strips crisp cooked bacon, chopped
⅓	cup poached chopped chicken breast (½ of whole breast)	⅓-½	cup 1000 Island dressing, p. 169, or vinaigrette, p. 170
⅓	cup chopped cooked beets,		

Garnish with 1 sprig of watercress

1. Chop all of the ingredients in small pieces, reserving each of them in individual bowls or cups.

2. Form a mound of chopped lettuce in the center of a large plate. Arrange the ingredients in wedges neatly from the peak of the lettuce mound down to its base. Garnish by placing a sprig of watercress on the center. Present the salad with the dressing on the side, then mix the dressing into the salad.

Tortellini Salad

SERVES 4 AS A MAIN COURSE

Tortellini has been very popular for centuries. The combining of cooked, cooled tortellini dressed with a vinaigrette is, however, something that is relatively new and until recently was unique to the United States. In this dish the accents provided by the fresh peppers, scallions, dill, parsley, and basil should convert even the most diehard old-world pasta purist.

1	pound tortellini (cheese or meat filled)	8-10	fresh, chopped basil leaves, or 2 tablespoons pesto sauce
1	pepper, red or green (or ½ of each) seeded and thinly sliced	2	tablespoons grated Parmigiano cheese (Reggiano or Grana Padano)
2	scallions, thinly sliced		
¼	cup finely chopped parsley	1	cup vinaigrette, p.170
3	tablespoons finely chopped fresh dill		Salt

Garnish with tomato wedges and toasted pine nuts

1. Bring 4 quarts of water and 3 tablespoons of salt to a boil. Add the tortellini, return to a boil and cook until tender (according to package instructions). Transfer the tortellini to cold water until cool, then drain well.

2. Transfer the tortellini to a large bowl. Add the peppers, scallions, parsley, dill, basil, Parmigiano, and vinaigrette. Toss gently and thoroughly.

3. Arrange the salad on a platter or on individual plates and garnish with marinated tomatoes, p. 186 . Sprinkle with toasted pine nuts. Serve.

NOTE: *Red and green peppers aren't separate varieties — most of the hundreds of varieties of peppers are harvested green (young) or red (mature). When choosing any kind of pepper, look for glossy skin and firm, unblemished walls. Sweet peppers and sharp peppers are available year-round but are particularly plentiful from August through September.*

Tortellin

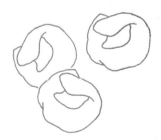

Cold Cassoulet Salad

SERVES 6-8 AS A MAIN COURSE

This is a great favorite of mine. When I have guests in the summer and I don't want a hot kitchen, yet I still want a substantial meal, this does the trick. Most of this dish (everything but the dressing) can be made a day in advance. And if you are preparing the duck and the pork especially for this cassoulet, they can be roasted in the same pan. The roasting techniques and times are the same. The lentils in vinaigrette, accented by roast pork and duck, make a spectacular combination. On a hot summer's night I serve this outstanding dish following a first course of cold curried carrot soup, p. 74, or leeks with remoulade, p.175. A dessert course of cold, fresh fruit or lemon meringue tart, p. 203, rounds out a superb meal.

Menu
Carrot Soup
Cold Cassoulet
Fruit

1	pound lentils	$1\frac{2}{3}$	pound pork loin roast, p. 132, cooled
2	cups chicken broth	$\frac{1}{2}$	cup finely chopped parsley
2	cups chopped yellow onion	$1\frac{1}{2}$-2	cups basic vinaigrette, p. 170
$\frac{1}{4}$	teaspoon thyme		
1	bay leaf		Salt
1	4-5-pound roast duck, p. 110, cooled		Pepper

1. Rinse the lentils well in a colander under running water and pick through the beans to remove any extraneous material. Add the lentils to a large saucepan with the broth, $2\frac{1}{2}$ cups water, onion, thyme and the bay leaf. Bring the liquid to a boil, reduce the heat and simmer the lentils until they are barely tender. This will take about $1\frac{1}{4}$ hours. Then drain the lentils, remove the bay leaf, and transfer the lentils to a large bowl. Cool to room temperature.

2. Remove the bones, skin, and sinew from the duck. Cut the meat into bite-size pieces and add to the lentils. Cut any crisp pieces of skin that are not too fatty into small pieces and add to the bowl. Remove the pork from the bones, trim away excess fat, and cut the meat into bite-size pieces. Add it to the bowl.

3. Add the parsley and the vinaigrette to the bowl and toss well. Add salt and pepper to taste. Let the salad stand at room temperature for a least 15 minutes before serving, so that the flavors blend well. This salad can be refrigerated, covered tightly with plastic wrap, for three or four days. Before serving, remove it from the refrigerator and let it come to room temperature

Potato Salad

SERVES 6-8

Steven Philips and I were experimenting with different salad recipes
and he suggested taking the traditional baked potato recipe made with
sour cream and chives and applying the ingredients to potato salad.
We were both delighted with the result.

4	large potatoes or 15 new potatoes (3-4 pounds)	2	hard-cooked eggs, finely chopped
5-6	scallions, chopped	⅓	cup sour cream
4	tablespoons balsamic vinegar	⅔	fresh mayonnaise, p.168
2	tablespoons fresh lemon juice	5	tablespoons chopped fresh chives
1	tablespoon Dijon mustard		Salt

OPTION: *Garnish with 4 ounces of crisply cooked and
crumbled bacon.*

1. Wash the potatoes well and place them in a large pot. Add cold
   water to cover by 1 inch. Add 2 tablespoons salt and bring to a boil.
   Then reduce the heat and simmer until the potatoes are tender but
   still firm (10-20 minutes. If they become too tender they will fall
   apart in the salad.) Pour off the water and fill the pot with cold
   water to stop the cooking.

2. Peel the potatoes (unless they are new potatoes which don't need
   to be peeled). The skins should slide off easily. Let them cool.

3. Combine the remaining ingredients in a large bowl. Cut the potatoes
   into cubes or slices, add them to the bowl and toss until well coated
   with the dressing. Cover with plastic wrap and refrigerate for at
   least one hour to let the flavor blend before serving.

NOTE: *There are many different kinds of potatoes; some are better
for certain dishes than others. Long Island and Maine potatoes, which
are waxy, are excellent for boiling as are the long white, round white
and round red potatoes grown in other parts of the country. Russet
potatoes are best for baking and frying, although they can also be boiled.
(Idaho potatoes are russets.) Any potato that is harvested when still
small and young is called a new potato and is excellent in this salad. (If
you use new potatoes, they needn't be peeled although large knots
or eyes should be removed with a paring knife.)*

Three Bean Salad

This is an excellent, hearty variation of the traditional three-bean salad. It keeps well in the refrigerator for one or two days. The recipe was developed for Pasta & Cheese by Jean-Claude Nédélec. He and Sean Driscoll own Glorious Foods — the outstanding New York and Washington D.C. caterers.

½   pound dried black beans

½   pound dried navy beans

½   pound dried flageolets

1   bay leaf

½   cup finely chopped onion

2   tablespoons olive oil

½   cup cooked ham, cut into ¼-inch julienne strips

⅓   finely diced peppers, (green, red, or yellow)

FOR THE DRESSING:

1   tablespoon finely chopped shallots

1   clove garlic, minced

½   teaspoon Dijon mustard

3   tablespoons tarragon vinegar

Pinch of cayenne or 2 drops Tabasco® sauce

3   tablespoons olive oil

3   tablespoons safflower oil

Chopped parsley or chives

Salt

White pepper

Navy Beans

Flageolets

Black Beans

1. Rinse the beans in a colander under running cold water. Pick through them to remove any extraneous materials. Add them to a large saucepan with the bay leaf and enough water to cover.

2. Bring the water to a boil, then lower the heat and simmer until the beans are tender (about 30 minutes). Drain, rinse with warm water, drain again and transfer the beans to a bowl, removing the bay leaf.

3. Sauté the onion in the oil over medium-high heat in a small frying pan, stirring frequently, until golden brown (about 5-8 minutes). Add the ham and sauté for another 2-3 minutes. Add the beans and toss in the peppers. Remove from heat and reserve.

TO PREPARE THE DRESSING:

4. Combine the shallots, garlic, mustard, vinegar, cayenne (or Tabasco®), 1 teaspoon salt, and ½ teaspoon pepper in a bowl. Then whisk in the oils and pour the dressing over the beans. Season to taste with salt and pepper and let the salad cool thoroughly before serving. Garnish with chopped parsley or chives and serve.

Sauteed Peppers

SERVES 4-6

The distinctive accent of basil and vinegar gives these peppers an outstanding taste. Store them in the refrigerator at least one day before serving to let the flavors mellow; I think they taste even better, however, if they are refrigerated for four or five days and served cold. Jean-Claude Nédélec gets credit for this marvelous recipe.

6   large peppers, seeded and sliced lengthwise into ½ inch strips (preferably 2 red, 2 yellow and 2 green)

4   cups coarsely chopped yellow onion

3   cloves garlic, minced (2 teaspoons)

Dash of tarragon vinegar

1   teaspoon fresh basil, finely chopped (½ teaspoon dried)

½   cup olive oil

Salt

Pepper

1. Heat 2 tablespoons of the olive oil in a large heavy pan over medium-high heat. Add the peppers to the pan and sauté, stirring frequently, until they are well browned. Transfer the peppers to a bowl.

2. Add 1 tablespoon of olive oil to the oil remaining in the pan and, over medium-high heat, sautè the onions, stirring frequently, for 10-15 minutes until they are lightly browned. Reduce the heat if they begin to burn. Then add the onions to the bowl with the peppers.

3. Add the garlic, vinegar, basil, 2 tablespoons of salt, and pepper to taste to the bowl with the onions and peppers. Stir well, pressing the ingredients down with a wooden spoon. Add the remaining tablespoon of olive oil to cover. Place a small plate or a saucer into the bowl atop the peppers and weight it with a filled can. Then cover the bowl tightly with plastic wrap and refrigerate for at least one day before serving.

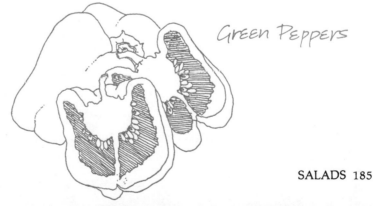

Green Peppers

Marinated Tomatoes

MAKES 16 WEDGES

Although tomatoes picked fresh at the peak of the season are best used without marinating, the majority of tomatoes that are available most of the year are markedly improved by this marinade. I like to substitute marinated tomatoes in recipes that call for fresh tomatoes when fresh tomatoes are not at their best.

½   medium shallot, finely minced

2   tablespoons balsamic vinegar

1   tablespoon olive oil

2   tomatoes, each cut into 8 wedges

Salt

Pepper

NOTE:
Only fully ripe tomatoes (rich red, slightly soft — not mushy) should be stored in the refrigerator — others should be kept at room temperature, away from direct sunlight, to ripen.

1. Combine the shallot, vinegar, ¼ tablespoon salt, and pepper to taste in a ceramic or stainless steel bowl. Whisk until smooth, then whisk in the oil.

2. With your fingers, gently remove as much of the tomatoes' juice and seeds as possible. Add the wedges to the bowl with the marinade, cover the bowl with plastic wrap, and refrigerate for 2 hours. Remove the wedges from the marinade and discard the marinade. Use in chopped tomato salad with roquefort, p. 177, or as a garnish for other salads or sandwiches.

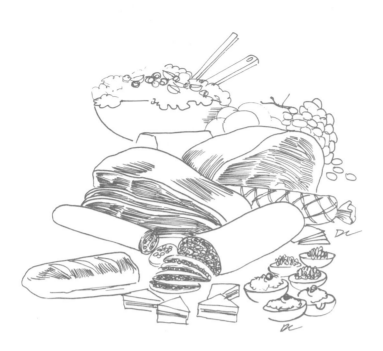

The Summer Spread

I often have a lot of people over for lunch at my
country house on summer weekends. And I've found,
through the years, that the easiest way to have an
exciting meal for 10-12 people (or more) is to serve
buffet style. Throughout this book there are dishes that
are both great taste experiences and visual delights. My
particular favorites for staging a "summer spread"
include a selection of cold cuts — a blend of Genoa
salami, Hungarian salami, prosciutto, Prague ham, and
mortadella. The salad selections include such dishes as
fettini, p. 176, the bratwurst and rice salads, p. 174, roasted
peppers, p.188, curried chicken salad, p.178,
mediterranian salad, p.178, broccoli salad, p.173, and the
cassoulet salad, p.182. The focus of the buffet, however,
is always a variety of stuffings in tomato and pepper
shells. The fillings can be made the night before. The
fresh pepper and the tomato shells can also be prepared
well in advance. Simply reserve the shells and the
stuffings separately. I stuff the shells, top them with the
cheese mixture, and bake them on the morning of
the buffet. Then I let them cool, uncovered, at room
temperature (up to two to three hours) until it's time to add
them to the buffet.

Stuffed Tomatoes and Stuffed Peppers

A selection of tomatoes and peppers with different stuffings served on a large, attractive platter, makes a spectacular focus for a buffet. Serve them at room temperature (they're also excellent served hot as an accent to a winter main course).

to prepare the Tomato Shells

FOR 6 SHELLS:

3   medium tomatoes

1. Wash and dry the tomatoes, trim off the stems, and place the tomatoes on a work surface, stem end up. Slice each tomato in half vertically, cutting from the top to the bottom. Then, using a paring knife or a spoon, remove the pulp and the seeds from the inside of the tomato halves. Take care not to break through the shell as you scoop out the insides. Drain and discard the juice. Neatly trim away any remaining bits of stem from the rim of each half.

to prepare the Pepper Shells

FOR 6 SHELLS:

6   small-medium peppers; (an assortment of green, red, and yellow)

1. Cut the tops from the peppers and discard. Then, using a paring knife or a spoon, remove and discard the seeds and the white membrane from the inside of each pepper. Cut each of the hollowed peppers crosswise on a line approximately 2½-inches from the bottom of the pepper. This bottom portion is the shell. Reserve the top pieces for another use.

to stuff, bake, and serve

1. Fill each tomato or pepper shell up to the rim with the stuffing of your choice. Top off with about 2 tablespoons of the topping mixture.

2. Preheat the oven to 350°. Place the tomatoes and/or the peppers in a baking pan. Bake until the cheese is golden brown on top (about 30 minutes). Remove the pan from the oven. Let the tomatoes and/or peppers return to room temperature and serve. These stuffed shells can be cooked several hours in advance and held at room temperature until needed.

The Stuffings

Spinach Stuffing

2   pounds fresh spinach, cleaned   Salt
     and stemmed
                                      Pepper
⅔   cup ricotta cheese

⅔   cup grated Parmigiano cheese
     (Reggiano or Grana Padano)

1. In a large pot, bring 4 quarts of water and 3 tablespoons of salt to a
    boil. Add the spinach, return to a boil and cook for 3 minutes.
    Drain in a colander and rinse under cold running water until the
    spinach is cold. Using your hands, squeeze all of the water from the
    spinach.

2. Add the spinach, ricotta cheese, and grated Parmigiano cheese to
    the bowl of a food processor fitted with the steel blade. Purée the
    cheese mixture. Then taste and season with salt and pepper.

Prosciutto and Vegetable Stuffing

5   tablespoons unsalted butter   ½   cup chopped eggplant

2   cups coarsely chopped onion   ¾   cup canned tomatoes,
                                            chopped, drained and peeled
5   ounces prosciutto (5 medium
     slices), chopped   ½   cup chopped toasted bread
                                            (2 slices)
½   cup chopped celery (2 stalks)
                                      Salt
½   cup chopped red or green
     peppers   Pepper

1. In a large, heavy pan sauté the onion in the butter over medium-
    high heat for 5 minutes. Add the prosciutto and sauté for 5 minutes
    more. Then add the celery, peppers, and eggplant, and sauté the
    combined mixture for an additional 5 minutes.

2. Add the chopped tomatoes to the mixture, continue sautéing for 5
    more minutes, then add the chopped bread. Continue to cook over
    medium-high heat for 30-60 seconds and then remove the pan
    from the heat. Cool the mixture to room temperature before
    adding to the pepper or tomator shells. If you're not using the
    stuffing immediately, transfer it to a bowl, cover with plastic wrap,
    and refrigerate. Serve at room temperature.

Mushroom Stuffing

MAKES 2 CUPS

3 slices white bread, crusts removed, lightly toasted

3 tablespoons unsalted butter

1½ cups chopped yellow onion

3 cloves garlic, minced

1½ pounds whole mushrooms, washed, dried, and finely chopped

1 cup white wine

1½ cups chicken broth

½ teaspoon nutmeg

¼ cup finely chopped parsley

Salt

Pepper

1. Break the bread into very small pieces or process briefly in the bowl of a food processor fitted with the steel blade.

2. In a saucepan, melt the butter and sauté the onions over medium heat for 10 minutes, stirring frequently. Add the garlic and sauté another 5 minutes, lowering the heat if necessary to prevent burning.

3. Add the mushrooms, raise the heat slightly, and sauté, stirring frequently, until the mushrooms have released their moisture. Raise the heat to high and let this mushroom liquid reduce until it is almost completely evaporated.

4. Add the wine and reduce again until barely any liquid remains. Then add the broth, breadcrumbs, nutmeg, parsley, and salt and pepper to taste. Reduce once more to evaporate the liquid, lowering the heat as necessary to prevent burning.

Topping

½ cup mozzarella cheese (about 3 ounces), cut into ½-inch cubes

½ cup grated Parmigiano cheese (Reggiano or Grana Padano)

Salt

Pepper

1. Combine the mozzarella and Parmigiano cheeses in the bowl of a food processor fitted with the steel blade. Pulse quickly 2 or 3 times until the mozzarella is cut into very small pieces and the cheeses are mixed. (Don't overprocess or the mixture will liquify.) Season with salt and pepper to taste. Pulse once more to blend in the seasonings and reserve.

Sandwiches

You don't need much culinary skill to make an outstanding and elegant sandwich. You need only some imagination and a willingness to experiment with a variety of breads and fillings. The sandwiches featured here and in the Pasta & Cheese cafes are tasty examples of how an assortment of ingredients can add up to sandwiches with a difference — sandwiches suitable for an elegant luncheon or a quick late-night snack. I have nothing against the old stand-bys such as roast beef or ham and Swiss on rye. But they can be boring, and I believe that with just a bit more time and effort something as basic as a sandwich can be turned into an excellent eating experience.

The 'Pasta & Cheese' Sandwich

SERVES 2-3

This is a delicious variation of the San Remo sandwich featured at the Pasta & Cheese Cafe on 3rd Avenue at 66th Street in Manhattan. The San Remo is named after the dried tomatoes it contains — here, they're replaced with fresh tomatoes. (If good dried tomatoes are available, try them — just replace the vinaigrette with sweet mustard.) As with all of the sandwiches in this book, fine ingredients are the key to its flavor. The tastes and textures of the individual ingredients add up to give you and your guests a superb dining experience.

3	English muffins (6 halves)	1	whole chicken breast (separated into 2 halves), poached as described on p. 104, each half cut into 3 thin slices.
3	tablespoons basic vinaigrette, p. 170		
2	fresh tomatoes, sliced, drained, and seeded	¼	pound ham, preferably Westphalian, thinly sliced
		3	ounces Swiss or Gruyère cheese, thinly sliced

1. Lightly toast the English muffins and arrange them, cut side up, on a baking tray. Drizzle each half with ½ tablespoon of vinaigrette. Divide the tomato slices among the muffins and top each with the chicken slices. Then divide the ham among the muffins and top each with cheese. Broil until the cheese is melted and golden brown. Serve.

Chicken, Avocado and Bacon Sandwich

Crisp bacon coupled with ripe avocado and tender, freshly poached chicken breast is a marvelous combination. I first tasted a version of this sandwich at the Stock Exchange in Los Angeles. It is spectacular.

FOR EACH SANDWICH

2	slices thin rye or white bread	2	slices poached chicken breast (½ of a whole breast), p. 104
1	tablespoon unsalted butter, softened	1	tablespoon Russian dressing
¼	avocado, thinly sliced		Salt
2-3	strips bacon, crisply cooked		Pepper

1. Spread ½ the butter on each slice of bread. Top one slice of bread with the ingredients in the following order: avocado slices, bacon, and chicken. Season with salt and pepper.
2. Spread the Russian dressing on the second slice of buttered bread. Place this slice, dressing side down, on top of the first slice. Cut and serve.

Pâté Sandwich

The individual ingredients — cheese, crisp bacon, and smooth pâté — in this sandwich combine to provide a unique eating experience. This recipe was inspired by a sandwich that is offered at the Beverly Hills Hotel in Los Angeles.

FOR EACH SANDWICH

2 thin slices rye bread

1 tablespoon unsalted butter, softened

2 thin slices pâté, p.52

2 ounces Swiss or Gruyère cheese, thinly sliced

2 heaping tablespoons basic coleslaw, p. 172

2 slices bacon, crisply cooked

1. Spread ½ the butter on each slice of bread. Layer the ingredients in the following order from bottom to top on one of the slices: 1 slice of pâté, 1 slice of cheese, coleslaw, then the bacon. Spread the remaining slice of pâté on the remaining slice of buttered bread. Place this slice, pâté side down, on top of the sandwich. Slice the sandwich in half or into 3 wedges and serve.

Tea Sandwiches

I can still remember being taken, as a child, to Schrafft's in New York, which featured a seemingly infinite variety of tea sandwiches. We have a selection of tea sandwiches on the menu at the Pasta & Cheese Cafe in Manhattan's Bergdorf Goodman and in our Cafe Marguery in the Park Avenue Plaza Building. The elegant sandwiches have been marvelously successful in both places. They are perfect for a light lunch or afternoon tea and it's refreshingly simple to make several varieties and serve an assortment on each plate, garnished with fruit such as grapes or apple slices or with raw vegetables such as celery stalks or tomato wedges.

When I make tea sandwiches at home, I begin by using a rolling pin to flatten the bread. Although this isn't essential, it does make the sandwiches more delicate.

Each recipe calls for quartering the sandwiches. You can make an attractive presentation by cutting some into squares and others diagonally to form triangles. If the sandwich ingredients become too soft after mixing, place them in the refrigerator or freezer for a few minutes to firm them up. The butter-mayonnaise mixture called for in the recipes gives all the sandwiches a surprising smoothness.

The Butter-Mayonnaise Mixture for the Sandwiches

MAKES 1¼ CUPS

1   cup mayonnaise, p. 168

4   tablespoons (½ stick) unsalted
    butter, softened

1. Put the mayonnaise in the bowl of a food processor fitted with
    the steel blade and start the machine. Add the butter, 1 tablespoon
    at a time, and mix until smooth. Transfer the mixture to a bowl
    and chill.

Watercress Sandwiches

MAKES 4 SANDWICHES (16 QUARTER SECTIONS)

⅓   cup mayonnaise/butter
    mixture, chilled

½   bunch watercress, washed,
    stems removed, and
    finely chopped

8   slices thin white bread, chilled

Salt

Pepper

1. In a mixing bowl, combine the mayonnaise/butter mixture,
    watercress, ⅛ teaspoon salt and ⅛ teaspoon pepper and mix well.
    Divide the mixture among 4 slices of bread and spread smooth.
    Top with the remaining bread and press together gently. Trim off
    the crusts and quarter each sandwich. Serve.

Cucumber Sandwiches

MAKES 4 SANDWICHES (16 QUARTER SECTIONS)

1   large cucumber

⅓   cup mayonnaise/butter
    mixture, chilled

1   tablespoon chopped dill

8   slices thin white bread, chilled

Salt

Pepper

1. Peel the cucumber and cut in half lengthwise. Remove the seeds
    and discard. Then cut each half crosswise into very thin slices and
    transfer to a colander. Add 1 teaspoon salt and toss to mix well.
    Let the cucumber drain for at least 30 minutes, then rinse well
    under cold running water and dry thoroughly with paper towels.
    Coarsely chop the dry cucumber.

2. Combine the cucumber with the mayonnaise/butter mixture,
    chopped dill, and ¼ teaspoon pepper and mix well.

3. Divide the cucumber mixture among 4 slices of bread and spread smooth. Top each with the remaining bread and press down gently. Trim the crusts and quarter each sandwich. Serve.

Chicken Sandwiches

MAKES 4 SANDWICHES (16 QUARTER SECTIONS)

½ whole poached chicken breast (separated into 4 halves), p. 104, chilled and finely chopped

1 tablespoon finely chopped parsley

8 slices white bread, chilled

⅓ cup plus ¼ cup mayonnaise/butter mixture, chilled

Salt

Pepper

1. Combine the chicken, parsley, ¼ teaspoon salt and ¼ teaspoon pepper in a bowl and mix well. Spread 4 slices of bread with ½ tablespoon each of the mayonnaise/butter mixture. Divide the chicken mixture among the 4 slices of bread. Top with the remaining slices of bread and press down gently. Remove the crusts and quarter each sandwich. Serve.

Egg and Tomato Sandwiches

MAKES 4 SANDWICHES (16 QUARTER SECTIONS)

2 hard-boiled eggs, p. 49, peeled and chilled

⅓ cup plus 2 tablespoons mayonnaise/butter mixture, chilled

1 ripe tomato, very thinly sliced, seeded and drained

8 slices white bread, chilled

Salt

Pepper

1. Combine the eggs, ⅓ cup mayonnaise/butter mixture, ¼ teaspoon salt and ¼ teaspoon pepper in the bowl of a food processor fitted with the steel blade. Pulse until the eggs are very finely chopped. Divide the egg mixture among 4 slices of bread and spread smooth. Arrange the tomato slices neatly on top of it. Spread the remaining 4 slices of bread with the remaining mayonnaise/butter mixture, using ½ tablespoon for each slice. Place these slices on top of the others and press down gently. Remove the crusts and quarter each sandwich. Serve.

Desserts

A good tart — one made of light pastry combined with a flavorful filling and garnished with fresh fruit — has always been one of my very favorite desserts. There is no hard and fast rule to assembling a tart; you can create an infinite number of desserts simply by combining different pastry doughs, fillings, and fruit. This section features, among other desserts, tarts made of flavor combinations that I've particularly enjoyed. I've included recipes for two basic yet extremely versatile pastries — quick puff pastry and sweet pastry — and four fillings — vanilla, lemon, almond, and zabaglione — as well as a recipe for a simple glaze that gives homemade tarts a professional look. These pastries and fillings are basics; feel free to combine them any way you'd like and top them with any fruit that appeals to you.

The quick puff pastry is actually a simple version of traditional puff pastry and can be made in a much shorter period of time. Although it is more complicated than the sweet pastry, it is also more delicate. And, because puff pastry is not sweet, it can be used in appetizers or with main dishes. Generally, the quick puff pastry is baked in a rectangular shape and the sweet pastry is baked in a tart pan, but if you want to use the puff pastry in a recipe that calls for a round crust, simply roll out the dough and cut it into a circle instead of a rectangle.

The sweet pastry is especially easy and quick to make in a food processor. I think it's an excellent pastry — its lemon base makes it more flavorful than many other sweet

pastries I've had. Whichever pastry you use, make sure you prebake it before filling and assembling the tart. Once the tart is assembled and glazed, it's best to leave it at room temperature before serving because when tarts are refrigerated the moisture condenses on the crust and can make it soggy. (The lemon meringue tart is an exception to this rule — it should be chilled before serving.)

In addition to the basic tarts in this section, I've included tarte tatin, a dessert similar to an open hot apple pie, which has always been a favorite of mine.
Although it is not easy to make, it is simpler than it first appears and is well worth a little extra effort. The apples in it are caramelized, which gives the tart a marvelous taste. The finished dessert, with the caramelized apples sitting on top of the pastry, is an attractive addition to any meal.

I find desserts made with chocolate irresistible. Many people share my taste for chocolate, and I think that the recipes for chocolate soufflé, chocolate mousse, and brownies that follow will satisfy anyone's craving for an intense chocolate flavor.

Dessert is also a great time to offer your guests something a little different. I sometimes like to serve palmyre leaves, dried apricots, or chocolate truffles in addition to a regular dessert. Obviously, I don't recommend that you serve truffles after a chocolate mousse or soufflé. But if you're having a fruit tart or other light dessert and are serving brandy and coffee afterwards, offer your guests an additional treat along with it.

Quick Puff Pastry
Pâté Feuilletée

MAKES TWO 5 x 12 TARTS

A simplified version of the classic puff pastry recipe which can require 4 hours or more to complete, this quick version gives you multi-layered flaky dough in 2½ hours (½ hour working with the dough; 2 hours chilling it). As you work, the dough is periodically chilled to make it easier to work with and to keep the butter between the layers from melting. Without chilling, the layers will merge, resulting in a less flaky crust. Once you've rolled out the finished dough, be sure to poke 10-15 holes in the bottom with a fork before baking or the dough will puff up uncontrollably during cooking. You can use this dough to make raspberry tart, p. 205, kiwi tart, p. 203, and palmyre leaves, p. 213, or in any tart combination.

2¼	cups flour	½	cup less 1 tablespoon water
1	teaspoon salt	1	egg, beaten
20	tablespoons (2½ sticks) unsalted butter (1½ stick softened; 1 stick cold)		

TO MAKE THE DOUGH:

1. Combine the flour, salt, and 1½ sticks of softened butter in a mixing bowl. Stir well with a wooden spoon until the mixture begins to bunch together. Add the water and stir until the mixture forms a ball. Using your hands, knead the dough a few times. Shape it into a square 1-inch thick, place on a baking tray, cover with wax paper and refrigerate for 1 hour.

2. Place the cold butter between 2 sheets of wax paper and flatten it into a ¼-inch thick rectangle with a rolling pin. (Don't worry if the butter breaks into pieces.) Refrigerate the flattened butter at least 10 minutes.

3. On a lightly floured board, roll the chilled dough into a ¼-inch thick rectangle. Lay the flat pieces of butter over two-thirds of the dough. Fold the uncovered third over the center third, then fold the other third over the center. Roll the dough into a new rectangle approximately 6 x 18 inches and just under ½-inch thick.

4. Make a "4-fold" by folding both sides into the center and then folding the resulting 2 sides in half as though you're closing a book. Roll the dough once again into a 6 x 18 inch rectangle, and make another 4-fold. Return the dough to the baking tray. Re-cover with wax paper and refrigerate for 1 hour.

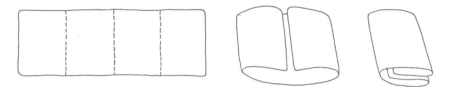

5. Roll the dough into a 6 x 18 inch rectangle and give it another 4-fold. Roll it again into a 6 x 18 inch rectangle and repeat the 4-fold one last time. The dough has now been given a total of four 4-folds, making an astounding 1280 layers out of the original 5 layers.

6. Chill the dough until ready to use. (The dough can be rolled immediately, but it will handle better after it's been chilled for ½ hour.)

TO ROLL THE DOUGH:

1. On a lightly floured board, roll a portion of the dough into a rectangle ⅛-inch thick and at least 2 inches wider than the tart pan you're using. (For example, for a 5 x 12 inch tart, roll the dough into at least a 7 x 12 inch rectangle.) Cut two 1-inch strips from the rectangle to use for the border.

2. Brush one side of each strip with the beaten egg and place on top of the rectangle, egg side down, along the edge to form a border. Pat the border gently in place with your fingers. Prick the dough with a fork everywhere except the border and place it on a cookie sheet.

3. Bake in a preheated 375° oven for 35 minutes or until golden brown. Check the dough during baking. If it puffs up in the center. poke it with a fork to release the air under the dough.

4. Remove the crust and allow it to cool. Add your choice of filling and top with fruit.

Sweet Pastry (Pâte Sucrée)

MAKES TWO 7-INCH TARTS

This dough is suitable for all desserts that call for a rich, sweetened dough. (See recipes for peach tart, p. 202, pear tart, p. 202, lemon meringue tarts, p. 203, apricot tart, p. 204, and tarte tatin, p. 206.) You can make the dough more durable and tear-resistant by folding it in half and pressing the halves together into a flat disk three times after it's been chilled but before it has been rolled out.

Although this recipe yields enough dough for two 7-inch tarts, it may also be used to make one large tart (up to 10 inches) or six 3½-inch individual tarts.

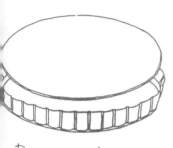

Be sure to use a tart pan with a removable bottom

2 cups all-purpose flour (1¼ for the dough, ¾ for dusting)	7 tablespoons cold unsalted butter, cut into 7 pieces
Zest of 1 lemon (see note below)	1 egg
	Pie weights, dry beans, or dry rice
3 tablespoons sugar	1½ tablespoons lemon juice
	Salt

NOTE: *To zest a lemon, remove the yellow part of the peel in strips with a vegetable peeler. Chop these strips finely for a fresh lemon flavor.*

TO MAKE THE DOUGH:

1. Place 1¼ cups flour, the lemon peel, sugar, ⅛ teaspoon salt, and butter in the bowl of a food processor fitted with the steel blade. Process the mixture until it resembles cornmeal.

2. Add the egg and lemon juice and process just until the mixture forms a ball. Remove the dough from the processor and shape it into a 1-inch thick disk. Place the dough on a plate, cover with plastic wrap and refrigerate for at least 15 minutes before rolling.

TO PREBAKE:

Hold the dough in place with pie weights, dry beans, or dry rice

1. Roll half the dough to a ¼-inch thick thickness. Line a tart pan with the dough, pressing it carefully into the edges. For best results, use a 7-inch tart pan with a removable bottom. Trim the excess.

2. Preheat the oven to 375°. Line the dough with aluminum foil or wax paper, being careful not to puncture the dough. Fill the foil or paper with pie weights, dry beans, or dry rice to keep the dough from puffing up in the center and sliding down the sides as it bakes. Place the dough in the preheated 375° oven and bake for 20 minutes. Remove the weights and paper or foil.

3. Return the crust to the oven and bake until it is golden brown, about 5-8 minutes. Remove and let cool. Fill with your choice of filling (see vanilla cream, p. 201, lemon filling, p. 201, and zabaglione, p. 208) and top with fruit.

Vanilla Cream Filling

MAKES TWO 7-INCH TARTS

This filling, known in France as "crème pâstissière" is a traditional filling for French pastries. Crème pâtissière may be used warm to bake in a crust, but it should be cool before use as filling in a prebaked crust. It can be refrigerated for about four days. Peach and pear tarts use this filling — feel free to experiment with any other fruit topping.

1	cup milk	1	egg yolk
1	teaspoon vanilla	⅓	cup sugar
1	egg	2	tablespoons flour

1. Bring the milk and vanilla to a boil in a covered saucepan. Remove it from the heat, still covered, and keep warm.
2. In a bowl, whisk the egg, egg yolk and sugar until the mixture turns a light yellow color and forms ribbons when you lift the whisk. This will take about 5 minutes. Add the flour and mix well.
3. Whisk the hot milk into the mixture slowly so that it doesn't curdle.
4. Return the mixture to the saucepan and cook over medium heat, stirring constantly, until it begins to thicken and just begins to simmer (about 2-3 minutes). Remove it from the heat and strain into a mixing bowl. Cover with plastic wrap and chill.

NOTE:
If you don't keep the milk covered, a skin will form.

Lemon Filling

MAKES ONE 7-INCH TART

This filling works well with any kind of berries, with kiwi fruit, or by itself topped with meringue. It also makes an excellent filling for white or spice cakes. See lemon meringue tart, p. 203, and kiwi tart, p. 203.

2	eggs	4	tablespoons unsalted butter, softened
2	egg yolks		
½	cup sugar	4	tablespoons lemon juice

Peel of 1½ lemons

1. Combine the eggs, egg yolks, sugar, and lemon peel in the top of a non-aluminum double boiler. and whisk for 1 minute to lighten the eggs and dissolve the sugar. Add the butter and lemon juice and mix well.
2. Set the pan over simmering water and cook, whisking constantly, until the mixture thickens to a pudding consistency (about 10-15 minutes).
3. Transfer the filling to a bowl, cover loosely with plastic wrap, and chill in the refrigerator at least 30 minutes. (If you need to use the filling immediately, chill it in the freezer for 15 minutes, stirring every 2 or 3 minutes.)

Pear Tart

SERVES 4-6

½ recipe vanilla cream filling, p. 201

½ recipe sweet pastry, p. 200 prebaked in a 7-inch tart pan and cooled

1 cup sugar

1 teaspoon vanilla extract

3 pears (Bosc if available), peeled, halved, and cored

½ cup apricot jelly

2 tablespoons Grand Marnier or other liqueur

1. Spread the filling in the prebaked crust, smoothing it evenly across the top with a spatula.

2. Bring 2 cups of water, the sugar, and vanilla to a boil in a saucepan over medium heat. Add the pears, return the liquid to a boil, lower the heat and simmer until the pears are tender (10-30 minutes). The cooking time will vary greatly according to the type of pear and its ripeness, so don't worry if the pears cook quickly or seem to take a long time. Test for doneness by inserting the tip of a knife into the thickest part of several pears to see that they are soft in the center. When they're done, remove the pan from the heat and let cool. Drain well on paper towels and arrange the fruit on top of the filling.

FOR THE GLAZE:

3. Combine the jelly and liqueur in a small saucepan and bring the liquid to a boil over medium-high heat, stirring frequently. Lower the heat to a simmer and continue stirring until the mixture is smooth. Let the glaze cool for 3-5 minutes until it begins to thicken, then brush it over the fruit.

4. Chill the tart for 5 minutes, then remove it from the refrigerator and leave it at room temperature until ready to serve.

Lemon Meringue Tart

SERVES 4-6

This tart is best made in advance because the meringue tends to turn out better if you're not in a hurry.

½ recipe sweet pastry, p. 200, prebaked and cooled

1 recipe lemon filling, p. 201

2 egg whites

¼ cup sugar

1. Add the chilled lemon filling to the cooled crust, spreading it into a smooth, even layer. Refrigerate the filled crust while making the meringue.

2. Preheat the oven to 500°. In a mixing bowl, whip the egg whites until they hold soft peaks. Add the sugar, sprinkling in a little at a time, and continue to whip until it is thoroughly mixed and the egg whites hold stiff peaks.

3. Remove the filled crust from the refrigerator and spread the meringue over the top of the filling, using a spatula or, for a more decorative pattern, pipe the meringue through a pastry bag fitted with a large star tip. Bake the tart in the preheated oven until the meringue is golden brown, about 3-5 minutes. Chill the tart for at least 15 minutes and let it come to room temperature before serving.

Kiwi Tart

SERVES 4-6

½ recipe quick puff pastry, p. 198, prebaked to a 5 x 12-inch tart and cooled

1 recipe lemon filling, p. 201

4 ripe kiwi

½ cup apricot jelly

2 tablespoons Grand Marnier or other fruit liqueur

1. Spread the filling over the prebaked crust and smooth the surface with a knife or rubber spatula. Peel the kiwi and cut them into ¼-inch thick slices. Arrange the fruit neatly over filling.

2. Combine the jelly and liqueur in a small saucepan and bring the liquid to a boil over medium-high heat, stirring frequently until the mixture is smooth. Let the glaze cool for 5 minutes, then brush it over the fruit. Chill the tart 10 minutes before serving.

Apricot Tart

SERVES 4-6

The almond filling used in this tart is to be baked in a tart shell to give it a nice crust. I think it makes a wonderful filling for an apricot tart. However, other types of fruit—fresh or canned—may be substituted. Fresh apples, pears, peaches or apricots should be peeled and poached until tender in a syrup of two cups water and one cup sugar, then cooled, drained, and sliced. If you're using canned fruits, be sure to drain them thoroughly on paper towels.

FILLING FOR TWO 7-INCH TARTS:

4   tablespoons (½ stick) unsalted butter, softened

¼   cup sugar

½   cup almond paste (4 ounces)

½   beaten egg

1   egg

3½   tablespoons flour

FOR THE CRUST:

½   recipe sweet pastry, p.200, unbaked

FOR THE FRUIT:

2   7-ounce cans apricots in syrup, drained

FOR THE GLAZE:

½   cup apricot jelly

2   tablespoons Grand Marnier or other fruit liqueur

FOR THE FILLING:

1. Cream the butter and sugar. In a bowl, soften the almond paste with ½ beaten egg by mixing with a fork until smooth. Add the almond paste to the butter-sugar mixture and blend well. Stir in the remaining egg until well mixed. Add the flour and stir until it is just blended.

TO COMPLETE THE TART:

2. Preheat the oven to 375°. Roll out the dough into a ¼-inch thick circle. Line a 7-inch tart pan with the dough, add ½ of the filling, and spread smoothly with a knife or rubber spatula. Dry the apricots thoroughly on paper towels and arrange them neatly over the filling.

FOR THE GLAZE:

3. Combine the jelly and liqueur in a small saucepan and bring to a boil, stirring frequently. Lower the heat to a simmer and continue stirring until the mixture is smooth. Let the glaze cool for 3–5 minutes, until it begins to thicken, then brush it over the fruit.

4. Bake the tart in the preheated 375° oven for 25-30 minutes or until the edges of the crust and filling are browned. Remove and cool.

Raspberry Tart

SERVES 4-6

This is a simple, elegant dessert that is rich yet light. When whipping the cream, it is important that the bowl, whisk, and cream are all clean and very cold. When the butterfat in the cream is warm, it will not support the air that is incorporated during the whipping process and the resulting whipped cream will not be as light as it should be, nor will it hold its consistency very long.

½	recipe quick puff pastry, p. 198	½-1	pint raspberries, well washed and drained
¾	cup heavy cream, chilled	1	cup raspberry sauce, recipe follows
3	tablespoons powdered sugar		
1½	tablespoons framboise or other fruit liqueur		

1. Roll out the dough to a ⅛-inch thick rectangle and, following the directions on p. 198, make a 5 x 12 inch tart crust with a 1-inch border. On a cookie sheet, prebake the crust according to directions and cool.

2. In a chilled bowl, whip the cream until it holds soft peaks. Sift the powdered sugar over the cream by measuring it into a strainer and pushing it through. Add the framboise.

3. Gently whip cream again with a whisk or with an electric beater at slow speed. Beat until the cream is stiff, then spread it over the tart, smoothing the top with a knife or rubber spatula.

4. Neatly arrange the raspberries over the cream. Refrigerate the tart for 15 minutes or longer before serving.

Raspberry Sauce

1	10-ounce package frozen raspberries	½	cup black currant or raspberry preserves

1. Defrost the frozen raspberries in a small saucepan over low heat. Add the preserves and cook until warmed through.

2. Pour the sauce through a strainer set over a mixing bowl and push through using a wooden spoon. Let it cool for 10 minutes, then serve with the tart.

Cold Lemon Soufflé

SERVES 8

2	envelopes unflavored gelatin	7	egg whites
½	cup cold water	2	tablespoons grated lemon zest
6	egg yolks	1	recipe raspberry sauce, p. 205
1½	cups sugar (¾ for the egg yolks, ¾ for the egg whites)	2	cups heavy cream
1	cup freshly squeezed lemon juice		Salt

1. Cut a strip of aluminum foil and fold it in half lengthwise. Oil one side of the foil and wrap it neatly around the outside of a 1½-quart soufflé dish, oiled side against the dish. Tie a string around it to hold it in place. This collar should stand about 3 inches above the top of the dish.

2. In a small bowl, sprinkle the gelatin over the cold water to soften.

3. In another bowl, lightly beat the egg yolks. Stir in ¾ cup sugar and ½ teaspoon salt. Add the gelatin mixture and pour into the top half of a double boiler. Set the pan over simmering water and cook, stirring constantly, until the mixture coats the back of a metal spoon.

4. Remove the egg yolk mixture from the heat and cool for 10 minutes. Add the lemon juice and grated rind and blend thoroughly. Refrigerate for 10 minutes or until the custard just starts to set.

5. Whip the egg whites until they hold soft peaks. Whisk in the remaining ¾ cup sugar and whip until the mixture forms a meringue with stiff, glossy peaks. Fold into the lemon custard mixture.

6. Whip the cream until it holds soft peaks and fold it into the lemon custard mixture.

7. Pour the mixture into the prepared soufflé dish. Refrigerate a minimum of 3 hours. Serve with raspberry sauce on the side.

Tarte Tatin

SERVES 4-6

This delightful variation of the standard apple tart is well worth the effort required to make it. When removing the seeds from the apples, make sure you remove the seed cases. These clear, often neglected pieces of cellulose are easily left in the apples and can give an unpleasant texture to the cooked fruit. Use a 9½-inch flameproof pie pan or a copper pan for the tart.

6-7   apples, (Golden Delicious, Cortland or Rome Beauty)

1   tablespoon flour

1-2   teaspoons cinnamon

½   recipe sweet pastry, p. 200

¾   cup sugar

3   tablespoons unsalted butter

FOR THE TOPPING: (OPTIONAL)

1   cup heavy cream

2   tablespoons confectioner's sugar

2   tablespoons cognac

1. Peel, core, and quarter the apples. Toss them in a large bowl with the flour and cinnamon to coat.

2. Roll out the dough to a 9-10 inch circle ⅛-inch thick and lay it on a baking sheet. Chill until ready to use.

3. In a small saucepan, combine the sugar and 1½ tablespoons water. Stir to dissolve the sugar and break up any lumps. Bring the mixture to a boil over medium-high heat. Do not stir. Let it continue to boil for about 5 minutes, until the bubbles rising to the surface turn golden brown. This is a caramel and it is very hot.

4. Immediately pour the caramel into the tart pan. Swirl the pan to spread the caramel evenly over the bottom. (If the caramel were to remain in the saucepan, the heat from the pan would continue to cook the caramel and burn the sugar. To clean the pan, immediately add water, bring to a boil and scrape the pan clean with a wooden spoon.)

5. Preheat the oven to 375°. Arrange a layer of apples close together, rounded side down, in the tart pan. Add a second layer, rounded side up. If there are any spaces remaining, cut the quartered apples to fit. There should be 2 layers of apples.

6. In a small saucepan, melt the butter and pour it over the apples. Cover the tart pan with aluminum foil and cook the apples on top of the stove over medium-low heat for 10 minutes. Loosen the foil so the steam can escape. Continue cooking until the bottom layer of apples is soft and the top layer is beginning to get tender. This will take another 10 minutes or more; the apples should just begin to smell burned. (If they smell burned before they are tender, lower the heat and sprinkle with 1 teaspoon of water.)

7. Remove the pan from the heat. Lay the reserved circle of dough over the apples and tuck the edges into the sides of the pan. Using the tip of a knife, poke about four 5½-inch slits in the dough to let the steam escape. Bake the tart in the preheated 375° oven for 40-45 minutes until the crust is well browned. Remove and let cool for 3-5 minutes.

8. Place a serving plate over the tart and invert. Carefully remove the tart pan. If any pieces of apple stick to the pan, gently loosen them and arrange on the tart. Serve warm or cold.

FOR THE TOPPING:

Whip the cream until it holds soft peaks. Then whip in the sugar and cognac until the mixture holds stiff peaks. Serve on the side.

Zabaglione

I've always loved zabaglione and marveled in Italian restaurants as waiters mixed zabaglione in copper bowls. When you discover how easy it is to make and how reasonable the price is compared to ordering it out, you'll become addicted to doing it yourself.

4	egg yolks	½	cup dry Marsala
3	tablespoons plus 2 teaspoons sugar	⅓	cup heavy cream

1. In the top of a double boiler off the heat, whisk the egg yolk with the sugar until smooth. Add the Marsala and whisk until smooth.

2. Place the mixture over a pot of simmering water and cook, whisking constantly, until the mixture is very thick. When you're able to see the bottom of the bowl while whisking, immediately remove from the heat, transfer to a clean bowl to stop the cooking, loosely cover, and refrigerate until chilled, about 1 hour.

3. Whip the cream until it holds stiff peaks. Fold the cream gently but thoroughly into the chilled Marsala mixture. Serve the zabaglione in glasses or dessert bowls with fruit, on a crust as a fruit tart filling, or in pear and zabaglione crepes, p. 212.

Chocolate Soufflé

SERVES 4

There are many versions of chocolate soufflé. I have experimented with a variety and I think this one gives the full, rich chocolate taste that I look for in a good chocolate soufflé.

4	tablespoons (½ stick) unsalted butter (1 to grease the dish)	1½	teaspoons instant coffee powder
½	cup sugar (to prepare dish)	1	tablespoon vanilla extract
3	ounces dark, semisweet or bittersweet chocolate	2	tablespoons liquor (cognac, brandy, Kahlua, or other)
3	tablespoons flour	4	egg yolks
1	cup milk	4	egg whites
5	tablespoons sugar (1½ for the sauce; 3½ for the egg whites)	4	tablespoons powdered sugar

1. Generously butter a 7-inch soufflé dish. Add ½ cup sugar and tilt the dish to coat evenly. Pour out the excess sugar and place the dish in the refrigerator until needed. Melt the chocolate in the top of a double boiler set over a pot of simmering water. Remove from the heat but leave over the hot water and cover with a lid or aluminum foil.

2. Melt the butter in a medium saucepan over medium heat. Add the flour, mix well with a whisk and cook for 5 minutes, stirring constantly, until the mixture is hot and bubbling but not yet browned. Remove from the heat and gradually whisk in the milk until smooth.

3. Add the 1½ tablespoons sugar, coffee, and vanilla to the pan and return the pan to the heat. Cook, stirring constantly, until the mixture gets very thick and begins to bubble. Lower the heat and cook for 1 minute, stirring constantly. Remove the pan from the heat.

4. Add the liquor and whisk until smooth. Add the egg yolks, blend well, and reheat the mixture, stirring vigorously, until the sauce re-thickens, about 1 minute. (Do not let it boil.) Transfer the sauce to a mixing bowl, add the melted chocolate, mix well and reserve.

5. Preheat the oven to 350°. Whip the egg whites until they hold soft peaks. Sprinkle 3½ tablespoons sugar over the whites and continue to whip until they hold very stiff peaks. Add ½ of the whites to the chocolate mixture and mix well. Add the remaining whites and fold in gently but thoroughly.

6. Very gently transfer the mixture to the soufflé dish and bake it in the center of the preheated 350° oven for 40 minutes. To test for doneness, shake the dish a little. The soufflé should not seem soupy, nor should it be as firm as a cake.

7. Place the powdered sugar in a strainer or sifter. Remove the soufflé to a serving plate and dust the top with the powdered sugar. Serve immediately.

Chocolate Mousse

SERVES 4

When you're making this recipe, remember that it is essential that all bowls, whisks, and other utensils that come into contact with the egg whites are clean and grease free. Any form of oil or grease can prevent the whites from whipping properly.

3 eggs	2 ½ tablespoons water
3 ounces good quality dark sweet chocolate	2 tablespoons liqueur (Grand Marnier, Kahlua, or other)
4 tablespoons sugar	1 cup heavy cream
2 tablespoons instant coffee granules	

1. Chill a bowl for whipping the cream. Separate the eggs into 2 bowls — whites in one, yolks in the other (the bowl the yolks are in should be heat-resistant) — and reserve at room temperature. Cut the chocolate into small pieces and melt in the top of a double boiler set over hot, but not boiling, water. Reserve.

2. Whisk 2 tablespoons sugar into the egg yolks. Then whisk the instant coffee, water, and liqueur into the sugar and yolk mixture. Place the bowl over a pot of simmering water or over low heat and cook, whisking constantly, until it is very thick. Remove from the heat.

3. Add the cream to the chilled bowl and whisk until it holds stiff peaks. Reserve. Whip the egg whites until they hold soft peaks. Sprinkle 2 tablespoons sugar over the whites and continue whisking until stiff. This is a meringue.

4. Using a rubber spatula, fold the chocolate into the egg yolk mixture. Fold this into the whipped cream. Add the meringue and fold in gently but thoroughly.

5. Gently transfer the mixture into a serving bowl or spoon it into individual serving dishes or glasses. Chill the mousse for a minimum of 3 hours before serving. To hold overnight, cover tightly.

Chocolate Truffles

MAKES ABOUT 2 DOZEN

Chocolate truffles should resemble the real, irregularly-shaped truffles which grow underground. They are the perfect chocolate to make at home as the dusting of cocoa powder eliminates the need for hand dipping and you don't have to spend a great deal of time creating uniform shapes. We sell chocolate truffles at Pasta & Cheese and have experimented with many varieties. I particularly like this one. The crème fraîche added to this recipe gives it a unique and smooth taste.

8	ounces dark, semisweet or bittersweet chocolate, Peters if available
½	cup crème fraîche, p. 83
2	tablespoons (¼ stick) unsalted butter, at room temperature
1	cup cocoa powder

1. Cut or break the chocolate into ½-inch pieces. In a medium saucepan, heat the crème fraîche over medium heat until it just begins to simmer. Add the chocolate and reduce the heat to very low. Stir until the chocolate has almost completely melted, then remove from heat.

2. Continue stirring the chocolate while you add the butter. Stir until the butter is melted and the mixture smooth, then spread on a baking sheet and chill in the refrigerator or freezer until it begins to firm. The mixture should be firm, but not hard. (You may want to turn the chocolate over with a spatula so that it cools evenly.)

3. Using a pastry bag or a spoon, form the mixture into 1-inch balls. There will be about 24–28 balls. Chill until firm, then roll each piece between the palms of your hands to form round shapes. Chill again, then dip into the cocoa. Remove and store tightly covered in the refrigerator.

Brownies

MAKES 12 LARGE BROWNIES

13	tablespoons (1⅝ sticks) unsalted butter (12 for the recipe; 1 to grease the pan)	4	eggs
		2	cups sugar
6	ounces unsweetened chocolate	1½	cups flour
1	tablespoon instant granulated coffee	½	teaspoon baking soda
1	teaspoon vanilla		

1. Grease a 9 x 12 inch baking pan with 1 tablespoon of butter. Preheat the oven to 375°.

2. In a medium saucepan over low heat, melt the remaining butter and unsweetened chocolate. Add the coffee and vanilla and mix well. Remove from the heat and reserve.

3. In a mixing bowl, whisk together eggs and sugar thoroughly (this should take about 3 minutes).

4. Add the chocolate mixture to the egg mixture and mix well.

5. Sift the flour and the baking soda into the mixture. Mix gently but thoroughly.

6. Pour the mixture into the prepared pan and bake on the lowest rack of the preheated oven for 20 minutes. Cool completely before cutting into individual brownies.

Pear and Zabaglione Crepes

SERVES 4-8

Zabaglione coupled with pears and wrapped in a crepe is a simple yet elegant dish that will surely delight your palate.

4	Bosc pears	1	recipe zabaglione, p. 208, at room temperature
2	cups red wine		
½	cup sugar	1	recipe crepes, p. 69, at room temperature

1. Prepare the crepes and zabaglione and reserve both. Chill the zabaglione in the refrigerator.

2. Peel the pears, halve them, and remove seeds and stems. In a medium saucepan, combine the pear halves with the wine and sugar. Bring to a boil, cover, and lower heat to a slow simmer. Let the pears simmer until they are tender (20-40 minutes, depending on the ripeness of the pears).

3. Drain the pears in a colander and cool. Cut them into cubes, about ½-inch square, and place in a bowl. Add enough zabaglione to thoroughly coat the pears. Reserve the remaining zabaglione. (This recipe may be prepared in advance up to this point. To hold, cover all ingredients with plastic wrap and refrigerate.)

4. Spread 8 crepes out on a table and divide the pear mixture among them. Roll up the crepes gently but tightly and arrange them on dessert plates or a platter. Serve with the remaining zabaglione on the side.

Palmyre Leaves

MAKES 2 DOZEN

Palmyre leaves are often found in the best French restaurants. They are an excellent and simple way to experiment with quick puff pastry dough. Make the palmyre leaves in advance and serve them with chocolate mousse or soufflé. Your guests will marvel at the range of your skills in the kitchen.

2   tablespoons (¼ stick) unsalted butter, melted

¼   cup sugar

¼   recipe quick puff pastry, p.198

Flour for dusting

1   teaspoon cinnamon

1. Spread half the butter over a jelly roll pan and add 3 tablespoons sugar. Shake the pan evenly to distribute sugar.

2. On a lightly floured work surface, roll the dough into a 6 x 10 inch rectangle, ⅛-inch thick. Brush the remaining butter onto the dough, then sprinkle the dough with 1 tablespoon sugar and the cinnamon. Roll dough tightly lengthwise from both sides toward the center.

3. Preheat the oven to 375°. Slice the roll of dough into ¼-inch slices and carefully lay them flat on the prepared pan, being careful not to let them unroll. Arrange the pieces at least ½-inch apart.

4. Bake on the lowest rack of the preheated 375° oven for approximately 20 minutes or until the sugar underneath the cookies has caramelized. Turn the cookies over and continue baking 5 minutes longer. Remove and cool before serving.

Weights and Measures

BASIC MEASURES

2 cups	= 1 pint
1 pint	= 16 ounces
½ pint	= 8 ounces
8 ounces	= 1 cup
4 cups	= 1 quart
1 quart	= 32 ounces
4 quarts	= 1 gallon
3 teaspoons	= 1 tablespoon
2 tablespoons	= 1 ounce (or $1/_8$ cup)
4 tablespoons	= ¼ cup
8 tablespoons	= ½ cup
16 tablespoons	= 1 cup

TEMPERATURE

Fahrenheit	Celsius
32	0
60	16
75	24
80	27
100	38
150	65
175	79
212	100
300	149
350	177
400	205
450	232

METRIC CONVERSION

LIQUID MEASURES

OUNCES	COOKING MEASUREMENTS	MILLILITERS
$1/_{16}$	1 teaspoon	4
½	1 tablespoon	15
1	2 tablespoons	30
2	¼ cup/4 tablespoons	59
4	½ cup	118
8	1 cup	237
10	1¼ cup	296
16	2 cups/1 pint	473
20	2½ cups	591
24	3 cups	710
32	4 cups/1 quart	946
128	4 quarts/1 gallon	3,800

WEIGHTS

OUNCES	POUNDS	GRAMS
¼		7
½		14
1		28
3½		100
4	¼	114
5		142
8	½	227
9		255
16	1	454

A

B

C